THE ARDEN SHAKESPEARE

GENERAL EDITOR: RICHARD PROUDFOOT

KING HENRY V

THE ARDEN SHAKESPEARE

THE ARDEN EDITION OF THE
WORKS OF WILLIAM SHAKESPEARE

KING HENRY V

Edited by
J. H. WALTER

ROUTLEDGE

LONDON and NEW YORK

The general editors of the Arden Shakespeare have been
W. J. Craig (1899–1906), R. H. Case (1909–44),
Una Ellis-Fermor (1946–58), Harold F. Brooks (1952–82),
Harold Jenkins (1958–82) and Brian Morris (1975–82)

Present general editor: Richard Proudfoot

This edition of *King Henry V*, by J. H. Walter,
first published in 1954 by
Methuen & Co. Ltd
Reprinted eleven times
Reprinted 1987

Reprinted 1988 by
Routledge
11 New Fetter Lane, London EC4P 4EE
29 West 35th Street, New York, NY 10001

ISBN (hardbound) 0 416 47340 7
ISBN (paperback) 0 415 02686 5

Printed and bound in Great Britain by
Richard Clay Ltd, Bungay, Suffolk

CONTENTS

PREFACE

In the present edition, footnotes, Introduction and Appendices, have been entirely rewritten. Here and there, however, a note from the first Arden has been retained.

The text is based on that of the *Cambridge Shakespeare* edited by W. Aldis Wright, 1891. It has been necessary, however, to make some departures from that edition: a few French spellings have been modernized, some entry notices and marks of punctuation have been altered, and a few new readings have been introduced; e.g. see II. i. 36; III. i. 7; IV. v. II. Apart from the French words the effect of the alterations has been to bring the text nearer to that of the Folio. Folio readings which for any reason have not been adopted are recorded in the notes, except in the scenes where the dialogue is mainly in French; there a selection of Folio readings is given.

F stands for the First Folio, 1623, Q for the first Quarto, 1600; only when it is necessary to distinguish readings from later Folios or Quartos are the terms F1, F2, etc., Q1, Q2 Q3 used.

References to Shakespeare's other plays follow the line numeration of the *Oxford Shakespeare*, 1916.

O Lord, thou knowest that mine intent hath been and yet is, if I might live, to build again the walls of Jerusalem.

Henry V (on his death-bed).

ACKNOWLEDGEMENTS

I am very grateful to the many friends and acquaintances who have helped me in various ways. The General Editor, Professor Una Ellis-Fermor, has been an ever-present help; her wise guidance and timely encouragement have been most generously given. My friend of many years, Mr J. H. P. Pafford, Goldsmiths' Librarian, University of London, has given me assistance beyond measure. I feel ashamed to think how greatly I have trespassed on his kindness and on the good nature of his staff. It is a pleasure to acknowledge Sir Walter Greg's kindness and helpfulness. His private comments on the textual theory put forward in the *Modern Language Review* (see below, p. xxxv) have been most valuable, and he has preserved me from at least one extravagantly ingenious emendation. My colleagues, Miss E. R. Crossley and Dr P. W. Packer, have kindly allowed me to discuss various points with them, and I have profited greatly from their knowledge and experience.

The note on scoring in tennis, I. ii. 263, owes much to the information very kindly given me by Mr. L. H. J. Dorey, Editor of *Lawn Tennis and Badminton*.

To the Editors of the *Modern Language Review* I am grateful for permission to use material from an article of mine, "With Sir John in it" (*MLR*, XLI. No. 3, 1946). Mr Alan Keen very generously lent me a copy of Hall's *Union of the Two Noble Families*, 1550, and his enthusiasm caused me to reread Hall with considerable benefit to this edition. Recently, Mrs J. Alder has helped me by acute criticism and by very kindly typing the Introduction.

My debt to the writings of Professor C. J. Sisson, Sir Edmund Chambers and J. Dover Wilson in textual matters will be obvious; so also to Lily B. Campbell, C. L. Kingsford, J. A. Wylie, whose work on the life of Henry V and on the Tudor view of history has been of the greatest value. I should like to thank, too, the many writers whose works, though not mentioned in this edition, have undoubtedly helped to shape my views; many of them, such as C.

Spurgeon, E. Dowden, G. Wilson Knight, A. Hart, Hardin Craig and Granville Barker will need no introduction to students of Shakespeare's plays.

Dr H. F. Brooks, the textual editor, whose most welcome help came when this edition was well advanced, has made valuable and illuminating suggestions, and he has helped to purge it of all too many faults.

To my wife I owe more than I can express: her clear, penetrating mind has saved me from grievous errors, and her encouragement and sympathetic foresight made easy and enjoyable a task that might have become tedious.

J. H. W.

INTRODUCTION

I. DATE OF COMPOSITION, PERFORMANCE AND PUBLICATION

Henry V was almost certainly written in the spring or summer of
1599. The evidence for this is an allusion in Act v. Chorus, ll.
30–2:

> Were now the general of our gracious empress,
> As in good time he may, from Ireland coming,
> Bringing rebellion broached on his sword . . .

"The general" clearly refers to the Earl of Essex, who led an expedition into Ireland to crush Tyrone's rebellion. Essex left
London on 27 March 1599 and returned on 28 September in the
same year having failed in his task. It is possible that the words
of the Chorus were written nearer March than September,
since long before the latter month it had become apparent
to everybody that Essex would not be making a return in
triumph.

Some support from external sources exists. Meres does not mention the play in his *Palladis Tamia*, 1598, and this is an indication
that it had not appeared before that date, although Meres' list is
not complete.

Again, some incidents and phrases in *The Life of Sir John
Oldcastle*, 1600, are derived without doubt from parallel incidents
in *Henry V*. The breaking of the angel between King Henry and
Sir John of Wrotham and the subsequent revealing of Henry's
identity (III. iv; IV. i) is taken from Henry's incognito adventures
and the glove incident; Harpoole's compelling of the Sumner to
eat his warrant (II. i. 1–127) is drawn from Pistol's ordeal of the
leek; and the conspiracy scenes in v. i. contain phrases that echo
phrases in the corresponding scene in *Henry V* (II. ii). *Henry V*
therefore must have been acted before 16 October 1599, for on
that date Henslowe records in his *Diary* that he disbursed ten
pounds to be paid to the authors of *Sir John Oldcastle*.[1]

In the following year it was entered in the Stationers' Registers:
"4 Augusti [1600] . . . Henry the ffift, a book} to be staied"
(Arber, III. 37), the entry being presumably an attempt by the
players to forestall the printing of an unauthorized and pirated

1. See Tucker Brooke, *Shakespeare Apocrypha*, 1918, xxvii.

copy.[1] However, a further entry ten days later shows that they were unsuccessful, and that Millington and Busby had already published Q1. The copyright was therefore transferred to Thomas Pavyer:

> "14 Augusti. Thomas Pavyer. Entered for his Copyes by direction of master White warden vnder his hand wrytinge. These Copyes followinge beinge thinges formerlye printed and sett over to the sayd Thomas Pavyer, viz . . . The historye of Henry the Vth with the battell of Agencourt vj^d" (Arber, III 169).

The unauthorized first quarto bears the following title-page:

> The Chronicle History of Henry the fift, With his battell fought at Agin Court in France. Togither with Auntient Pistoll. As it hath bene sundry times playd by the Right honorable the Lord Chamberlaine his seruants. [Creede's device] London Printed by Thomas Creede, for Tho. Millington, and Iohn Busby. And are to be sold at his house in Carter Lane, next the Powle head. 1600.

Apart from the general statement that the play "hath bene sundry times played", there is no recorded performance of the play until the entry in the Revels Accounts on 7 January 1605, when the King's Majesty's Players presented it at Court.

Although this quarto was twice reprinted in 1602 and 1619,[2] the first authoritative edition is that of the First Folio, 1623.

2. THE DIVERSITY OF CRITICAL OPINIONS

We have no reason to doubt that *Henry V*, even without Falstaff, that "globe of sinful continents", was a popular play. It is only later that criticism becomes doubtful, uncertain and confused, particularly when it is directed at Henry. Johnson found fault with him in Act v:

> "I know not why Shakespeare now gives the king nearly such a character as he made him formerly ridicule in *Percy* . . . The truth is, that the poet's matter failed him in the fifth act, and he was glad to fill it up with whatever he could get."

Bradley, *Oxford Lectures on Poetry*, 1926, pp. 256–7, sums up Henry's virtues:

> ". . . he is, perhaps the most *efficient* character drawn by Shakespeare, unless Ulysses, in *Troilus and Cressida*, is his equal.

---

1. For evidence that players' companies did attempt to control publication see *Malone Soc. Collections*, II (3) 384–5 and Alexander, *Shakespeare's Life and Art*, p. 34, n. 1.

2. See below, p. xxxiv.

And so he has been described as Shakespeare's ideal man of action; nay, it has even been declared that here for once Shakespeare plainly disclosed his own ethical creed, and showed us his ideal, not simply of a man of action, but of a man."

Then, rejecting this latter view, he continues:

". . . we shall discover with the many fine traits a few less pleasing . . . he is still his father's son, the son of the man whom Hotspur called a 'vile politician'. Henry's religion, for example, is genuine, it is rooted in his modesty; but it is also superstitious—an attempt to buy off supernatural vengeance for Richard's blood; and it is also in part political, like his father's projected crusade. Just as he went to war chiefly because, as his father told him, it was the way to keep factious nobles quiet and unite the nation, so when he adjures the Archbishop to satisfy him as to his right to the French throne, he knows very well that the Archbishop *wants* the war, because it will defer and perhaps prevent what he considers the spoliation of the Church. This same strain of policy is what Shakespeare marks in the first soliloquy in *Henry IV*, where the prince describes his riotous life as a mere scheme to win him glory later. It implies that readiness to use other people as means to his own ends which is a conspicuous feature in his father."

That is a severe indictment. On the other hand, Charles Williams in his "Henry V" in *Shakespeare Criticism*, 1919–35, pp. 187–8, writes thus of Henry on the eve of Agincourt:

"Henry then has made of his crisis an exaltation of his experience; he has become gay. This gaiety—a 'modest' gaiety, to take another adjective from the Chorus—lasts all through the Act. It lightens and saves the speech on ceremony; more especially, it illuminates the speech to Westmoreland. In view of the King's capacity the stress there may well be on the adjective rather than the substantive: 'We few, we *happy* few.' His rejection of all those who have no stomach for the fight, his offer of crowns for convoy, is part of the same delight: so far as possible he will have no one there who does not love to be there. He makes jokes at the expense of the old men's 'tall stories' of the battle, and at the French demand for ransom. We are clean away from the solemn hero-king, and therefore much more aware of the Harry of the Chorus, and of the thing he is—the 'touch of Harry in the night'. The very last line of that scene—'how thou pleasest, God, dispose the day'—is not a prayer of resignation but a cry of complete carelessness. What does it matter what *happens*? . . .

"[Henry] deserves more greatly than has perhaps always been allowed. The Muse, *entertaining conjecture* of a new and dreadful world, conjectured also a touch in the night, the thawing of fear, a royal captain of a ruined band, and conjectured the nature of the power of love and consequent lightness that thrills through the already poring dusk."

Masefield, *Shakespeare*, 1911, p. 121, is scornful, "Henry V is the one commonplace man in the eight plays"; but to Moore Smith, Warwick ed., p. 31, Shakespeare "loves this 'plain soldier' from the bottom of his heart, and means us to do the same". Van Doren, *Shakespeare*, 1941, p. 176, is contemptuous, "The king whom he has groomed to be the ideal English king, all plumes and smiles and decorated courage, collapses here into a mere good fellow, a hearty undergraduate with enormous initials on his chest". And while there are some who consider that Henry was merely doing on a large scale what Bardolph did on a small scale, Dover Wilson, New Cambridge ed., p. xli, writing of the lines, "How thou pleasest, God, dispose the day", rises to opposing heights, "It is a statement of the ultimate heroic faith, a faith which, like that of the martyrs, put him who holds it beyond reach of mortal man". The debate continues.

3. THE EPIC NATURE OF THE PLAY AND ITS IMPLICATIONS—THE IDEAL KING

Poor Henry! the chorus of critics sings both high and low, now as low as "Mars, his idiot", now as high as "This star of England". It is strangely ironical that a play in which the virtue of unity is so held up for imitation should provoke so much disunity among its commentators.

More recently Tillyard, *Shakespeare's History Plays*, 1944, and Dover Wilson have examined the play from fresh aspects. Tillyard considers that the weight of historical and legendary tradition hampered Shakespeare too greatly; that the inconsistencies of Henry's miraculously changed character, the picture of the ideal king and the good mixer were "impossible of worthy fulfilment". Dover Wilson praises Shakespeare's attempt to deal with the epic form of the story, and he writes with justice and with moving eloquence on the heroic spirit that informs the play. Both pose important questions without following up the implications of their own terms. It is necessary, therefore, to make some general observations on the relationship of *Henry V* to epic poetry, to the ideal king and, very briefly, to the view of history in the intellectual fashions of the day.

The reign of Henry V was fit matter for an epic. Daniel omits apologetically Henry's reign from his *Civil Wars*, but pauses to comment,

> O what eternal matter here is found
> Whence new immortal *Iliads* might proceed;

and there is little doubt that this was also the opinion of his contemporaries, for not only was its theme of proper magnitude, but it also agreed with Aristotle's pronouncement that the epic fable should be matter of history. Shakespeare, therefore, in giving dramatic form to material of an epic nature was faced with difficulties. Not the least was noted by Jonson, following Aristotle, "As to a *Tragedy* or a Comedy, the Action may be convenient, and perfect, that would not fit an *Epicke Poeme* in Magnitude" (*Discoveries*, ed. 1933, p. 102). Again, while Shakespeare took liberties with the unity of action in his plays, insistence on unity of action was also a principle of epic construction (*Discoveries*, p. 105) and could not lightly be ignored. Finally, the purpose of epic poetry was the moral one of arousing admiration and encouraging imitation. Sidney writes,

"as the image of each action styrreth and instructeth the mind, so the loftie image of such Worthies most inflameth the mind with desire to be worthy, and informes with counsel how to be worthy" (*Apologie*, p. 33).

Shakespeare's task was not merely to extract material for a play from an epic story, but within the physical limits of the stage and within the admittedly inadequate dramatic convention to give the illusion of an epic whole. In consequence *Henry V* is daringly novel, nothing quite like it had been seen on the stage before. No wonder Shakespeare, after the magnificent epic invocation of the Prologue, becomes apologetic; no wonder he appeals most urgently to his audiences to use their imagination, for in daring to simulate the "best and most accomplished kinde of Poetry" (*Apologie*, p. 33) on the common stage he laid himself open to the scorn and censure of the learned and judicious.

Dover Wilson points out that Shakespeare accepted the challenge of the epic form by writing a series of historic tableaux and emphasizing the epical tone "by a Chorus, who speaks five prologues and an epilogue". Undoubtedly the speeches of the Chorus are epical in tone, but they have another epical function, for in the careful way they recount the omitted details of the well-known story, they secure unity of action. Shakespeare, in fact, accepts Sidney's advice to follow the ancient writers of tragedy and "by some *Nuncius* to recount thinges done in former time or other place" (*Apologie*, p. 53). Indeed, it is possible that the insistent emphasis on action in unity in I. ii. 180–213, with illustrations drawn from music, bees, archery, sundials, the confluence of roads and streams, is, apart from its immediate context, a reflection of Shakespeare's concern with unity of action in the structure of the play.

The moral values of the epic will to a large extent depend on the character and action of the epic hero, who in renaissance theory must be perfect above the common run of men and of royal blood, in effect, the ideal king. Now the ideal king was a very real conception. From Isocrates onwards attempts had been made to compile the virtues essential to such a ruler. Christian writers had made free use of classical works until the idea reached its most influential form in the *Institutio Principis*, 1516, of Erasmus. Elyot and other sixteenth-century writers borrowed from Erasmus; indeed, there is so much repetition and rearranging of the same material that it is impossible to be certain of the dependence of one writer upon another. Shakespeare knew Elyot's *Governor*, yet he seems closer in his general views to the *Institutio* and to Chelidonius' treatise translated from Latin into French by Bouvaisteau and from French into English by Chillester as *Of the Institution and firste beginning of Christian Princes*, 1571. How much Shakespeare had assimilated these ideas will be obvious from the following collection of parallels from Erasmus,[1] Chelidonius and *Henry V*.

It is assumed that the king is a Christian (I. ii. 241, 2 Chorus 6; Chel. p. 82; Eras., *Prefatory Letter*, p. 177, etc.) and one who supports the Christian Church (I. i. 23, 73; Chel., p. 82; Eras., *passim*). He should be learned (I. i. 32, 38–47; Chel., p. 57, c. VI.; Eras., *Prefatory Letter*) and well versed in theology (I. i. 38–40; Eras., p. 153). Justice should be established in his kingdom (II. ii; *2 Henry IV*, v. ii. 43–145; Chel., p. 42, c. X; Eras., pp. 221–37) and he himself should show clemency (II. ii. 39–60; III. iii. 54; III. vi. 111–18; Chel., pp. 128–37; Eras., p. 209) not take personal revenge (II. ii. 174; Chel., p. 137; Eras., pp. 231–3) and exercise self-control (I. ii. 241–3; Chel., p. 41; Eras., pp. 156–7). He should allow himself to be counselled by wise men (I. ii.; II. iv. 33; Chel., c. VI; Eras., p. 156), and should be familiar with humble people (IV. i. 85–235; Chel., pp. 129, 131; Eras., p. 245) though as Erasmus points out he should not allow himself to be corrupted by them (p. 150). The king seeks the defence and preservation of his state (I. ii. 136–54; II. ii. 175–7; Chel., p. 148;

1. For convenience the translation of the *Institutio*, by L. K. Born, *The Education of a Christian Prince*, 1936, has been used.

Eras., pp. 160, 161, etc.), his mind is burdened with affairs of state (IV. i. 236–90; Eras., p. 160) which keep him awake at night (IV. i. 264, 273–4, 289; Eras., pp. 162, 184, 244). The kingdom of a good king is like the human body whose parts work harmoniously and in common defence (I. ii. 178–83; Chel., p. 166; Eras., pp. 175–6) and again like the orderly bee society (I. ii. 183–204; Chel., pp. 18–21; Eras., pp. 147, 165) with its obedient subjects (I. ii. 186–7; Chel., p. 21; cf. Eras., p. 236). He should cause idlers, parasites and flatterers to be banished or executed (the fate of Bardolph, Nym, Doll, etc.; Chel., *Prologue;* Eras., p. 194 etc.). The ceremony and insignia of a king are valueless unless the king has the right spirit (IV. i. 244–74; Eras., pp. 150–2); some titles are mere flattery (IV. i. 269; Eras., p. 197); at all costs flattery is to be avoided (IV. i. 256–74; Chel., *Prologue;* Eras., pp. 193–204). Although it is customary to compare kings with great men of the past, the kings must remember that as Christians they are far better than such men as Alexander (IV. vii. 13–53; Eras., pp. 153, 203; cf. Chel., denunciation of Alexander for murdering Cleitus, p. 129). The king should consider his responsibility in war for causing the deaths of so many innocent people (IV. i. 135–49; Eras., pp. 253–4). The evils of war are described (II. iv. 105–9; III. iii. 10–41; V. ii. 34–62; Chel., pp. 169–71; Eras., pp. 253–4). It is a good thing for a king to enter into the honourable estate of matrimony (V. ii; Chel., p. 179).[1] Erasmus regards marriage for the sake of an alliance as liable to create further strife (pp. 241–3).

There are, too, some small points of resemblance. Chelidonius gives a full account of the society of bees (pp. 18–21) taken mainly from Pliny, *Nat. Hist.*, XI, and St Ambrose, *Hexaemeron*, and his opening phrasing is similar to Shakespeare's, "they have their King, and seeme to keepe a certaine forme of a kingdome", and he too stresses obedience as a civic virtue. The episode of the man who railed against Henry has a close parallel. Chelidonius, p. 137, refers to a story of Pyrrhus, king of Epirus, who pardoned some soldiers who spoke "uncomly and indecēt wordes of him" because they were drunk with wine.[2]

4. THE CONVERSION OF PRINCE HENRY

It is just this portrait of Henry, the ideal king, that most commentators have found difficult to reconcile with Prince Hal, and to describe Henry as Hal "grown wise" is to avoid the issue. If

---

1. This part of the *Institution* was added by Bouvaisteau.
2. Shakespeare, however, may have remembered the incident in Plutarch.

Henry V is the end that crowns *1* and *2 Henry IV*, then King Henry V must come to terms with Prince Hal. The heart of the matter is the nature of the change that came over Henry at his coronation, and this must be examined in detail.

Shakespeare gives only one observer's account of what happened, that by the Archbishop of Canterbury I. i. 25–34:

> The breath no sooner left his father's body,
> But that his wildness, mortified in him,
> Seem'd to die too; yea, at that very moment,
> Consideration like an angel came,
> And whipp'd th' offending Adam out of him,
> Leaving his body as a Paradise,
> T'envelop and contain celestial spirits.
> Never was such a sudden scholar made;
> Never came reformation in a flood,
> With such a heady currance, scouring faults.

This deftly intricate passage is based mainly on the Baptismal Service from the *Book of Common Prayer*. Compare,

"he being dead unto sin . . . and being buried with Christ in his death, maye crucifye the olde man, and utterlye abolyshe the whole bodye of sinne",

and,

"graunt that the olde Adam in this child may be so buryed, that the new man may be raised up in him",

and,

"that all carnall affections maye dye in him, and that all thynges belonginge to the Spirite may lyve and growe in him".[1]

Again the baptismal "washing away of sins" is almost certainly responsible for the flood imagery in ll. 33–4. Not only is Baptism the "only true repentance" in Jeremy Taylor's phrase, but it is also a means of "spiritual regeneration".

This, however, is not all. Lines 28–30, besides containing an obvious allusion to the casting forth of Adam and Eve from the Garden of Eden (*Gen.* iii. 23–4), have a deeper significance. The word "consideration" is usually glossed as "reflection" or "contemplation", but this is surely an unsatisfactory gloss here. Its usage in this period points to another connotation. In the *Authorized Version* the verb "consider" is frequently used where it is almost equivalent to an exhortation to repent from evil doing or

1. *Boke of Common Prayer*, London, 1560.

at least in association with evil doing (*Deut.* xxxii. 29; *Ps.* l. 22; *Hag.* i. 5; *Isa.* i. 3; *Jer.* xxiii. 20; xxx. 24, etc.). In Donne's sermons "consideration" appears again with similar associations (*Sermons* XLV, LIV. § 2, LXIII, etc.), as it does in Hooker (*Works*, 1850, II. 242). Jeremy Taylor, *Holy Living* and *Holy Dying* uses "consideration" in numerous section headings with the meaning of spiritual contemplation, and again in the general context of turning away from sin to the good life or the good death. It is evident that the word was associated with intense spiritual contemplation, and self-examination, and not with merely thought or reflection.

Centuries earlier Bernard of Clairvaux, called upon to write an exhortation that would encourage corrupt members of the Church to repent and reform their lives, wrote *De Consideratione*. "Consideration" for St Bernard is one of the "creatures of Heaven" [1] dominated on earth by the senses. He notes that St Paul's ecstasies (*2 Cor.* xii. 4) were departures from the senses and therefore forms of consideration or divine contemplation in which men were "caught up to Paradise". Consideration, when the help of heavenly beings is given—and such angelic help is given to those who are the "heirs of salvation" (*Heb.* i. 14)—becomes perfection in the contemplation of God. There is no evidence that Shakespeare knew Bernard's work, although it was regarded as one of his most important writings and was very highly esteemed in the Middle Ages. But the linking of significant words "consideration", "angel", "paradise", "celestial spirits", indicates that Shakespeare was undoubtedly thinking of repentance and conversion in the religious sense.

In a later comment on the Prince's reformation, Canterbury says,

> for miracles are ceas'd;
> And therefore we must needs admit the means
> How things are perfected.

Had it been doctrinally admissible Canterbury would have acknowledged a miracle; as it is, he has to admit that to the Prince by the revelation of divine grace is "made known the supernatural way of salvation and law for them to live in that shall be saved" (Hooker, *Eccles. Polity*, I, xi. 5).

Was there any suggestion of a religious conversion in the historical sources? Hall and Holinshed both state briefly that the Prince "put on the new man", a phrase that had become proverbial even in the sixteenth century and may therefore have lost

1. Quotations taken from the translation of G. Lewis, 1908, pp. 130–7.

its original scriptural significance. With two exceptions the earlier chroniclers are not very informative on this point; the exceptions are Elmham's *Liber Metricus* (p. 100), which gives a mere hint in the line "rex hominem veterem sic renovare", and the *Vita et Gesta Henrici Quinti*, written some thirty years after Henry's death. In this latter work, Henry, upon his father's death, spent the day in profound grief and repentance, he shed bitter tears and admitted his errors. At night he went secretly to a man of perfect life at Westminster and received absolution. He departed completely changed, "felici miraculo convertitur" (pp. 14–15). The writer of the *Vita et Gesta* has no doubt that there was a miraculous conversion.

It is not certain that Shakespeare was acquainted with the *Vita et Gesta*, but it is highly probable (see notes on sources, p. xxxiv) at least as probable as that he knew the *Gesta*.

It may be objected that this does not solve the problem, but only introduces almost literally a *deus ex machina*. Yet if we had read *1* and *2 Henry IV* with imagination, this turn of events would not appear arbitrary and inconsistent. Let us reconsider some of Hal's speeches and actions in these two plays. In *1 Henry IV*, I. ii. 217–39, Hal's declaration that he would throw off his unyoked idle humour when the time was ripe and thereby gain wide approbation has earned him accusations of cold-hearted, selfish scheming. Admittedly the speech is a clumsy dramatic device which Shakespeare also used in *Richard III* to let Gloucester announce that he was "determined to prove a villian". But it is not cold-blooded scheming, it is a piece of self-extenuation, a failure to reform which Hal justifies as unconvincingly as Hamlet does his failure to run Claudius through while he was at prayer. It is no more and no less than St Augustine's youthful prayer of repentance, "O God, send me purity and continence—but not yet". Henry's interview with his father brings about a partial change of his attitude, but he does not see beyond physical and material ends; his atonement is to match himself in battle with Hotspur, in which he succeeds brilliantly. These taken with Vernon's praise of him, *1 Henry IV*, v. ii. 51–68, suggest perhaps not altogether fancifully, that Henry had reached physical perfection, the first of Aristotle's three ways of perfection.

In *2 Henry IV*, II. ii. 51–61, we are given a clear warning not to think that Henry is a hypocrite, and in IV. iv. 67–78 Warwick's defence of the Prince's essential integrity. At the same time the Prince and Falstaff are moving farther apart, Hal has nothing to do with Falstaff's night of venery, nor with his capture of Coleville. The soliloquy on the cares of kingship shows the Prince beginning to realize his responsibilities; his profound grief (mentioned twice it should be noted), his reconciliation with his father, his committal of the powers of the law into the hands of the Lord Chief Justice, suggest again that he is attaining the second Aristotelian perfection, intellectual perfection, or as Hooker phrased it, "perfection civil and moral" (*Eccles. Polity*, I. xi. 4).

Finally, Canterbury's account in *Henry V* shows Henry's perfection, physical, intellectual and spiritual completed, he is now the "mirror of Christendom".

It could not be otherwise. Medieval and Tudor historians saw in the events they described the unfolding of God's plan, history for them was still a handmaid to theology, queen of sciences. Henry V, the epic hero and the agent of God's plan, must therefore be divinely inspired and dedicated; he is every bit as dedicated as is "pius Aeneas" to follow the divine plan of a transcendent God.

Within this all-embracing Christian Providence there was an acceptance of classical beliefs of the innate tendency of states to decay, and of the limitations and repetitions of human thoughts and emotions throughout the ages consequent on the sameness of the elements from which human bodies were formed. It was hoped that men would return to the brilliance of pagan achievement in classical times, that highest peak of human endeavour, since the conception of progress had not yet come to birth. In the meantime classical writers were models for imitation and touchstones of taste, classical figures were exemplars of human actions and passions, and the language of Cicero and Virgil, still current, foreshortened the centuries between. The modern was naturally compared with the ancient, Henry with Alexander. Calvary apart there could be no greater praise.

Only a leader of supreme genius bountifully assisted by Fortune and by the unity of his people could arrest this civic entropy and raise a state to prosperity. We do less than justice to Henry if we do not realize that in Elizabethan eyes he was just such a leader whose exploits were greater than those of other English kings, in Ralegh's words, "None of them went to worke like a Conquerour: saue onely King *Henrie* the fift".

5. SHAKESPEARE'S HENRY V

This is the man, and this his background. Let us now look more closely at Shakespeare's presentation of him in the major incidents of the play.

The conversation of Canterbury and Ely in the opening scene

establishes economically the religious conversion of Henry on the highest authority in the country, Henry's support of the Church as a true Christian monarch, and his desire for guidance from learned churchmen, a procedure warmly recommended to kings by Erasmus, Chelidonius and Hooker. Later Canterbury demolishes the French objections to Henry's claim to the throne of France, and by his authority encourages Henry to undertake a righteous war. The characters of the two prelates have been heavily assailed, but Dover Wilson is surely right in his vindication of their integrity. Hall's bitter attack on the churchmen who sought to divert Henry's attention from the Bill by advocating war with France was followed more moderately by Holinshed.[1] Shakespeare, however, alters the order of events. Canterbury on behalf of Convocation offers Henry a subsidy to help him in the war with France which is already under consideration. His speech on the Salic Law is made at Henry's request to discover the truth behind the French objections to claims already presented, and not as in Hall and Holinshed thrust forward to divert his attention from the Lollard Bill by initiating a war with France. In 1585 in very similar circumstances the Earl of Leicester asked Archbishop Whitgift whether he should advise Queen Elizabeth to fight on the side of the Low Countries against Spain. There was talk, too, of seizing Church revenues to pay for the war, but nevertheless the Church encouraged the war and offered a substantial subsidy.[2] Moreover, to portray Henry as the dupe of two scheming prelates, or as a crafty politician skilfully concealing his aims with the aid of an unscrupulous archbishop, is not consistent with claiming at the same time that he is the ideal king; indeed it is destructive of the moral epic purpose of the play.

Yet Henry has been so calumniated. His invasion of France has been stigmatized as pure aggression—though the word is somewhat worn—and Henry himself charged with hypocrisy. Now Henry does not, as Bradley alleges, adjure "the Archbishop to satisfy him as to his right to the French throne", he urges that the Archbishop should

> justly and religiously unfold
> Why the law Salic that they have in France
> Or should, or should not, bar us in our claim

1. Christopher Watson, *The Victorious actes of Henry the fift*, " coarcted out of Hall" goes further than Hall. He refers to the "panchplying porkheads" who to divert Henry's attention from the bill seek to "obnebulate his sences with some glistering vaile" (p. 100).

2. Strype, *Life and Acts of Archbishop Whitgift*, I. 434. See L. B. Campbell, *Shakespeare's Histories*, p. 268.

and the remaining twenty lines of his speech are a most solemn
warning to the Archbishop not to

> wrest, or bow your reading,
> Or nicely charge your understanding soul
> With opening titles miscreate, whose right
> Suits not in native colours with the truth.

This does not sound like hypocrisy or cynicism. The Archbishop
discharges his duty faithfully, as it stands his reasoning is im-
peccable apart from any warrant given by the precedent of
Edward III's claims. Henry is not initiating aggression, in fact
Shakespeare omits from Exeter's speech in Hall the one argument
that has a predatory savour, namely, that the fertility of France
makes it a desirable addition to the English crown. And if
Shakespeare did consider Henry's claims justified, he was thinking in agreement with Gentili, the greatest jurist of the sixteenth
century, who quite uninvited expressed his opinion that the claim
of the English kings to the French throne was legal and valid:

"... as the kings of England wished to retain their rights in the
kingdom of France ... calling themselves their kings ... and
thus they preserve a kind of civil possession. ... And that title
is not an empty one. ..."

De Iure Belli, p. 110.

Henry accepts the advice of his counsellors, but he it is who
displays his foresight by asking the right questions. Shakespeare
again adapts his sources to make Henry the first to raise the
possibility of a Scottish invasion—not merely the incursion of
marauding bands—during his absence in France, and then to
assure himself of the essential unity of the country and its capacity
to deal with such a threat.

In the presentation of the tennis balls by the French ambassadors Shakespeare has made a significant change from both Hall
and Holinshed. Holinshed places the incident before Archbishop
Chichele's speech in the Parliament of 1414, before there has been
any suggestion of invading France; Hall places it after the
speeches of Chichele, Westmoreland and Exeter, adding that,
though he cannot be certain, this "vnwise presente" among other
things may have moved Henry to be "determined fully to make
warre in Fraunce". In the play it is placed *after* Henry has determined to make war in France, it makes no difference to the issue.
Shakespeare uses it to show Henry's Christian self-control. To the
French ambassadors, uneasy lest their message may cost them
their lives, he declares:

> We are no tyrant, but a Christian king;
> Unto whose grace our passion is as subject
> As is our wretches fetter'd in our prisons.

The message itself he receives with unruffled urbanity:

> We are glad the Dauphin is so pleasant with us;
> His present and your pains we thank you for . . .

and wittily turns the jest on the sender. Henry, the ideal king, is not to be incited to war by a personal insult; he reveals remarkable self-restraint, at the same time warning the Dauphin that his refusal to treat the English claims seriously will bring about bloodshed and sorrow.

While with some insensitiveness to irony we in this modern age may excuse Henry's invasion of France as arising from his limited medieval horizons, many are less inclined to pardon his rejection of Falstaff. Although Shakespeare's original intention was to portray Falstaff larding the fields of France, no doubt discreetly distant from Henry, he must accept responsibility for the play as it is. If he were prohibited from introducing Falstaff in person into *Henry V*, why was it necessary to mention Falstaff at all? In some slight way it might be regarded as fulfilling the promise in the epilogue of *2 Henry IV* that Falstaff might "die of a sweat", or as containing a topical reference to the Oldcastle affairs, or as the best conclusion that could be made to cover the results of official interference; any or all of these might be offered as explanation. Surely the truth lies deeper. The "finer end" that Falstaff made changes the tone of the play, it deepens the emotion; indeed, it probably deepened the tone of the new matter in Act IV. The play gains in epic strength and dignity from Falstaff's death, even as the *Aeneid* gains from Dido's death, not only because both accounts are written from the heart with a beauty and power that have moved men's hearts in after time, but because Dido and Falstaff are sacrifices to a larger morality they both ignore. Some similarities too between Aeneas and Henry may be noted; both neglect their duties for pleasant dalliance; both are recalled to their duty by divine interposition; thenceforth both submit to the Divine Will—it is significant that in *Aeneid*, IV, 393, immediately after Dido's denunciation of him, Aeneas is "pius" for the first time in that book—both display a stoic self-control for which they have been charged with coldness and callousness.

Falstaff has given us medicines to make us love him, he has bewitched us with his company just as Dido bewitched the imagination of the Middle Ages. We have considered him at once too lightly and too seriously: too seriously in that we hold him in the balance against Henry and England, and too lightly in that as a corrupt flatterer he stands for the overthrow of the divinely ordained political order. Erasmus expresses the opinion of the age when he reserves his severest censures for those flatterers who corrupt a prince, the most precious possession a country has (p. 194), and whom he would punish with death. Falstaff is such a one. If Henry's conversion and acceptance of God's will mean anything at all, they must be viewed in the light of the period to see Henry's full stature, even as a reconsideration of Virgil's religion enlarges and dignifies the character of Aeneas. The medieval habit of mind did not disappear with the Renaissance and Copernicus, on the contrary it is no longer a paradox that the Renaissance was the most medieval thing the Middle Ages produced. For both Middle Ages and Renaissance religion was planned, logical and integrated with everyday life, not as it is for many of their descendants a sentimental impulse to an occasional charity. So while a place may have been found for Falstaff with his crew of disreputable followers with Henry's army, there could be no room for him in Henry's tent on the eve of Agincourt.

It has been suggested that Henry deals with the conspirators with cat-like cruelty. Now Shakespeare has deliberately added to his immediate sources the pardoning of the drunkard who reviled Henry and the merciless attitude of the conspirators towards this man. While the latter may owe something to Le Fèvre, there is nothing of the kind in Hall or Holinshed. The reason is clear enough. Henry is to be shown as the ideal prince magnanimous enough to pardon offences against his person like Pyrrhus, king of Epirus, and the conspirators are to blacken themselves by their contrasting lack of mercy. Even when to high treason Scroop adds the personal disloyalty of a beloved and trusted friend, a treachery that disgusted Henry's nobles, Henry, consistent with his mercy to the drunkard, seeks no personal revenge:

> Touching our person seek we no revenge;
> But we our kingdom's safety must so tender,
> Whose ruin you have sought, that to her laws
> We do deliver you.

Henry's threats to Harfleur sound horrible enough, but he was precisely and unswervingly following the rules of warfare as laid down by Vegetius, Aegidius Romanus and others. Harfleur he regards as his rightful inheritance, and those who withhold it from him are "guilty in defence", because they wage an "impious war".[1] He allows the besieged time to discover whether a relieving force is on its way, then warns them to surrender before he begins his main assault, which could not then be halted and which would have inevitable evil consequences. All this was in strict accord with military law:

> "This also is the reason for the law of God which provides that cities which do not surrender before they are besieged shall not be spared" (Gentili, *De Iure Belli*, p. 217).

Henry again exercises his royal clemency by requiring Exeter to "use mercy to them all".

It is in Act IV that we see the full picture of Henry as the heroic leader. The devotion and enthusiasm he inspires indeed begin earlier, before he sets foot in France. His personality has united England as never before (I. ii. 127), and already "the youth of England are on fire" eager to follow the "mirror of all Christian kings". Something of the expectation in the air of 1598, when Essex was preparing his forces for Ireland has infected the spirit of these lines. A contemporary describes such a gathering:

> "They were young gentlemen, yeomen, and yeomen's sons and artificers of the most brave sort, such as did disdain to pilfer and steal, but went as voluntary to serve of a gaiety and joyalty of mind, all which kind of people are the force and flower of a kingdom."[2]

The heavy losses before Harfleur by battle and dysentery, the "rainy marching in the painful field", the frightening size of the French army which might well have disheartened Henry's men, only united them closer still. Henry shares their dangers and is accepted into their fellowship which his exhilaration and leadership had made so strong. He shares too in the grim jesting of men bound in spirit in the eye of danger, who hobnob sociably with the Almighty, of Lord Astley at Edgehill and of the English soldier at Fontenoy, who, as the French troops levelled their firearms at the motionless English ranks, stepped forward and exclaimed, "For what we are about to receive may the Lord make us truly thankful". Henry's men are "taking no thought for raiment" for if God gives them victory they will have the coats off the Frenchmen's backs, and if not He will otherwise provide robes for them in Heaven.

Nobleman and common soldier alike are inspired by Henry's

1. See note to III. iii. 15.
2. Quoted without reference, P. Alexander, *Shakespeare's Punctuation*, 1945, p. 1.

gay and gallant spirits. Among the English nobles there is a courteous loyalty to each other quite unlike the sparrow squabbling of the French nobles, their preoccupation with vain boasting and their lack of foresight and order. Salisbury, the "winter lion" of *2 Henry VI*, goes "joyfully" into battle, and Westmoreland unwishes five thousand of the men he had previously desired. Henry himself sums up the heart of the matter in the memorable words,

"We few, we happy few, we band of brothers",

words that have come to stand for so much that is English. Dover Wilson recalls Churchill's famous epitaph on those who "left the vivid air signed with their honour" in the summer of 1940, "Never in the field of human conflict was so much owed by so many to so few", as coming from the same national mint. But it is older than Shakespeare, it is pure Hall. Listen to his last words on Henry V:

"yet neither fyre, rust, nor frettying time shall amongest Englishmen ether appall his honoure or obliterate his glorye whiche in so fewe yeres and brief daies achived so high adventures and made so great a conquest".

The words are English but the mood is older and universal, it is the note of epic heroism that sounded at Thermopylae, at Maldon, and in a pass by Rouncesvalles.

While Henry infuses courage into his men, he is not without unease of soul. The conversation with Bates, Court and Williams forces him to examine his conscience on his responsibility for those who are to die in the coming battle, and to complain how little his subjects understand the hard duties of a king in their interests. Militarily his position is desperate: his enemy has selected the time and place for battle, his men are heavily outnumbered, tired and weakened by disease and lack of food. His faith in the righteousness of his cause is strained to the uttermost, and in prayer he pleads that his father's sin of usurpation may not be remembered against him. His courage is magnificent, and his extraordinary self-control has not always been acknowledged. He does not unpack his heart and curse like a drab, nor flutter Volscian dovecots, nor unseam his enemies from the nave to the chaps, he is no tragic warrior hero, he is the epic leader strong and serene, the architect of victory.

For all his self-control he is moved to rage by the treacherous attack on the boys and lackeys in his tents, and, fearing for the safety of his army, gives the harsh order to kill the prisoners. Dover Wilson's comment is valuable:

> "The attack is historical; and Fluellen's exclamation, 'Tis expressly against the law of arms, 'tis as arrant a piece of knavery, mark you now, as can be offert!', is in accordance with much contemporary comment on the battle, which shows that the treacherous assault left a deep stain upon the chivalry of France. Thus any lingering doubt about Henry's action is blotted from the minds of even the most squeamish in the audience . . .".

Gower's remark, "the king most worthily hath caused every soldier to cut his prisoner's throat. O! 'tis a gallant king", shows wholehearted approval of Henry's promptness in decision and his resolute determination. The rage of the epic hero leading to the slaughter of the enemy within his power is not without Virgilian precedent (see *Aeneid*, X and XII).

Exeter's account of the deaths of York and Suffolk also touches Henry to tears. The purpose of the description, for which there is no warrant in any of the sources of the play, seems to have been overlooked. It is not, as has been supposed, an imitation of the moving and presumably successful description of the heroic deaths of Talbot and his son in *1 Henry VI*, iv. vi. and vii. York and Suffolk die in the right epic way, their love "passing the love of women" is fulfilled in death. The surviving heroes, in epic style, mourn their death at once so fitting, so sadly beautiful, so "pretty and sweet", a phrase recalling at once that other pair of heroes who "were lovely and pleasant in their lives, and in their death they were not divided".

The Henry of Act v is to many a disappointment, indeed the whole act, it is suggested, is an anticlimax. Dover Wilson defends it rather unconvincingly as a good mixture, and, following Hudson, praises Henry's overflowing spirits and frankness in the wooing scene as a convincing picture of the humorous-heroic man in love. This is so, but the truth lies deeper. The Christian prince to complete his virtues must be married. Bouvaisteau, following Aegidius Romanus, is most emphatic on this point. Erasmus agrees, though he discounts the value of alliances secured by marriage; in this he differs from other theorists. The brisk and joyous wooing promises a happy marriage, though both Henry and Katharine have themselves well under control. In fact, Henry's remark that the eloquence of Kate's lips moves him more than the eloquence of the French Council may be a glance at what some chroniclers openly stated, that Katharine's beauty was used to try to make Henry lessen his demands. Henry's earlier proverbial reference to himself as the king of good fellows may show that he fully appreciates this point that Katharine proverbially is the queen of beggars.

This marriage in particular seals the union of two Christian countries with momentous possibilities for Christendom then divided by schism. Henry's letter to Charles as related by Hall puts the matter clearly:

> "Sometymes the noble realmes of Englande & of Fraunce were united, whiche nowe be separated and deuided, and as then they were accustomed to be exalted through the vniversall worlde by their glorious victories, and it was to theim a notable vertue to decore and beautifye the house of God . . . and to set a concorde in Christes religion" (xliiiʳ).

The Treaty of Troyes saw Henry as the most powerful monarch in Europe, he had built unity by force of arms, by his inspiring military genius, and by the grace of God. He was now the complete Christian monarch, "the mirror of christendom". It is this completion that necessitated Act v, it was not implicit in Agincourt.

The character of Henry has not, of course, been "deduced" from the writings of Erasmus, Chelidonius and others, but it is significant that where Shakespeare adds to his historical sources, the intruding passage or episode has an apt parallel with passages from these writers. Even some of his omissions, notably the absence of reference to the English archers to whom the victory was mainly due, can be construed as helping to enlarge the stature of Henry. It is also not without significance that the Henry of *Henry V* is a complete and balanced contrast in character and appearance with Richard II in the first play of the tetralogy.

If Henry has proved less interesting a man than Richard, it is because his problems are mainly external. The virtuous man has no obvious strife within the soul, his faith is simple and direct, he has no frailties to suffer in exposure. It is just this rectitude and uprightness, this stoicism, this unswerving obedience to the Divine Will that links both Aeneas and Henry, and has laid them both open to charges of priggishness and inhumanity. Both are complete in soul:

> omnia praecepi atque animo mecum ante peregi.

Of Henry as of Aeneas can it truly be said,

> rex erat . . . quo iustior alter
> nec pietate fuit, nec bello maior et armis.
>
> (*Aeneid*, I. 554–5).

6. FLUELLEN

Although Hotson has praised Pistol highly,[1] the only other character of any significance is Fluellen.

Fluellen, whatever his origin, whether he is a gentle caricature of Sir Roger Williams as Dover Wilson thinks (though Hotson has pointed out that he is on the wrong side in the ancients versus moderns dispute), or whether, as seems more likely, he owes a great deal to Ludovic Lloyd,[2] is a well-conceived and endearing figure. The description of Parolles, "the gallant militarist . . . that had the whole theorick of war in the knot of his scarf, and the practice in the chape of his dagger" (*All's Well*, IV. iii. 162–5) fits Fluellen admirably. His quaint pedantry and self-conscious dignity link him at once with his fellow-countrymen Glendower and Sir Hugh Evans, in what may have been national traits, but his essential manliness and love for Henry shine through his oddities. Indeed, he underlines Henry's virtues, and if the ancestry of Falstaff be Riot as has been suspected, Fluellen in the uncensored version of *Henry V* may have performed with his cudgel a service that in earlier plays would have required a dagger of lath.

7. THE SPIRITUAL SIGNIFICANCE OF THE PLAY

As for the play itself it has been roundly condemned as lacking spiritually significant ideas. This is curious. In hardly any other play of Shakespeare is there such interweaving of themes of the highest value to an Elizabethan. References, explicit and implicit, to "breed", "unity", "honour" (fame), "piety" abound throughout the play. It is noteworthy that the French display degenerate breeding, disunity, dishonour and impiety in waging a "bellum impium" against Henry the rightful inheritor. Shakespeare's description of the evils and devastation of war as having befallen or as likely to befall the French, it should be observed, is part of his insistence that war is God's scourge for securing justice among the nations: defeat and despoiling is the portion of those nations whose cause is unrighteous.

What does seem to have escaped notice is the unfolding of Henry's character. At the outset of the play his virtue after his conversion, complete though it may be, is yet cloistered, it has not sallied forth into the dust and heat. Though he makes decisions, he is dependent on the advice of others, and in spite of his self-control, the treachery of Scroop, his bedfellow, obviously hurts him and he finds it necessary to ease his mind in speech.

1. In the *Yale Review*, 1948.
2. See E. Owen, *Ludovic Lloyd*, 1931.

At Harfleur his speech is an incitement to battle, very skilfully done, but with no deeper note. By Agincourt he no longer seeks advice, he acts, he directs. His physical courage, long since proved on Shrewsbury field, is again apparent but not stressed. Shakespeare might have shown the famous combat with Alençon, but he did not; physical prowess in Henry was not at this point the most important quality. It is Henry's spiritual strength, his faith and moral courage which inspire and uphold his whole army. By sheer exaltation and power of spirit he compels his men to achieve the impossible. And this inspired mood does not leave him again, it carries him exuberantly through v. ii. to the union of England and France. No spiritual significance? Surely,

> The gods approve
> The depth, and not the tumult, of the soul.

8. HISTORICAL SOURCES

It is customary to assume that Holinshed's *Chronicles*, 1587, provided the main source from which Shakespeare drew his historical material for *Henry V*, and there are certain passages, such as Canterbury's speech on the Salic Law and part of Henry's speeches to the conspirators (ii. ii. 166–81), in which this assumption is demonstrably true. Shakespeare has taken a phrase from Holinshed which does not occur in the chronicles of other historians, or he has followed him in a historical error of which other writers are innocent.

Holinshed, as is well-known, used Hall's *Union of the Two Noble Houses of Lancaster and York*, 1548, as a source-book; some passages from Hall he used almost without changing a single word, others he summarized. There are, therefore, some passages in *Henry V* in which it is impossible to tell whether Shakespeare has used Hall or Holinshed. Most of the historical matter in the play is common to both chroniclers, but of the two Holinshed alone contains the effect of the countermining (iii. ii. 64–8), Westmoreland's wish for more men (iv. iii. 16–18), the Constable's seizing of a banner from a trumpeter (iv. ii. 61–2), and Henry's threat to the French horsemen (iv. vii. 57–67). Generally speaking, Shakespeare's use of Holinshed suggests that he was working with a copy of the *Chronicles* open before him. Canterbury's speech on the Salic Law, for example, is a verse paraphrase in which the least possible alteration has been made to the words of the original.

But Shakespeare used Hall and not Holinshed for the conversation between Henry and his nobles (i. ii. 136–70), and for the Constable's description of the English soldiers (iv. ii. 16–24, 33–4).

In various other places occur phrases or lines obviously based on Hall (see notes to i. i. 4, 72; ii. 102, 125–7, 146–62, 250–97, 263; 2 Chorus 6; ii. iv. 106–9; iii. vii. 150–4; iv. i. 295–98; iii. 91–4, 113). Shakespeare, in fact, knew his Hall so well that odd phrases and scraps of information came spontaneously into his thought and reappeared in the play. Even when he is paraphrasing Holinshed, his pen sets down a spelling peculiar to Hall (i. ii. 45, 52). In short, by far the greater part of the historical matter in the play derives from Hall either directly or at second hand through Holinshed with very little alteration.

Shakespeare too caught something of Hall's ardent spirit. Hall's stress on the theme of unity—a second title for the play might well be the "Union of the two noble Kingdoms of England and France"—is not to be found in Holinshed.

In Hall the theme of honour, one of the leading themes of the play, is strongly emphasized, particularly in Henry's oration before Agincourt. The contrast between Richard II and Henry V implicit in the balance of the four plays is put forward by Hall (xxxiii^v).[1] Shakespeare's debt to Holinshed is in effect superficial, Hall is the source of his inspiration.

There are a few other chronicles and some early biographies of Henry from which Shakespeare must in some way have drawn information.

The *Henrici Quinti Angliae Regis Gesta*, usually called the *Gesta*, was written by a chaplain who accompanied Henry on his first campaign. Traces of a possible knowledge of the *Gesta* occur at iii. vi. 46; iv. i. 76; iv. iii. 17, 76. Dover Wilson suggests further traces at iii. ii. 62–63; iii. iii. 1–43; iv. iii. 111; v. 19, but they do not seem convincing.

Another biography written approximately thirty years after Henry's death was the *Vita et Gesta Henrici Quinti*, at first errone-ously attributed to Elmham and now usually referred to as by Pseudo-Elmham. This work has already been mentioned in con-nexion with Henry's conversion (p. xx). Shakespeare's phrasing at ii. ii. 111–12 recalls a phrase in this work. Although the claims of Stowe's *Annals* and of Titus Livius' *Vita* have been pressed as sources for the description of Henry's arrival at Dover, 5 Chorus 9–13, Pseudo-Elmham gives an account much nearer to Shake-speare's than either. Finally, the episode of the kiss in the wooing scene v. ii. 265, may have been suggested by Pseudo-Elmham's account of the Melun meeting.

There are two rather doubtful occasions on which material may

1. Tillyard, p. 234, mentions this contrast, but it is susceptible of much more detailed treatment than he gives it.

have been drawn from Elmham's *Liber Metricus* (see notes to III. i. 33–4 and IV. iii. 111).

Similarly, the references that Dover Wilson finds to Titus Livius, *Vita Henrici Quinti*, the Frenchmen's boasts of the excellence of their horses and armour, III. vii. 1 ff; the Constable's seizing of a banner from a trumpeter, IV. ii. 60; and the description of Henry's arrival at Dover already mentioned, 5 Chorus 9–13, all seem doubtful whether they are drawn direct from the Latin version or from the English translation of 1513, *The First English Life of King Henry the Fifth*. On the other hand, a much more likely borrowing occurs in 4 Chorus 28–47.

A few possible borrowings remain: from the *Brut* in I. ii. 255; from Fabyan's *Chronicle*, 1516 in IV. i. 307; and from the French chronicler Le Fèvre. Le Fèvre's chronicle has already been mentioned (p. xxv) as a possible source for Henry's treatment of the conspirators. Le Fèvre was present with Henry at Agincourt, and his comparison of Henry's discipline with that of the Romans is curiously parallel to Fluellen's views in IV. i. 66–84.

9. PREVIOUS PLAYS ON HENRY V

The history of Henry V had been dramatized before 1599. We know nothing of the play Nashe had in mind when he referred to "Henrie the fifth . . . represented on the Stage, leading the French king prisoner, and forcing both him and the Dolphin to sweare fealty" (*Works*, ed. McKerrow, 1904, I. 213), nor of "harey the Vth", a new play which the Admiral's men were acting from the winter of 1595 to July 1596 (Chambers, *Eliz. Stage*, II. 144–5). It is impossible to say, therefore, whether Shakespeare was in any way influenced by these plays. But it has been claimed that he was indebted to another play, the *Famous Victories of Henry V*, though recent criticism inclines to the belief that his debt was not to the *Famous Victories* as we have it, but to the original play on which the *Famous Victories* was based.

The *Famous Victories*, entered in the Stationers' Registers on 14 May 1594, survives in an edition dated 1598, which states on its title page, "As it was plaide by the Queenes Maiesties Players". It is clearly a "bad quarto". With the exception of the scene between Henry and Katharine, the text is so corrupt and full of repetitions that it may even have been reconstructed from an author's plot of the kind represented by the so-called *Philander, King of Thrace*.

The general soundness of the wooing scene may be accounted for by supposing that the boy who took Katharine's part helped in the reconstruction. The original play was probably the one referred to in *Tarlton's Jests*, 1638, Sig. C 2-3 in which Tarleton himself took down the clown's part and deputized on one occasion for the Lord Chief Justice. This would put the play before 1588, the year in which Tarleton died.

Dover Wilson considers that the *Famous Victories* is a version of two plays belonging to the Queen's men which were compressed into one for performance in the provinces. The original two plays, he suggests, were acquired about 1592 by Lord Strange's men in the same way as they had acquired Greene's *Orlando Furioso*. Shakespeare, therefore, could have drawn upon these two original plays for *1* and *2 Henry IV* and *Henry V*. However this may be, the *Famous Victories* and the first quarto of *Henry V* came into being in a similar way to earn a little money for dishonest members of the company.

The play covers the same historical period as Shakespeare's trilogy, but makes no mention of the Percy rebellion, the conspiracy against Henry V, and the siege of Harfleur. It is closest to *Henry V* in the tennis balls incident and in the wooing scene (see Appendix, p. 165). There are a few verbal and other similarities (I. ii. 239, 255, 306; IV. vii. 83–5), but rather fewer than between it and *1* and *2 Henry IV*. The scene between Dericke and the French soldier has obvious resemblances to Pistol's capture of M. le Fer.

On the whole, it seems best to adopt the view first put forward by Morgan (*Some Problems of Shakespeare's 'Henry IV'*, 1924) that resemblances between Shakespeare's three plays and the *Famous Victories* have arisen because all four plays have borrowed in varying measure from an earlier play now lost.

10. THE NATURE OF THE QUARTO AND FOLIO TEXTS— EVIDENCE OF ALTERATIONS IN THE FOLIO TEXT— FALSTAFF ORIGINALLY INCLUDED

Four early texts of *Henry V* exist, three quarto editions Q1 (1600), Q2 (1602), Q3 (1619, title page 1608), and the First Folio, F1 (1623). Q2 and Q3 are reprints with some few corrections of Q1, and the nature of the corrections indicates that they were set up independently from Q1.

Although the origin and nature of the Q text has aroused much discussion, it seems evident that it is derived from the same text that was later printed in the Folio. It is a "bad" quarto, that is a corrupt version of the play presumably concocted by one or two members of the company from memory. In spite of Price's contention to the contrary,[1] there is no convincing evidence that shorthand played a part in the transmission of the Q text; on the contrary, there is a great deal of evidence that the text was compiled from memory.[2]

The speeches of Exeter and Gower are much closer to the text than those of any others, and it has been suspected that the actors taking parts in the play were the ones who put together the Q text and betrayed the Company by selling it to Millington and Busby. Certain omissions show that the play had been cut for compression, possibly for censorship, and to reduce the number of actors' parts. Generally there is a lowering of pitch, a substitution of cliché and the common currency of daily speech for the more heightened style of the Folio.

In brief, the Q version may well be based on a cut form of the play used by the company for a reduced cast on tour in the provinces.

Readings from the Q text, therefore, cannot be relied upon to correct the Folio, though occasionally Q may, by preserving the general sense of a passage, lead to an improved reading of a passage that is doubtful in the Folio (see note to II. i. 36, "here").

The Folio text forms the basis of all modern editions. It has certain characteristics which suggest that it was set up from Shakespeare's own draft, or "foul papers", from which the playhouse scribe frequently made an acting or "prompt" copy. Thus there is no scene division (the erroneous act division was undoubtedly added in the printing house).[3] One or two unusually descriptive stage directions, "scaling ladders at Harfleur", "the king with his poore soldiers", together with some unusual spellings ("mervailous", II. i. 46; "Deules", II. iii. 32; "Deule", II. iii. 36; "aunchiant", III. ii. 82; "moth", IV. i. 186; "vawting", V. ii. 139, etc.) are presumably the work of the author, since a professional playhouse scribe would tend to simplify unusual spellings in his copy for the sake of clarity. Finally, there are a number of misprints and errors which can be corrected by reference to Shakespeare's style of letter formation[4] ("mare" (name), II. i. 25; "here" (hewne), II. i. 36; "pasterns" (postures), III. vii. 12).

On the other hand, these spellings and errors together with some colloquialisms and oaths are scattered unevenly throughout

1. *Text of Henry V*, 1920.

2. Duthie's view that there are bibliographical links between Q and F texts is inconclusive. See his *The Bad Quarto of Hamlet*, p. 53, n. 2.

3. E. E. Willoughby, *The Printing of the First Folio of Shakespeare*, 1932.

4. Cf. J. Dover Wilson, *The Manuscript of Shakespeare's "Hamlet"*, 1934.

the play. Of colloquialisms in the sixty-three lines of II. iii. there
are about six, while in the whole of Act I there are about four.
Some inequality of distribution is due to the comic or formal
nature of the scenes, but inequality in the comic scenes which are
otherwise comparable is unexpected. Again, there are a few
errors that are more likely to be committed by a scribe than by a
compositor: the anticipation of a word or part of a word, "th",
I. ii. 74; "And", I. ii. 212; "Noblish", III. i. 17; "with", IV. vii.
80; and the misplacing of two lines, IV. iii. 13–14.

While the assumption that the copy was the author's "foul
papers" is generally acceptable, it is not impossible that some
portions may have been a playhouse transcript.

There is one other complicating factor, for the evidence points
clearly to some use of Q text, and particularly of Q3, in the copy
for F. The correspondences between Q3 and F are small and
various, but cumulatively convincing. There are agreements in
unusual or erroneous words or phrases ("brother of", II. iv. 75);
identity or close similarity in stage directions ("*Enter the Boy*", II. i.
80); anomalous lineation (the positioning of "*Nym*, Pish" within
the last line of the preceding speech, II. i. 40); the unnecessary
indentation of IV. viii. 108 in F, explicable only in terms of a
deleted speech-heading in Q2, 3; common variations in speech
headings (*Pi*, II. i. 101); common mislineation (II. iv. 129–30);
common variations in the use of italics and roman for proper
names in the text; common peculiar spellings ("owse", I. ii. 164);
and common unusual punctuation ("quoth I?", II. iii. 18).

It is not easy to see how F combined its use of Q3 with the
manuscript which served as its main authority. A. S. Cairncross,
who has pointed out these correspondences, argues that the manuscript was used to correct the quarto by someone in the printing-
house, and that the corrected quarto was then used as copy for F.
He goes further in suggesting that copies of two quartos, Q3 and
Q2, were used for this purpose, but the evidence presented for
the use of Q2 is slight. A more detailed treatment of Cairncross's
views will be found in Appendix IV.

There are signs that the play may have undergone alterations
in those parts involving Pistol and his "irregular humorists",
Fluellen, the "internationals", and the three soldiers, Bates,
Court and Williams. The evidence is of various kinds and may
perhaps best be dealt with in the order in which it appears in the
play.

The Chorus to Act II states that the scene is now transferred to
Southampton, thence to France and finally back once more to
England (ll. 35–8) ending with a couplet:

for if we may,
We'll not offend one stomach with our play.

Then a further couplet, obviously added later, warns the audience
that the move to Southampton is not to take place "till the king
comes forth", i.e. II. ii. What may be called the original Chorus
describes an act of three scenes, (i) in Southampton, (ii) in France,
(iii) in England, but as the act is now, there are four scenes, (i) in
London, (ii) in Southampton, (iii) in London, (iv) in France, so
that even the final couplet does not accurately describe the course
of events. Now there are in II. i and iii, a number of spellings of the
kind Shakespeare used[1] ("Mervailous", II. i. 46; "Deules", II.
iii. 32) together with errors perhaps due to the misreading of
Shakespeare's hand ("mare", II. i. 25; "hewne", II. i. 36; "Table",
II. iii. 17) and the frequent use (fourteen times) of the colloquial-
ism "a' " (he) by the Hostess and the Boy in II. iii. The only
other place where "a' " is used with frequency is in the Boy's
soliloquy in III. ii (four times). This suggests that II. i. and iii.
are very close to Shakespeare's autograph, and that they are
additions taking the place of an original scene iii some of which is
perhaps incorporated in the present II. i.

Fluellen's appearance at III. ii. 20 raises difficulties. He cannot
remain on the stage during the Boy's soliloquy, yet he is given
no re-entry notice with Gower (l. 57), and this failure to indicate
the re-entry of a character does not occur elsewhere in the play.
He is unannounced, and the abject terror in Pistol's appeal (ll.
22–5) loses much of its humour unless the audience knows who
Fluellen is. Ancient Pistol, it will be remembered, is a sutler (II. i.
111–12) and it is certainly odd to find him in the breach with
assault troops.

All this suggests that the scene as far as the Boy's soliloquy
(l. 28) has been altered, and that the Boy's soliloquy itself has
been added, probably to prepare the audience for the deaths of
Bardolph and Nym.

The "international" episode that immediately follows is probably additional. It includes oaths which would not have escaped
the eye of the Master of Revels unless the passage had been added
after he gave his licence to act. Fluellen's speeches here contain
only one "p" for "b", although elsewhere with one exception
(III. vi. 1–60), he uses it freely. Moreover, the scene has no links
with anything else in the play, and Jamy and Macmorris do not
appear again.

1. On this see Greg, "Elizabethan Printer and his Copy", *Library*, 4th
Series, IV. 1924, pp. 102–18.

III. vi. 1–60 mentioned above contains Pistol's plea for Bardolph's life and Fluellen's discourse on Fortune. Again the lack of "p's" for "b's" suggests that it has been added.

Duthie and Wilson note that IV. i. 30–2 are a preparation for a soliloquy which in fact does not take place until l. 295, closely after another soliloquy ll. 236–90. At l. 293 Henry gives Erpingham the same order he had previously given to his brothers, ll. 25–7.

Finally, the resolution of the glove episode is confused, for Fluellen should surely have recognized Williams and remembered the challenge upon which his opinion had been asked only a few moments before.

v. i. contains Pistol's eating of the leek. It is self-contained in that it does not arise out of Pistol's insults to Fluellen in III. vi, but out of some subsequent offence (v. i. 5–12). But its conclusion is astonishing. Pistol threatens revenge, "all hell shall stir", yet the moment Fluellen and Gower have gone, he cringes in abjectness and unexpectedly complains:

> Doth Fortune play the huswife with me now?
> News have I that my Doll is dead i' the spital
> Of malady of France;
> And there my rendezvous is quite cut off.
> Old I do wax, and from my weary limbs
> Honour is cudgelled.

It was Doll indeed who went to the spital (II. i. 74–7), but Pistol, married to Nell, can hardly claim as his the lady who had already tartly informed him that she was "meat for" his master, Falstaff. So far there has been no reference to Pistol's age, and he has given no indication that would justify the statement, "Old I do wax". The one person in whose mouth this speech would be appropriate is Sir John Falstaff.

All this suggests the conclusion that Falstaff originally accompanied Henry to France, and that for some reason or other it was decided to change this and to kill him off. Act II. iii was then written and II. i, perhaps embodying part of an earlier scene, was written to prepare for it. The rest of the underplot was adapted so that Pistol could assume much of the mantle of his master. It is possible that Act III contained a comic scene before Harfleur of which we have left some portions of the opening dialogue; the rest has been replaced by the Boy's soliloquy and the "international" scene. Act IV may have contained nocturnal, incognito adventures of Henry which brought him into conflict with Falstaff. How far the conversation with the soldiers and the glove episode contain matter from the original form of the play is impossible to say. Falstaff, true to his form in *1* and *2 Henry IV*, captured M. le Fer and in v. i. was humiliated by Fluellen.

II. THE "REJECTION OF FALSTAFF"—A LINK WITH THE *Merry Wives*.

Shakespeare then did fulfil the promise in the epilogue of *2 Henry IV* to continue the story "with Sir John in it". But why was Falstaff's part removed? It is most unlikely that the removal was made for artistic and moral reasons, or because Shakespeare's company were, from 1598 to 1602, without the comedian Kemp who presumably played Falstaff in the two earlier plays. The only possible answer lies in the continued opposition of Oldcastle's descendants, the Brooke family. There is much evidence that the name Oldcastle persisted in the mind of the public in spite of the alterations to *1* and *2 Henry IV*, and it is probable that the Brooke family, realizing that they could not stop people from calling Falstaff Oldcastle, determined to prevent Falstaff appearing on the stage in a third play, and in this they were successful.

This, however, is not quite the end of the affair. It is safe to assume that Shakespeare's audience was well acquainted with the Oldcastle–Falstaff story. It must have been one of the best jokes of the decade in London. One suspects that the players let it be known that *Henry V* had also run counter to the wishes of the Brooke family, and that any shortcomings were to be attributed to the activities of its members. In this way they both advertised the play and safeguarded themselves.

The illness and death of Falstaff look like the result of an agreement with the Brookes that Shakespeare should not introduce Falstaff in person, but would be permitted to give the old rogue an ending that might, in some measure of the letter if not in the spirit, fulfil the promise in the Epilogue to *2 Henry IV*, "for anything I know Falstaff shall die of a sweat." The Hostess's description is immortal, and the whole play is deepened in tone as a result. Yet the temptation to have one last jest at the expense of Oldcastle was irresistible. There could be no doubt that the audience would be breathlessly savouring every word for a topical hit. It came. The hostess, admitting in reply to the Boy, that Falstaff "did in some sort, indeed, handle women", adds magnificently "but then he was rheumatic, and talked of the whore of Babylon". The F spelling "rumatique" gives the pronunciation ū (compare the quibble in *Julius Caesar*, I. ii. 155, on "room" and "Rome"). The insulting reference to the Church of

Rome in "whore of Babylon" completes the last glance at the Lollard Oldcastle.

This continued opposition of the Brooke family gives significance to the story of Queen Elizabeth's interest in the *Merry Wives*: "This comedy was written at her command, and by her direction, and she was so eager to see it acted that she commanded it to be finished in fourteen days" (Dennis, Epistle Dedicatory, *The Comical Gallant*, 1702). In other words, the Queen, well aware of what had happened to *Henry V*, and perhaps yielding to requests, so far over-ruled the protests of the Brooke family as to give royal authority for the revival of Falstaff in a setting of domestic comedy. The result was the *Merry Wives*, in which Shakespeare rang the last changes on the Oldcastle jest. To Simple who has asked to speak with Falstaff the Host replies, "There's his chamber, his house, his castle . . ." (IV. v. 6–7). But the joke that must have brought the house down was the jealous Ford's selection of a nom de guerre by which to be known to Falstaff, "tell him my name is Brook, only for a jest". And the Host's reply drives the point home, ". . . and thy name shall be Brook. It is a merry knight. . . ."

One can imagine, too, the fun that the actor who played Falstaff extracted from the latter's toying with the name Brook (II. ii. 152–61). Indeed one wonders whether there is not some sly allusiveness in the pursuit of Falstaff by the jealous Ford-Brook in defending the honour of his house.[1]

12. BIBLIOGRAPHICAL NOTE

A number of books and periodicals are referred to by using either the name of the author or a shortened title. Normally the name of the author is used. In the list of full titles below shortened titles used are given in square brackets:

APPERSON, G. L. *English Proverbs and Proverbial Phrases*, 1929.

BALDWIN, T. W. *William Shakespeare's Small Latine and Lesse Greek*, 2 vols, 1944.

Brut, The, ed. F. W. D. Brie, Early English Text Soc. Original Series. 131, 136, 1906, 1908. [*Brut*.]

CHAMBERS, SIR EDMUND. *Elizabethan Stage*, 4 vols., 1923. [*Eliz. Stage*.]

CHELIDONIUS, T. *A most excellent Hystorie of the Institution and firste beginning of Christian Princes . . . Whereunto is annexed a treatise of Peace and Warre, and another of the dignitie of Mariage*, tr. James Chillester, 1571.

1. Were the Brookes responsible for the change of Q Brooke to Broome in F?

COOPER, T. *Thesaurus linguae Romanae et Britannicae*, 1584.

DANIEL, S. *The first fowre books of the civile wars*, 1595.

ELMHAM, T. *Liber Metricus de Henrico Quinto*, ed. C. A. Cole in *Memorials of Henry V*. Rolls Series, 1858. [*Liber Metricus*.]

ERASMUS, D. *Institutio Principis Christiani, Opera*, vol. iv., 1703. *The Education of a Christian Prince*, tr. L. K. Born, 1936.

Famous Victories of Henry V, The, 1598. Students' Facsimile Edition, 1912. [*Famous Victories*.]

Gesta Henrici Quinti, ed. B. Williams, English Hist. Soc., 1850. [*Gesta*.]

GILES, C. W. SCOTT-, *Shakespeare's Heraldry*, 1950.

GREG, SIR WALTER. "Principles of Emendation in Shakespeare." *Aspects of Shakespeare*, Brit. Academy, 1933. [Greg, *Principles*.]

HALL, E. *The Union of the two noble Families of Lancaster and York*, 1548.

HOLINSHED, R. *Chronicles*, 1587.

JACOB, E. F. *Henry V and the Invasion of France*, 1947.

KINGSFORD, C. L. *The First English Life of King Henry the Fifth*, 1911 (see Titus Livius).

LE FÈVRE, J. *Chronique*, 2 vols. ed. F. Morand, 1876, 1881.

Modern Language Review. [*MLR*]

MONSTRELET, F. DE. *Chronique*, tr. T. Johnes, 1810.

MORGAN, A. E. *Some Problems of Shakespeare's "Henry IV"*, 1924.

NOBLE, RICHMOND. *Shakespeare's Biblical Knowledge*, 1935.

PRICE, H. T. *The Text of Henry V*, 1920.

PSEUDO-ELMHAM. *Vita et Gesta Henrici Quinti*, ed. Hearne, 1727.

Review of English Studies. [*RES*]

SIDNEY, SIR P. *Apologie for Poetrie*, ed. Collins, 1924. [*Apologie*.]

TITUS LIVIUS. *Vita Henrici Quinti*, ed. Hearne, 1716.

WYLIE, J. H. *The Reign of Henry the Fifth*, 3 vols. (vol. 3 completed by W. T. Waugh), 1914–29.

Reference in the textual footnotes to earlier editions of Shakespeare is made by citing the name of the editor. A few later editions such as the Warwick and the first Arden are referred to by the name of the editor of *Henry V*, i.e. Moore Smith and Evans respectively.

The following is a list of earlier editions of Shakespeare to which reference is made:

ROWE, N. *Works*. 7 vols. 1709–10 (3rd ed., 1714).

POPE, A. *Works*. 7 vols. 1723–5 (2nd ed., 1728).

THEOBALD, L. *Works*. 7 vols. 1733 (2nd ed., 1740).

HANMER, T. *Works*. 6 vols. 1743–4.

WARBURTON and POPE. *Works.* 8 vols. 1747.

JOHNSON, S. *Plays.* 8 vols. 1765.

STEEVENS, G. *Plays.* 4 vols. 1766 (ed. Reed. 1778).

CAPELL, E. *Comedies, Histories and Tragedies.* 10 vols. 1768.

RANN, J. *Plays.* 1786–94.

MALONE, E. *Plays and Poems* (ed. J. Boswell). 21 vols. 1821.

KNIGHT, C. *Works,* 8 vols. 1842.

DELIUS, N. *Shakespeares Werke.* 2 Bde. (3rd ed. 1872).

DYCE, A. *Works.* 6 vols. 1857.

STAUNTON, H. *Works.* 3 vols. 1858–60.

CLARK, W. G., GLOVER, J. and WRIGHT, W. A. *Cambridge Shakespeare.* 9 vols. 1863–6.

KEIGHTLEY, T. *Plays.* 1864.

HUDSON, H. N. *Works.* 20 vols. 1881.

MOORE SMITH, G. C. *Henry V.* Warwick Shakespeare (Gen. ed., C. H. Herford). 1893, etc.

CRAIG, W. S. *Works.* (Oxford Shakespeare.) 1904 (ed. 1916.)

EVANS, H. A. *Henry V.* Arden Edition. 1903.

WILSON, J. DOVER. *Henry V.* New Shakespeare. 1947.

KING HENRY V

DRAMATIS PERSONÆ

KING HENRY THE FIFTH.
DUKE OF GLOUCESTER, } *Brothers to the King.*
DUKE OF BEDFORD,
DUKE OF EXETER, *Uncle to the King.*
DUKE OF YORK, *Cousin to the King.*
EARLS OF SALISBURY, WESTMORELAND *and* WARWICK.
ARCHBISHOP OF CANTERBURY.
BISHOP OF ELY.
EARL OF CAMBRIDGE.
LORD SCROOP.
SIR THOMAS GREY.
SIR THOMAS ERPINGHAM, GOWER, FLUELLEN, MACMORRIS, JAMY,
    Officers in King Henry's Army.
BATES, COURT, WILLIAMS, *Soldiers in the same.*
PISTOL, NYM, BARDOLPH.
Boy.
A Herald.

CHARLES THE SIXTH, *King of France.*
LEWIS, *the Dauphin.*
DUKES OF BURGUNDY, ORLEANS, BRETAGNE *and* BOURBON.
The CONSTABLE *of France.*
RAMBURES *and* GRANDPRÉ, *French Lords.*
MONTJOY, *a French Herald.*
GOVERNOR *of Harfleur.*
Ambassadors to the King of England.

ISABEL, *Queen of France.*
KATHARINE, *Daughter to Charles and Isabel.*
ALICE, *A Lady attending on the Princess.*
*Hostess of a tavern in Eastcheap, formerly Mistress Quickly, and now
    married to Pistol.*

*Lords, Ladies, Officers, French and English Soldiers, Citizens, Mes-
    sengers, and Attendants.*

CHORUS.

SCENE: *England; afterwards France.*

Henry V] born in 1387 at Monmouth, the eldest son of Henry IV. He may have been educated at Queen's College, Oxford. During his father's banishment Richard II took him into his own household and showed him favour. For most of his father's reign he was active in campaigns against the Welsh and the rebels. On his accession, 1413, he demanded the restoration of certain French territories to the English crown, and in pursuit of his claim made three separate campaigns against the French, the first ending with the victory of Agincourt, 1415, the second ending in the Treaty of Troyes, 1420, by which he became regent and heir to the French throne, and was married to Katharine, the third ending with Henry's death from dysentery at Bois de Vincennes in 1422.

Duke of Gloucester] born 1391, the fourth and youngest son of Henry IV. Unprincipled in character yet with scholarly tastes. He was felled by Alençon at Agincourt, but saved by Henry V in person and was later present at Troyes. He died in prison, 1447.

Duke of Bedford] John of Lancaster, born 1390, the third son of Henry IV. He was appointed Lieutenant of England during the first French campaign, but took over reinforcements to Henry during the second campaign. He was an extremely able general and of great integrity of character. He died at Rouen in 1435.

Duke of Exeter] Thomas Beaufort, youngest son of John of Gaunt by Catherine Swynford. In 1410 he was Chancellor and after Henry V's accession he went on an embassy to France. After the capture of Harfleur he was made governor of it; there is some doubt whether he was present at Agincourt. He was made Duke of Exeter in 1416 and was present at the signing of the Treaty of Troyes, 1420. He died at Greenwich, 1427.

Duke of York] Duke of Aumerle, born *c.* 1373, eldest son of Edmund, Duke of York and brother of Richard, Earl of Cambridge. Henry IV pardoned him for treason and for complicity in the murder of Gloucester (Shakespeare gives a further story in *R2*). He was killed at Agincourt.

Earl of Salisbury] Thomas Montacute, born 1388, eldest son of John Montacute, Earl of Salisbury. He was employed in negotiations with the French by Henry V and was present at Agincourt. He was an extremely skilful commander and a popular leader. He was killed at the siege of Orleans, 1428.

Earl of Westmoreland] Ralph Neville, born 1364, son of John, Earl of Westmoreland. He became Warden of the West Marches, and supported Bolingbroke against Richard II and the Percies. He remained in England to defend the Marches during Henry's French campaigns, and died in 1425.

Earl of Warwick] Richard Beauchamp, born 1381. He accompanied Henry to Harfleur, and then returned to England with prisoners and spoils. He was present at the meeting at Troyes. After Henry's death the infant Henry VI was committed to his care. He died at Rouen, 1439.

Archbishop of Canterbury] Henry Chichele, born 1362, bishop of St. David's 1408, was employed as an ambassador to France by Henry V in 1413. A year later he was elevated to the Archbishopric of Canterbury, and so did not sit as Archbishop in the Leicester Parliament as Hall alleges. He founded All Souls College, Oxford and made benefactions to that university and to Canterbury Cathedral. He died in 1443.

Bishop of Ely] John Fordham, Bishop of Durham, 1382. In 1388 he was translated to Ely, where he died in 1435.

Earl of Cambridge] Richard, the second son of Edmund, Duke of

York. He was created Earl of Cambridge by Henry V in 1414. In 1415 he plotted to place the Earl of March on the throne, but the plot was discovered and he was executed.

Lord Scroop] Henry, third Baron Scroop of Masham, born *c*. 1376. For a time he was Treasurer, but after Henry V's accession he was sent on an embassy to France. He was executed in 1415.

Sir Thomas Grey] of Heton, Northumberland, the son-in-law of the Earl of Westmorland. He was executed in 1415.

Sir Thomas Erpingham] of Erpingham, Norfolk, born 1357. A distinguished soldier and a Steward of the Royal Household. He ordered the English battle-line at Agincourt, and gave the signal to attack. After bestowing many benefactions on Norwich, he died 1428.

Charles VI] King of France, born 1368. He became insane, and this incapacity led to strife for power between the dukes of Burgundy and Orleans. He was not present either at Agincourt or at Troyes. He died in 1422, two months after the death of Henry V.

Lewis, the Dauphin], the eldest son of Charles VI. He was not present at Agincourt, and died soon afterwards in 1415.

Duke of Burgundy] The Duke of Burgundy mentioned in III. v. 42 and IV. viii. 99, is John the Fearless, born 1371, murdered in 1419. His son, Philip the Good, born 1396, the "Charolois" of III. v. 45, and the Duke of Burgundy of v. ii, was not present at Agincourt. After the murder of his father at the instigation of the Dauphin Charles, he supported the English and helped to bring about the Treaty of Troyes. He died in 1467.

Duke of Orleans] Charles, the nephew of Charles VI, born 1391. In 1406 he married Isabella, widow of Richard II. He was involved in the factions and disputes with the Burgundians. At Agincourt he was taken prisoner and spent twenty-five years in captivity at Windsor and Pomfret, during which time he wrote some delightful French lyrics. He was ransomed in 1440 and died in 1465.

Duke of Bourbon] John, uncle of Charles VI. He was captured at Agincourt, and died in England in 1433.

Duke of Bretagne] John V de Montfort, actually step-brother to Henry by Henry IV's second wife, John's mother. He was present at Agincourt. Died 1442.

Constable of France] Charles de la Bret, son of Charles, king of Navarre and half-brother of Henry V. He commanded the French army at Agincourt, where he was killed.

Lord Grandpré] A French noble killed at Agincourt.

Lord Rambures] Master of the Crossbows at Agincourt, where he was killed.

Isabel, Queen of France], daughter of Stephen II of Bavaria, born 1370. She was present at the negotiations for the Treaty of Troyes. Her character was dissolute, and she died in poverty, 1435.

Katharine] of Valois, daughter of Charles VI, Queen of England, 1420–22, born 1401 and mother of Henry VI. By her second marriage to Owen Tudor she became the grandmother of Henry VIII.

These notes have been drawn from various sources, but I should like to acknowledge a particular debt to W. H. Thomson, *Shakespeare's Characters*, 1951.

THE LIFE OF KING HENRY
THE FIFTH

Enter PROLOGUE

O, for a Muse of fire, that would ascend
The brightest heaven of invention;
A kingdom for a stage, princes to act
And monarchs to behold the swelling scene!
Then should the warlike Harry, like himself,   5
Assume the port of Mars; and at his heels,
Leash'd in like hounds, should famine, sword, and fire
Crouch for employment.   But pardon, gentles all,

Enter Prologue] i.e. the actor who spoke the prologue. He normally wore a long black velvet cloak. See Heywood, *Four Prentices of London*, 1615, Prologue 2, " Doe you not know that I am the Prologue? Do you not see this long blacke velvet cloke upon my backe?" Later, l. 32, he announces that he is also to play the Chorus. Moore Smith, and Creizenach, *English Drama in the Age of Shakespeare*, 1916, p. 276, have both noted that in mood and substance the choruses in *H5* are unique in Elizabethan plays.

1–2. *O . . . invention*] Fire, believed to be the lightest of the four elements composing man, was associated with poets whose " erected wit " was naturally urged by a " desire, lift upward and divine ". In the Ptolemaic cosmology fire ascended in its purest and brightest form to the ninth and highest sphere, the empyrean, loosely called Heaven by Christian writers.

Shakespeare's epic-like invocation embraces the fiery, warlike nature of his theme, the divine origin of poetry, and the sublimity of the conception he hopes to achieve. More profoundly, however, the imagery symbolizes and emphasizes the theme of

royalty explicit in ll. 4–5. Chelidonius (see Introduction, p. xvi) notes that the imperial heaven is the prince " above all other heauens ", and fire has " in it a certain similitude of Royaltie " (p. 17).

2. *invention*] (*a*) A rhetorical term for the discovery of topics, (*b*) a work of the imagination. Here = poetic creation. Cf. " The Poet . . . citeth not authorities of other Histories, but euen for hys entry calleth the sweete Muses to inspire into him a good inuention " (Sidney, *Apologie*, p. 39).

4. *swelling*] magnificent.

5. *like himself*] presented in a manner worthy of his incomparable greatness. H. T. Price (*R.E.S.*, 1940, XVI, 178–81) distinguishes two main meanings of this phrase, (i) incomparable, unique, (ii) worthy of such a person

6. *port*] bearing

7–8. *Leash'd . . . employment*] A leash consisted of three hounds fastened by one thong. Cf. Holinshed, p. 567. Henry replying to the ambassadors from Rouen " declared that the goddesse of battell, called Bellona, had three handmaidens, ever of necessitie attending upon hir, as blood, fire, and famine ". Talbot,

5

The flat unraised spirits that hath dar'd
On this unworthy scaffold to bring forth   10
So great an object: can this cockpit hold
The vasty fields of France? or may we cram
Within this wooden O the very casques
That did affright the air at Agincourt?
O, pardon! since a crooked figure may   15
Attest in little place a million;
And let us, ciphers to this great accompt,
On your imaginary forces work.

9. *spirits that hath*] F; *spirits that have* Staunton; *Spirit, that hath* F 4.

1H6 IV. ii. 10–11, threatens Bourdeaux with his "three attendants, Lean famine, quartering steel, and climbing fire".

9. *flat unraised spirits*] dull, uninspired actors and playwright.

9. *hath*] Shakespeare frequently uses a singular form of the verb with a plural subject (see Abbott, *Sh. Grammar*, §§ 247, 332–6).

10. *scaffold*] a technical term for a stage. Cf. *Troil.* I. iii. 156, "scaffolage".

13. *this wooden O*] this small wooden circle. As Dover Wilson notes, this was probably the Curtain Theatre and not the Globe. The Essex references in the Chorus to Act V can hardly have been written later than June 1599, while the Globe was not completed until August or September of that year (see Introduction, p. xi).

13. *O*] a round spot or small circle.

13. *the very casques*] "even the casques or helmets; much less the men by whom they were worn" (Malone).

14. *affright the air*] Cf. *Troil.* IV. v. 4, "appalled air", and Susenbrotus, *Epitome Troporum*, 1565, p. 17, "Coelum territat armis".

15. *O, pardon!*] Part of the playful quibble on "O", "crooked figure" and "ciphers" (ll. 13, 15, 17). Perhaps it may be interpreted freely: "O", did I say, I crave your pardon for mentioning so worthless a figure (theatre) but, as you all know, a mere nought. . . .

15–16. *since . . . million*] since a mere nought may in the humble unit's position increase the value of a number to the million range. Dover Wilson quotes Peele, *Edward I* (Malone Soc.), ll. 204–5, "'Tis but a Cipher in Agrum [= a cipher in algorism or arithmetic = o], And it hath made of *10000* pounds, *100000* pounds". Cf. also *Wint.* I. ii. 6–9.

Baret, *A briefe Instruction of Arythmetike* (in *Alvearie*, 1580) makes the line of thought clear. Sig. A 8ʳ, ". . . o called a ciphre, which is no Significatiue figure of it selfe, but maketh the other figures wherewith it is joined, to increase more in value by their place . . . on euerie Compound, or Digit number the first place is from the right hand to the left, and there you must first begin to count the value of your number."

17. *ciphers . . . accompt*] mere nothings (noughts) "in comparison with this great (*a*) sum total (*b*) story" (Dover Wilson).

18. *imaginary forces*] powers of imagination. Aldis Wright notes a parallel in the Chorus to *Captain Thomas Stukely* (acted 1596):
"Your gentle favours must we needs
    entreat

Suppose within the girdle of these walls
Are now confin'd two mighty monarchies,   20
Whose high upreared and abutting fronts
The perilous narrow ocean parts asunder:
Piece out our imperfections with your thoughts;
Into a thousand parts divide one man,
And make imaginary puissance;   25
Think, when we talk of horses, that you see them
Printing their proud hoofs i' th' receiving earth;
For 'tis your thoughts that now must deck our kings,
Carry them here and there, jumping o'er times,
Turning th' accomplishment of many years   30
Into an hour-glass: for the which supply,
Admit me Chorus to this history;
Who prologue-like your humble patience pray,
Gently to hear, kindly to judge, our play.   [*Exit.*

21. *high upreared*] Pope; *high, up-reared* F.

For rude presenting such a royal
   fight
Which more imagination must supply
Than all our utmost strength can
   reach unto."
22. *perilous narrow ocean*] the English Channel. Its reputation for shipwrecks was well known, cf. *Mer.V.* III. i. 2–6; *John* v. iii. 11; *Weakest Goeth to the Wall*, ll. 2306–9.
25. *puissance*] army, forces. Here it is trisyllabic.

27. *proud*] spirited. A term frequently used of a horse. Cf. *R2*, v. v. 83; *Ven.*, l. 300.
28. *deck*] array, equip.
29 *them*] variously interpreted as referring to (*a*) thoughts, (*b*) kings. The former seems preferable but see 5 Chorus, 8–9.
30. *many years*] the events of the play extend from 1414 to 1420.
31. *for the which supply*] to aid you in which.

ACT I

SCENE I.—*London.   An Antechamber in the King's Palace.*

Enter the Archbishop of CANTERBURY *and the Bishop of* ELY.

Cant. My lord, I'll tell you; that self bill is urg'd,
Which in the eleventh year of the last king's reign
Was like, and had indeed against us pass'd,
But that the scambling and unquiet time
Did push it out of farther question.   5
Ely. But how, my lord, shall we resist it now?
Cant. It must be thought on.   If it pass against us,
We lose the better half of our possession;
For all the temporal lands which men devout
By testament have given to the Church   10
Would they strip from us; being valu'd thus:
As much as would maintain, to the king's honour,
Full fifteen earls and fifteen hundred knights,
Six thousand and two hundred good esquires;
And, to relief of lazars and weak age,   15
Of indigent faint souls past corporal toil,

ACT I

Scene 1

Act 1] Actus Primus.   Scoena prima F.   London . . . Palace] Pope.
Enter . . . Ely] Rowe;   Enter the two Bishops of Canterbury and Ely F.
8. *half*] F 1; *part* F 2.   15–16. *age, Of*] Capell; *age Of* F.

ACT I

Scene 1

The act divisions are erroneous: see Introduction, p. xxxv.   The scene divisions are the work of various editors.

London] According to Holinshed the presentation of the tennis balls was made at Kenilworth, while the other incidents in the scene took place at Leicester, 1414.   As there is no indication of locality, it seems better to follow Pope's suggestion and place it in London.

1. *self*] same.

1–19. These lines closely follow Holinshed.   See Appendix, p. 159.

2. *eleventh year*] i.e. 1410.

4. *scambling*] unruly, disordered, Cf. v. ii. 213.

15. *lazars*] lepers.

8

A hundred almshouses right well supplied;
And to the coffers of the king beside,
A thousand pounds by the year. Thus runs the bill.

Ely. This would drink deep.

Cant.   'Twould drink the cup and all.   20

Ely. But what prevention?

Cant. The king is full of grace and fair regard.

Ely. And a true lover of the holy Church.

Cant. The courses of his youth promis'd it not.
The breath no sooner left his father's body,   25
But that his wildness, mortified in him,
Seem'd to die too; yea, at that very moment,
Consideration like an angel came,
And whipp'd th' offending Adam out of him,
Leaving his body as a Paradise,   30
T' envelop and contain celestial spirits.
Never was such a sudden scholar made;

25–34. *The breath . . . faults*] see Introduction, p. xviii. *The breath . . . too* is an echo of Henry's words to his brothers in *2H4* v. ii. 123–4,

"My father is gone wild into his grave,

For in his tomb lie my affections". While the chronicles generally and the *Famous Victories* refer to Henry's change of heart on his accession as a "rebirth" or "putting on the new man", only Elmham's *Liber Metricus* has anything resembling Shakespeare's treatment of the matter. It describes the change, "rex hominem veterem sic renovare". Canterbury's speech with its elegant transitions is clearly, and most appropriately, based on the Baptismal Service of the *Book of Common Prayer*. Cf. "he, being dead unto sin . . . & being buried with Christ in his death, maye crucifye the olde man, and utterlye abolyshe the whole bodye of sinne, . . .". Again, "graunt that the olde Adam in this child may be so buryed, that the new man may be raised up in him". And, ". . . that all carnall affec-

tions maye die in him, and that all thynges belonghynge to the Spirite maye lyve and growe in him" (edn. 1560).

28. *Consideration*] See Introduction, p. xviii.

28–30. *like . . . paradise*] see *Genesis* iii. 23–4.

29. *offending Adam*] (a) the Adam of the Garden of Eden, (b) the "old Adam" or innate wickedness.

30. *Paradise*] (a) Eden, also called Paradise, (b) Paradise or Heaven, the home of celestial spirits. In Renaissance views man was a small world (microcosm) which epitomized the ninefold shell of the heavens (macrocosm) around him. Canterbury, following his quibble over Adam, ingeniously introduces the Christian Paradise in place of the normal macrocosm, and suggests that the new Henry now imbued with the Heavenly Spirit epitomises Paradise itself.

32. *scholar*] Cf. Nenna, *Nennio, or a Treatise of Nobility*, 1595, pp. 87–8, "It is certaine that the value & excellency of men, proceedeth either

Never came reformation in a flood,
With such a heady currance, scouring faults;
Nor never Hydra-headed wilfulness   35
So soon did lose his seat—and all at once—
As in this king.

Ely.   We are blessed in the change.

Cant. Hear him but reason in divinity,
And, all-admiring, with an inward wish
You would desire the king were made a prelate: 40
Hear him debate of commonwealth affairs,
You would say it hath been all in all his study:
List his discourse of war, and you shall hear
A fearful battle render'd you in music:
Turn him to any cause of policy,   45
The Gordian knot of it he will unloose,
Familiar as his garter; that, when he speaks,
The air, a charter'd libertine, is still,

---

34. *currance*] F 1 ; *currant* F 2 ; *current* F 4.

from learning or armes ". The stock
Renaissance phrase was " Tam Marti
quam Mercurio " (*I Return from
Parnassus*, l. 929).

33–4. *flood . . . faults*] Possibly an
allusion to the cleansing of the
Augean stables by Hercules who
diverted a river through them.

34. *heady currance*] headlong tor-
rent. " Currance " is an interesting
nonce word. Cf. " congreeing ", I. ii.
182, and M.F. " courance ", a flux.

35. *Hydra-headed*] many-headed,
persistent. The Hydra of Lerna
was a nine-headed monster slain by
Hercules. Each time a head was cut
off two grew in its place until Iolaus,
Hercules' companion, thrust a burning torch into the bleeding stump.

36. *seat*] throne, power.

38. *reason in divinity*] Probably a
reminiscence of Henry's theological
discussions with the imprisoned Lollard, Oldcastle, before the events of
the play. Holinshed records that
Henry " right earnestlie exhorted
him, and louinglie admonished him

to reconcile himselfe to God and to
his laws " (III. 544).

44. *render'd . . . music*] narrated
with moving eloquence.

45. *cause of policy*] intricate problem
of statecraft.

46. *Gordian knot*] To cure their misfortunes, the Phrygians by the advice
of the oracle, elected as king the first
man to approach the temple of
Jupiter in a wagon. This was the
peasant Gordius, who thereupon
dedicated his wagon to Jupiter. The
knot which fastened the yoke to the
shaft of the wagon was extremely
intricate, and it was believed that
whoever untied it would rule over
Asia. Alexander the Great cut the
knot with his sword and declared
that the legend referred to him
(Arrian, *Anabasis*, II. iii.).

48. *charter'd libertine*] licensed free-
man. Cf. *AYL* II. vii. 47–8,
        " I must have liberty
Withal, as large a charter as the
    wind ".

And the mute wonder lurketh in men's ears,
To steal his sweet and honey'd sentences;   50
So that the art and practic part of life
Must be the mistress to this theoric:
Which is a wonder how his grace should glean it,
Since his addiction was to courses vain;
His companies unletter'd, rude, and shallow;   55
His hours fill'd up with riots, banquets, sports;
And never noted in him any study,
Any retirement, any sequestration
From open haunts and popularity.

Ely. The strawberry grows underneath the nettle,   60
And wholesome berries thrive and ripen best
Neighbour'd by fruit of baser quality:
And so the prince obscur'd his contemplation
Under the veil of wildness; which, no doubt,
Grew like the summer grass, fastest by night,   65
Unseen, yet crescive in his faculty.

49. *wonder*] F; *wand'rer* Staunton's conjecture.

49–50. *mute . . . sentences*] i.e. the sound that was actually recreated in the ear.

49. *wonder*] wonderer.

51. *art and practic part of life*] practice and experience of living.

52. *mistress*] authoress, patroness.

59. *open haunts*] places frequented by common people.

59. *popularity*] mingling with the common people. Used in a derogatory sense. Cf. *1H4* III. ii. 68–9.

60. *strawberry . . . nettle*] Cf. T. Hill, *The Profitable Arte of Gardeninge*, 1572, fol. 124, "Strawberye . . . aptly groweth in shadowie places, and rather ioyeth vnder the shadow of other herbes, than by growing alone". Modern horticultural research has verified the accuracy of this observation. An apt analogy in the mouth of Ely, whose strawberry garden at Ely Place, Holborn, was well known. Cf. *R3* III. iv. 31–2.

61–2. *wholesome berries . . . quality*] Moore Smith quotes from Florio's translation of Montaigne's *Essays* (p. 581): "If it hapned (as some gardners say) that those Roses and Violets are ever the sweeter & more odoriferous that grow neere vnder Garlike and Onions, for so much as they suck and draw all the ill-sauours of the ground vnto them." Prothero, in *Shakespeare's England*, I. 373 gives a different explanation.

65–6. *Grew . . . faculty*] Steevens noted a parallel in Horace, *Odes*, Bk. I, 12, ll. 45–6,

"crescit occulte velut arbor aevo
    fama Marcelli".

The simile was well-known and appeared in several sixteenth century collections. Baldwin, II. 500–3, suggests that Shakespeare's adaptation was influenced by the gloss in Lambinus' edition of *Horace*, 1567, I. 47.

66. *Unseen . . . faculty*] Unseen by us although we know it is its nature to grow.

66. *crescive*] growing.

66. *his faculty*] its inherent power.

Cant. It must be so; for miracles are ceas'd;
     And therefore we must needs admit the means
     How things are perfected.

Ely.   But, my good lord,
     How now for mitigation of this bill   70
     Urg'd by the commons?   Doth his majesty
     Incline to it, or no?

Cant.   He seems indifferent,
     Or rather swaying more upon our part
     Than cherishing th' exhibiters against us;
     For I have made an offer to his majesty,   75
     Upon our spiritual convocation,
     And in regard of causes now in hand,
     Which I have open'd to his grace at large,
     As touching France, to give a greater sum
     Than ever at one time the clergy yet   80
     Did to his predecessors part withal.

Ely. How did this offer seem receiv'd, my lord?
Cant. With good acceptance of his majesty;
     Save that there was not time enough to hear,
     As I perceiv'd his grace would fain have done,   85
     The severals and unhidden passages
     Of his true titles to some certain dukedoms,
     And generally to the crown and seat of France,
     Deriv'd from Edward, his great-grandfather.

86. *severals*] F; *several* Pope.

67–9. *for   miracles . . . perfected*]
Protestant doctrine asserted that
miracles ceased to occur after the
revelation (see Scot, *Discoverie of
Witchcraft*, VIII. i. 25; Wm. Perkins,
Works, I. 156, 574; III. 608). Any
apparent miracles, even those " leading to the perfection of nature "
were the work of demons. Canterbury's point is that Henry's conversion proves the validity of the doctrine
that a man by purifying his mind can
attain heavenly perfection without
the aid of evil powers. (See Agrippa,
Occult Philosophy I. i.) Cf. *All's W.*
II. iii. 1–4.

72. *indifferent*] unbiased. Cf. the
phrase used by Chichele to Henry in
Hall, xxxvi[r], " Now with indeferente
eares if you wyll note . . . ".

74. *exhibiters*] introducers of the
bill. Cf. *Wiv.* II. i. 29, " Why, I'll
exhibit a bill in the parliament for
the putting down of men ".

75–81. *For . . . withal*] Sh. closely
follows Holinshed, who follows Hall
almost verbatim. The significant
phrases and words are in both.

86. *severals*] details. Cf. *Troil.* I.
iii. 180, " severals and generals ".

86. *unhidden passages*] clear and un-
disputed descent.

Ely. What was th' impediment that broke this off?   90
Cant. The French ambassador upon that instant
     Crav'd audience; and the hour I think is come
     To give him hearing: is it four o'clock?
Ely. It is.
Cant. Then go we in to know his embassy;   95
     Which I could with a ready guess declare
     Before the Frenchman speak a word of it.
Ely. I'll wait upon you, and I long to hear it.   [*Exeunt.*

SCENE II.—*The Same. The Presence Chamber.*

Enter KING HENRY, GLOUCESTER, BEDFORD, CLARENCE,
WARWICK, WESTMORELAND, EXETER, *and Attendants.*

K. Hen. Where is my gracious lord of Canterbury?
Exe. Not here in presence.
K. Hen.   Send for him, good uncle.
West. Shall we call in th' ambassador, my liege?
K. Hen. Not yet, my cousin: we would be resolv'd,
     Before we hear him, of some things of weight   5
     That task our thoughts, concerning us and France.

Enter the Archbishop of CANTERBURY *and
the Bishop of* ELY.

Cant. God and his angels guard your sacred throne
     And make you long become it!
K. Hen.   Sure, we thank you.
     My learned lord, we pray you to proceed,
     And justly and religiously unfold   10

Scene II

Enter . . . Attendants] Ed.; Enter the King, Humfrey, Bedford, Clarence,
Warwick, Westmerland, and Exeter F.   6. Enter . . . Ely] Rowe;
Enter two Bishops F.

Scene II

S.D. Clarence in F has no speaking
part, nor does he appear elsewhere in
the play.

     4. *my cousin*] Westmoreland mar-
ried Joan Beaufort, the daughter of
John of Gaunt, Henry's uncle.

Why the law Salic that they have in France
Or should, or should not, bar us in our claim.
And God forbid, my dear and faithful lord,
That you should fashion, wrest, or bow your reading,
Or nicely charge your understanding soul   15
With opening titles miscreate, whose right
Suits not in native colours with the truth;
For God doth know how many now in health
Shall drop their blood in approbation
Of what your reverence shall incite us to.   20
Therefore take heed how you impawn our person,
How you awake our sleeping sword of war:
We charge you, in the name of God, take heed;
For never two such kingdoms did contend
Without much fall of blood; whose guiltless drops 25
Are every one a woe, a sore complaint
'Gainst him whose wrongs gives edge unto the swords
That makes such waste in brief mortality.
Under this conjuration speak, my lord,
For we will hear, note, and believe in heart   30
That what you speak is in your conscience wash'd
As pure as sin with baptism.

Cant. Then hear me, gracious sovereign, and you peers,
That owe yourselves, your lives, and services
To this imperial throne.   There is no bar   35
To make against your highness' claim to France

---

27. *gives*] F; *give* Malone.   28. *makes*] F; *make* Rowe.

14. *That . . . reading*] A topical point. One of the main charges brought against the Puritans was their false interpretation of the Scriptures (see J. Bridges, *A defence of the government* . . . , 1587, p. 13).

15–16. *nicely . . . miscreate*] by subtle reasoning lay guilt upon your soul—which knows the truth to be otherwise—by putting forward illegitimate claims.

15. *understanding soul*] Possibly a glance at the " rational " soul as distinct from the souls of " growth " and " sense ". Cf. *Tw.N.* II. iii. 63, "drew three souls out of one

weaver ", and Donne, *To the Countess of Bedford*, ll. 34–5,
" But as our Soules of growth and Soules of sense
Have birthright of our reason's Soule ".

19. *approbation*] support.

21. *impawn*] pledge.

27. *wrongs*] wrong-doings.

27. *gives*] Cf. Prologue 9.

31–2. *wash'd . . . baptism*] An interesting comment in view of Canterbury's words in I. i. 25–34.

32. *sin*] original sin.

33–95. This speech follows Holinshed very closely. See Appendix, p. 160.

But this, which they produce from Pharamond,
In terram Salicam mulieres ne succedant,
" No woman shall succeed in Salic land: "
Which Salic land the French unjustly gloze   40
To be the realm of France, and Pharamond
The founder of this law and female bar.
Yet their own authors faithfully affirm
That the land Salic is in Germany,
Between the floods of Sala and of Elbe;   45
Where Charles the Great having subdu'd the Saxons,
There left behind and settled certain French;
Who, holding in disdain the German women
For some dishonest manners of their life,
Establish'd then this law; to wit, no female   50
Should be inheritrix in Salic land:
Which Salic, as I said, 'twixt Elbe and Sala,
Is at this day in Germany call'd Meissen.
Then doth it well appear the Salic law
Was not devised for the realm of France;   55
Nor did the French possess the Salic land
Until four hundred one and twenty years
After defunction of King Pharamond,
Idly suppos'd the founder of this law;
Who died within the year of our redemption   60
Four hundred twenty-six; and Charles the Great
Subdu'd the Saxons, and did seat the French
Beyond the river Sala, in the year

---

38. succedant] F 2; succedaul F 1.

45, 52. *Elbe*] Capell; *Elue* F.

37. *Pharamond*] a legendary king of the Salian Franks.

38–9. The Salic Law was actually a collection of folk laws and customs and had nothing to do with the right of succession. The French nobles who elected Philip of Valois to the throne did so to prevent the kingdom falling into the hands of a woman. They further rejected Edward III's claim through his mother, Isabella. The name Salic Law seems to have become attached to this principle later on.

40. *gloze*] gloss, interpret.

45, 52. *Elbe*] So Holinshed. The Folio reading " Elue " appears in Hall.

49. *dishonest*] unchaste. Holinshed (1587) uses " dishonest " for " un-honest " (1578). One of the indications that Shakespeare was using the second edition.

57. *four hundred one and twenty*] So Holinshed. Actually it was 379 years later, i.e. four hundred less one and twenty.

Eight hundred five.   Besides, their writers say,
King Pepin, which deposed Childeric,   65
Did, as heir general, being descended
Of Blithild, which was daughter to King Clothair,
Make claim and title to the crown of France.
Hugh Capet also, who usurp'd the crown
Of Charles the Duke of Lorraine, sole heir male   70
Of the true line and stock of Charles the Great,
To find his title with some shows of truth,
Though, in pure truth, it was corrupt and naught,
Convey'd himself as heir to th' Lady Lingare,
Daughter to Charlemain, who was the son   75
To Lewis the emperor, and Lewis the son
Of Charles the Great.   Also King Lewis the Tenth,
Who was sole heir to the usurper Capet,
Could not keep quiet in his conscience,
Wearing the crown of France, till satisfied   80
That fair Queen Isabel, his grandmother,
Was lineal of the Lady Ermengare,
Daughter to Charles the foresaid Duke of Lorraine:
By the which marriage the line of Charles the Great
Was re-united to the crown of France.   85
So that, as clear as is the summer's sun,
King Pepin's title, and Hugh Capet's claim,
King Lewis his satisfaction, all appear

72. *find*] F; *fine* Q, Pope.   74. *as heir*] Q, Pope; *as th' Heire* F.

66. *heir general*] "one who in-
herits whether his descent be through
the male or the female" (Moore
Smith).

72. *find*] furnish, provide. The Q
reading "fine" is preferred by some
editors who render it as "furbish".
This is rather strained, and it seems
better to retain the F reading, although Shakespeare does not use
"find" elsewhere in this sense.

74. *Convey'd himself*] dishonestly
gave himself out to be. Cf. *Wiv.*
I. iii. 30–1, "'Convey', the wise it
call 'Steal'! foh! a fico for the
phrase".

74. *as heir*] The F reading "as th'
Heir" is probably due to an anticipation of the following "the".

74. *Lingare*] "Lingard" in Holinshed.   Probably an "e": "d" misprint in the play.

75. *Charlemain*] Actually Charles
the bald.   The error is in Holinshed
and Hall.

76, 77. *Lewis*] a monosyllable.

77. *Lewis the Tenth*] Historically the
ninth as in Hall.   The error is
Holinshed's.

82. *Ermengare*] Ermengard in
Holinshed.   Cf. l. 74, "Lingare".

88. *his satisfaction*] see l. 80.

To hold in right and title of the female:
So do the kings of France unto this day;   90
Howbeit they would hold up this Salic law
To bar your highness claiming from the female;
And rather choose to hide them in a net
Than amply to imbar their crooked titles
Usurp'd from you and your progenitors.   95

K. Hen. May I with right and conscience make this claim?

Cant. The sin upon my head, dread sovereign!
For in the book of Numbers is it writ:
" When the man dies, let the inheritance
Descend unto the daughter." Gracious lord,   100
Stand for your own; unwind your bloody flag;
Look back into your mighty ancestors:
Go, my dread lord, to your great-grandsire's tomb,
From whom you claim; invoke his war-like spirit,
And your great-uncle's, Edward the Black Prince,   105
Who on the French ground play'd a tragedy,
Making defeat on the full power of France;
Whiles his most mighty father on a hill
Stood smiling to behold his lion's whelp

94. *imbar*] F 3, Camb.; *imbarre* F 1; *imbare* Theobald following
Warburton's conjecture; *imbace* Q 1.

93–4. *And . . . titles*] They therefore
chose to take refuge in a transparent
tangle of contradictions rather than
to admit that the law places an
absolute bar on their own claims.

94. *imbar*] Most modern editors
read " embare ", expose, as an anti-
thesis to " hide ", l. 93. This interpretation, however, misses the point
of the Archbishop's skilful oratory.
He takes up the word " bar " (l. 12)
from Henry and adroitly plays on it
(ll. 35, 42, 92). Then, having de-
molished the arguments of the French,
he shows that as they still uphold
this " bar ", they by their own
showing completely bar the claims
of their own kings. " imbar " is a
variant of " embar " (Evans), " em "
an intensive prefix.

99–100. *when . . . daughter*] Numbers

xxvii. 8: " When a man dyeth &
hath no sonne, ye shall turne his
enheritaunce vnto his daughter."
Here taken from Holinshed.

102–19. *Look . . . veins*] Probably
based on a passage in Hall,
xxxvii^r: " diminishe not youre
title, whiche your noble progenitors
so highly haue estemed. Where
fore auaunce forth your banner, . . .
conquere your inheritaunce."

103. *great-grandsire's*] Edward III's.
Henry derived his claim to the
French throne through Edward III
whose mother, Isabella, was the
daughter of Philip IV of France.

107. *defeat*] Cressy, 1346.

108. *on a hill*] Cf. Holinshed, III.
171, " he stood aloft on a windmill-
hill ".

Forage in blood of French nobility.   110
O noble English, that could entertain
With half their forces the full pride of France,
And let another half stand laughing by,
All out of work, and cold for action!

Ely. Awake remembrance of these valiant dead,   115
And with your puissant arm renew their feats:
You are their heir, you sit upon their throne,
The blood and courage that renowned them
Runs in your veins; and my thrice-puissant liege
Is in the very May-morn of his youth,   120
Ripe for exploits and mighty enterprises.

Exe. Your brother kings and monarchs of the earth
Do all expect that you should rouse yourself,
As did the former lions of your blood.

West. They know your grace hath cause and means and
        might;   125
So hath your highness; never king of England
Had nobles richer, and more loyal subjects,
Whose hearts have left their bodies here in England
And lie pavilion'd in the fields of France.

Cant. O, let their bodies follow, my dear liege,   130
With blood and sword and fire to win your right;
In aid whereof we of the spiritualty
Will raise your highness such a mighty sum

---

131. *blood*] F 3; *Bloods* F 1.

110. *Forage in*] prey on.

112. *half*] The English army was
arranged in three divisions, one of
which remained with Edward in
reserve.

114. *cold for action*] i.e. for lack of
action.

119. *thrice-puissant*] i.e. a reckoning
of the three points of relationship in
the preceding two lines.

120. *May-morn . . . youth*] Henry
was 27. Shakespeare follows the
convention, derived from classical
sources, in which youth (juventus) is
defined as the period from 17 or 23
to 46 or 42 years of age. Some
authorities divide this period into

youth and manhood.   Even so Henry
was still a youth. Cf. Ferne, *Blazon
of Gentrie*, 1586, p. 171, "Lusty green
youth from 20. till 30. yeeres."

125-7. *They . . . subjects*] Cf. Hall,
xi[r], "But sithe God hathe sent
you people, riches, municiõs of warre
and all thynges necessary . . .".

128-30. *Whose . . . follow*] Cf. Hall,
xli[r].   "[Westmoreland's] opinion
was muche noted and well digested
with the kynge, but in especiall with
his thre brethren and diuerse other
lordes beynge yonge and lusty, desir-
ous to win honor and profite in the
realme of Fraunce. . . . So that now
all men cried warre, warre, Fraunce,
Fraunce".

As never did the clergy at one time
Bring in to any of your ancestors.   135
K. Hen. We must not only arm t' invade the French,
But lay down our proportions to defend
Against the Scot, who will make road upon us
With all advantages.
Cant. They of those marches, gracious sovereign,   140
Shall be a wall sufficient to defend
Our inland from the pilfering borderers.
K. Hen. We do not mean the coursing snatchers only,
But fear the main intendment of the Scot,
Who hath been still a giddy neighbour to us;   145
For you shall read that my great-grandfather
Never went with his forces into France
But that the Scot on his unfurnish'd kingdom
Came pouring, like the tide into a breach,
With ample and brim fullness of his force,   150
Galling the gleaned land with hot assays,
Girding with grievous siege castles and towns;
That England, being empty of defence,

137. *lay . . . proportions*] estimate the number of troops required.

137–9. Note that Henry is the first to raise the threat of Scottish invasion, in Hall and Holinshed it is Westmoreland.

139. *With all advantages*] with everything in his favour.

140–2. *They . . . borderers*] Cf. Hall, xi^r, " and leue my Lorde of Westmerlande and other graue capitaines of the Northe with a conuenient nombre to defende the Marches if the subtill Scottes . . . will any thyng attempt durynge your voyage and absence ".

140. *marches*] borders.

143. *coursing snatchers*] swift-riding raiders, thieving hounds. The metaphor is derived from the sport of coursing in which hares were pursued by greyhounds. The " snatch " was the term used to describe the act of seizing the quarry.

144. *main intendment*] general hostile purpose.

145. *still*] ever.

146–65. *For . . . treasuries*] Cf. Hall, xxxix^v: " Let men reade the Chronicles and peruse oure Englishe Chronographiers, & you shall finde that the Scottes haue seldom of their owne mocion inuaded or vexed England. . . . And wher they haue inuaded, as I can not deny but they have dooen, what glory or what profite succeeded of their enterprise. . . . Dauid le Bruse also entered Englande, your greate graundfather kyng Edward the third liyng at the siege of Caleis. Was not . . . kyng Dauid taken beside Durrham."

148. *unfurnish'd*] unprovided with defences.

150. *brim fullness*] so written in Shakespeare's time. Dover Wilson quotes Folio reading of *Tp.* v. i. 14.

151. *gleaned*] stripped of its defenders.

Hath shook and trembled at th' ill neighbourhood.

Cant. She hath been then more fear'd than harm'd, my
    liege;   155
    For hear her but exampled by herself:
    When all her chivalry hath been in France
    And she a mourning widow of her nobles,
    She hath herself not only well defended,
    But taken and impounded as a stray   160
    The King of Scots; whom she did send to France,
    To fill King Edward's fame with prisoner kings,
    And make her chronicle as rich with praise
    As is the ooze and bottom of the sea
    With sunken wrack and sumless treasuries.   165

Ely. But there's a saying very old and true;
        If that you will France win,
        Then with Scotland first begin:
    For once the eagle England being in prey,
    To her unguarded nest the weasel Scot   170
    Comes sneaking and so sucks her princely eggs,
    Playing the mouse in absence of the cat,

---

163. *her*] Capell following Johnson's conjecture; *their* F; *your* Q, Steevens.
166. Ely] Ed.; Bish. Ely. F; West. Capell and most modern editions.

---

154. *neighbourhood*] neighbourliness.
155. *fear'd*] frightened.
160. *impounded as a stray*] put in the parish pound (cattle pen) like a stray beast.
161. *The King . . . France*] David II was captured at Nevill's Cross, 17 October 1346, during Edward III's absence in France. He was not actually taken to France, although in the play of *Edward III* (pr. 1596) v. i. 63 ff., John Copland, his captor, is represented as bringing him to Edward at Calais.
163. *her*] The Q reading " your " was adopted by Steevens and has been approved by Price (p. 45) and Greg (*Principles*, p. 174). The F " their ", spelt " ther " (Wilson), is a possible misreading of either " her " or " your ", spelt " yor ".

The adoption of " her ", however, seems more consistent with the trend of the speech.
164. *ooze and bottom*] oozy bottom (hendiadys).
164–5. *As . . . treasuries*] Cf. *R3* i. iv. 27–8, " Inestimable stones, unvalu'd jewels All scatter'd in the bottom of the sea ".
166. Ely] The corresponding speech in Holinshed and Hall is assigned to Westmoreland. As Shakespeare has already diverged from Holinshed (see note to ll. 137–9), and as both lords and prelates are equally enthusiastic in favour of a French war, it seems unnecessary to change the F reading.
169. *in prey*] in pursuit of her prey.

To tame and havoc more than she can eat.

Exe. It follows then the cat must stay at home:
Yet that is but a crush'd necessity,   175
Since we have locks to safeguard necessaries
And pretty traps to catch the petty thieves.
While that the armed hand doth fight abroad
Th' advised head defends itself at home:
For government, though high and low and lower,   180
Put into parts, doth keep in one consent,
Congreeing in a full and natural close,
Like music.

Cant.   Therefore doth heaven divide
The state of man in divers functions,
Setting endeavour in continual motion;   185
To which is fixed, as an aim or butt,

173. *tame*] F, Dover Wilson after Greg; *tear* Rowe (ed. 3); *taint* Theobald.

173. *tame*] pierce, cut into, broach. The F reading was established by Greg (*Principles*, p. 171), who pointed out that it was an aphetic form of "attame".

174 ff. In Hall and Holinshed Exeter argues that since France conspires with Scotland against England and sends her money for that purpose, to cut off the main trunk (France) would automatically ensure the destruction of the branch (Scotland). In the play, however, Exeter merely extends Canterbury's view (ll. 155–65), and then makes an easy transition to the latter's description of the bees which is clearly the climax of the discussion. See Introduction, p. xxiii.

175. *crush'd necessity*] the need (for staying at home) is greatly diminished. Cf. *Cym.* I. i. 26–7, "Crush him together rather than unfold His measure duly".

177. *pretty*] good, ingenious.
179. *advised*] prudent, wise.
180–3. *For . . . music*] Grether, *Das Verhältnis von Shakespeares Heinrich V zu Sir T. Elyot's "Governour"*,

1938, draws attention to a passage in the *Governor* (ed. Croft, 1880) I. 42: "[the tutor] shall commende the perfecte understandinge of musike, declaringe how necessary it is for the better attaynyne the knowledge of a publike weale: which as I before have saide, is made of an ordre of astates and degrees, and, . . . conteineth in it a perfect harmony." Theobald, however, noted an even older parallel in Cicero's *De Republica* II. *De Republica* was not available in the sixteenth century, but the passage Theobald referred to was quoted by St. Augustine in *De Civitate Dei*, and thus would have been available to Shakespeare. Here is the passage in *De Civitate Dei* II, 21 (ed. Dombart), p. 80: ". . . isque concentus ex dissimillimarum vocum moderatione concors tamen efficitur et congruens: sic ex summis et infimis et mediis interiectis ordinibus, ut sonis moderata ratione civitatem consensu dissimillimorum concinere, et quae harmonia a musicis dicitur in cantu, eam esse in civitate concordiam. . . ."

Obedience: for so work the honey-bees,
Creatures that by a rule in nature teach
The act of order to a peopled kingdom.
They have a king and officers of sorts;   190
Where some, like magistrates, correct at home,
Others, like merchants, venture trade abroad,
Others, like soldiers, armed in their stings,
Make boot upon the summer's velvet buds;
Which pillage they with merry march bring home   195
To the tent-royal of their emperor:
Who, busied in his majesty, surveys
The singing masons building roofs of gold,
The civil citizens kneading up the honey,
The poor mechanic porters crowding in   200
Their heavy burdens at his narrow gate,
The sad-ey'd justice, with his surly hum,

189. *act*] F; *art* Pope.   197. *majesty*] Q, Rowe; *Maiesties* F.
199. *kneading*] F; *lading* Q.

187–204. *for so . . . drone*] It is likely
that Shakespeare is more indebted
to the description of the bees in the
fourth book of Virgil's *Georgics*, ll.
152 ff. than to Pliny, *Nat. Hist.* XI. or
to any of the innumerable borrowers
from them such as St Ambrose,
Chelidonius, Elyot or Lyly. Baldwin, II. 472–8, claims that Shakespeare was indebted to Willichius'
commentary at the beginning of the
Georgics, Bk. IV, *Opera*, Venice,
1544, pp. 141–3 since "Shakespeare
has used the same classifications and
in the same order as Willichius".
He adds that a compendious edition
containing the notes of other commentators as well was probably
used by Shakespeare since there are
some details not accounted for by
Willichius' Virgil. There are later
editions of Virgil which include
Willichius' commentary with those
of other writers.

188. *rule in nature*] instinctive polity
(Dover Wilson).

189. *act of order*] orderly action.

190. *king*] A common belief derived from Aristotle.

190. *of sorts*] of various ranks. Cf.
Chelidonius, p. 18, " they have their
king, and seeme to keepe a certaine
forme of a kingdome ".

191. *correct*] administer justice.

194. *boot*] booty, prey.

195–6. *which . . . emperor*] Cf. *Troil.*
I. iii. 81–3,
" When that the general is not like the
hive
To whom the foragers shall all repair,
What honey is expected? "

197. *busied . . . surveys*] Dover
Wilson quotes Pliny, *Nat. Hist.* XI.
17, " when all his people are busie in
labor, himselfe . . . overseeth their
workes ".

198. *singing masons*] Baldwin notes
Willichius', " Aliae sunt σειρῆνες ".

199. *kneading*] a normal term for
moulding wax according to Cooper's
Thesaurus and Baret's *Alvearie*. Probably a recollection of Virgil's earlier
passage, *Georgics* IV. 56 " et mella
tenacia fingunt ".

Delivering o'er to executors pale
The lazy yawning drone.　I this infer,
That many things, having full reference　　　　205
To one consent, may work contrariously;
As many arrows, loosed several ways,
Come to one mark; as many ways meet in one town;
As many fresh streams meet in one salt sea;
As many lines close in the dial's centre;　　　　210
So may a thousand actions, once afoot,
End in one purpose, and be all well borne
Without defeat.　Therefore to France, my liege.
Divide your happy England into four;
Whereof take you one quarter into France,　　　　215
And you withal shall make all Gallia shake.
If we, with thrice such powers left at home,
Cannot defend our own doors from the dog,
Let us be worried and our nation lose
The name of hardiness and policy.　　　　220

K. Hen. Call in the messengers sent from the Dauphin.

　　　　　　　　　　　　[Exeunt some Attendants.

Now are we well resolv'd; and by God's help,
And yours, the noble sinews of our power,
France being ours, we'll bend it to our awe
Or break it all to pieces: or there we'll sit,　　　　225
Ruling in large and ample empery
O'er France and all her almost kingly dukedoms,
Or lay these bones in an unworthy urn,
Tombless, with no remembrance over them:
Either our history shall with full mouth　　　　230

---

212. *End*] Q, Pope; *And* F.
Exeunt . . .] added Capell.

221. *Dauphin*] *Dolphin* F and elsewhere.
222. *well*] F 1; *all* F 3.

203. *executors*] executioners.
205–6. *having . . . consent*] being fully related by a common aim.
207. *loosed several ways*] shot from different directions.
210. *dial's*] sundial's.
212. *End*] The F "And" was probably an anticipation of "and" later in the line.
212. *borne*] sustained.

220. *policy*] statesmanship.
224. *ours*] i.e. by the right of inheritance.
224. *bend . . . awe*] bring it in awe of us, subdue it to our authority.
226. *empery*] sovereignty.
228. *urn*] grave.
229. *Tombless*] without a monument.

Speak freely of our acts, or else our grave,
Like Turkish mute, shall have a tongueless mouth,
Not worshipp'd with a waxen epitaph.

Enter Ambassadors of France.

Now are we well prepar'd to know the pleasure
Of our fair cousin Dauphin; for we hear   235
Your greeting is from him, not from the king.

Amb. May't please your majesty to give us leave
Freely to render what we have in charge;
Or shall we sparingly show you far off
The Dauphin's meaning and our embassy?   240

K. Hen. We are no tyrant, but a Christian king;
Unto whose grace our passion is as subject
As is our wretches fetter'd in our prisons:
Therefore with frank and with uncurbed plainness
Tell us the Dauphin's mind.

Amb.   Thus then, in few. 245
Your highness, lately sending into France,
Did claim some certain dukedoms, in the right
Of your great predecessor, King Edward the Third.
In answer of which claim, the prince our master
Says that you savour too much of your youth,   250

---

233. *waxen*] F; *paper* Q, Malone.

232. *Turkish mute . . . mouth*] To
ensure secrecy certain kinds of
slaves in the Turkish royal household
had their tongues cut out.

233. *Not . . . epitaph*] without the
honour even of a waxen epitaph,
much less one of stone or brass
(Evans). Shakespeare may be using
"waxen" in the sense of "frail" or
"perishable". Cf. *R2* I. iii. 75.

233. Enter . . .] Shakespeare com-
bines two separate embassies in one.

239. *sparingly show you far off*]
discreetly indicate in general terms.
Cf. *R3* III. v. 93, "But touch this
sparingly, as't were far off". The
Archbishop of Burges, the ambassador
in the *Famous Victories*, shows a similar
hesitancy (Sig. D3^r).

243. *is*] F; *are* Q, Rowe.

243. *is*] A singular verb followed
by a plural subject is not uncommon.
Cf. II. iv. 1, "comes the English".

250–97. Shakespeare follows Hall
in placing this incident after the
proroguing of Parliament 1414;
Holinshed reports that it took place
earlier, in fact before Henry had
considered invading France. The
text also seems closer to Hall: "the
Dolphin thinkynge Kyng Henry to
be geuen still to suche plaies and light
folies as he exercised & vsed before
the tyme that he was exalted to the
croune sente to hym a tunne of tennis
balles to plaie with, as who saied that
he coulde better skil of tennis then of
warre, and was more expert in light
games then marciall pollicy" xliv.

And bids you be advis'd: there's nought in France
That can be with a nimble galliard won;
~~You cannot revel into dukedoms there.~~
He therefore sends you, meeter for your spirit,
This tun of treasure; and, in lieu of this,　　255
Desires you let the dukedoms that you claim
Hear no more of you.　This the Dauphin speaks.

K. Hen. What treasure, uncle?

Exe.　　　　　　　　　Tennis-balls, my liege.

K. Hen. We are glad the Dauphin is so pleasant with us;
His present and your pains we thank you for:　260
When we have match'd our rackets to these balls,
We will in France, by God's grace, play a set
Shall strike his father's crown into the hazard.

---

251. *be advis'd*] consider, take care. Those editors who omit the F colon after " advis'd " interpret " informed ". Cf. 2 Chorus 12.

252. *galliard*] a lively dance (Fr gaillarde, merry). See Davies *Orchestra*, 1596, stanzas 67, 68.

255. *tun of treasure*] The word " tun " is used in Hall, xii^v, the *Famous Victories*, and in various accounts of the legend early in the fifteenth century, e.g. the *Brut*, p. 374, and Lydgate's *Poem on Henry V's Expedition* (Nicolas, *Chronicle of London from 1089 to 1483*, 1827, p. 216).

259. *so . . . us*] so given to pleasantries at our expense. Cf. *Famous Victories*, Sig. D3^v, " My lord prince Dolphin is very pleasant with me ".

261–6. *When . . . chases*] Tennis, from which modern lawn tennis is derived, was a popular game among the Elizabethan nobles. The oblong court was paved and enclosed by walls, the two shorter walls being pierced by holes or galleries called " hazards ". Netted string rackets were used to drive a leather ball stuffed with hair over a low net or rope halfway along the two longer walls. Points were scored when a ball was driven into a " hazard " or when it bounced twice (" chase "). A modified form of the game is still played.

262. *in France*] (a) the country, (b) a tennis court. Cf. Dekker, *Gull's Horn-book*, ed. 1905, p. 51, " how often you have sweat in the tennis-court with that great Lord; for indeed the sweating together in France (I mean the society of tennis) . . . ", and *Famous Victories*, Sig. D3^r,

" Yea such balles as never were tost in France,
The proudest Tennis Court shall rue it ".

263. *strike . . . hazard*] (a) score a winning point (see note ll. 261–6), (b) place his father's crown in jeopardy.

263. *crown*] (a) coin (stake money), (b) French throne. The method of scoring in royal tennis is apparently derived from the practice of betting on the game in the reign of Louis X, 1289–1316. The normal stake was a " couronne " (crown) or " paume " worth 60 sous (cf. Florio, *Second Frutes*, 1591, pp. 25–7). Each scoring point was calculated as a denier d'or (15 sous) until the first player to reach 60 sous won the final point, which was called " couronne ". Cf.

Tell him he hath made a match with such a wrangler
That all the courts of France will be disturb'd   265
With chases.   And we understand him well,
How he comes o'er us with our wilder days,
Not measuring what use we made of them.
We never valu'd this poor seat of England;
And therefore, living hence, did give ourself   270
To barbarous licence; as 'tis ever common
That men are merriest when they are from home.
But tell the Dauphin I will keep my state,
Be like a king and show my sail of greatness
When I do rouse me in my throne of France: 275
For that I have laid by my majesty
And plodded like a man for working-days,
But I will rise there with so full a glory
That I will dazzle all the eyes of France,
Yea, strike the Dauphin blind to look on us.   280
And tell the pleasant prince this mock of his
Hath turn'd his balls to gun-stones; and his soul
Shall stand sore charged for the wasteful vengeance
That shall fly with them: for many a thousand widows

Hall, xliiv, " I truste to make the hyghest croune of your countreye stoupe ".

264. *wrangler*] (*a*) opponent, (*b*) disputant in an academic exercise.

265. *courts*] (*a*) royal, (*b*) tennis, (*c*) law.

266. *chases*] (*a*) points in tennis, (*b*) disputes over claims to the crown, (*c*) hunting of the Chevy Chase variety.

267. *comes o'er us with*] throws in our face.

269–72. *We . . . home*] Ironical.

269. *seat*] throne.

274. *my sail of greatness*] the swelling powers of my greatness. Cf. *Sonnet* 86, " Was it the proud full sail of his great verse ".

275. *rouse me*] raise myself up, ascend. Cf. *2H4* IV. i. 118, " Being mounted and both roused in their seats ".

276–80. *For that . . . us*] Cf. *1H4* I. ii. 217–39, particularly the sun-image of royalty in both.

277. *like . . . working-days*] like a common man on working days.

282. *gun-stones*] Not in Hall or Holinshed but mentioned by Lydgate (Nicolas, *Chronicle of London*, 1827, p. 220) and in the *Brut*, p. 375 " and anon lette make tenysballis for the Dolfyn in alle the haste that thay mygte be maade, & that thei were harde & grete gune-stonys, for the Dolfyn to play with-alle ". At Harfleur, p. 376, " he played at tenys with his hard gune-stonez ". Nicolas, *History of the Battle of Agincourt*, 1827, p. 120, states, " an order occurs during this reign, for the forming a certain number [of gun stones] from the quarries of Maidstone ".

Shall this his mock mock out of their dear husbands;
Mock mothers from their sons, mock castles down; 286
And some are yet ungotten and unborn
That shall have cause to curse the Dauphin's scorn.
But this lies all within the will of God,
To whom I do appeal; and in whose name   290
Tell you the Dauphin I am coming on,
To venge me as I may and to put forth
My rightful hand in a well-hallow'd cause.
So get you hence in peace; and tell the Dauphin
His jest will savour but of shallow wit   295
When thousands weep more than did laugh at it.
Convey them with safe conduct. Fare you well.
                              [*Exeunt Ambassadors.*

Exe. This was a merry message.
K. Hen. We hope to make the sender blush at it.
    Therefore, my lords, omit no happy hour   300
    That may give furth'rance to our expedition;
    For we have now no thought in us but France,
    Save those to God, that run before our business.
    Therefore let our proportions for these wars
    Be soon collected, and all things thought upon   305
    That may with reasonable swiftness add
    More feathers to our wings; for, God before,
    We'll chide this Dauphin at his father's door.
    Therefore let every man now task his thought,
    That this fair action may on foot be brought.   310
                              [*Exeunt. Flourish.*

310. *Flourish*] before " Enter Chorus " F.

290–3, 303. Note Henry's insistence on the righteousness of his cause, and his frequent prayers.

292. *as I may*] See note to II. i. 15–16.

300. *omit . . . hour*] lose no favourable occasion.

304 *proportions*] forces. See l. 137.

306. Henry's speed is noted elsewhere. Cf. II. iv. 68 and *Famous Victories*, Sig. D3ᵛ, Sig. E1ᵛ.

306–7. *with . . . wings*] Cf. 2 Chorus 7; IV. iii. 112, and *Troil.* II. ii. 43–5,

              " if he do set
The very wings of reason to his heels,
And fly like chidden Mercury from Jove ".

307. *God before*] with God guiding us.

Handwritten notes at top: "From R Goss with Simon W. enter with lance / Bring on hand lights — to / foot of stage."

ACT II

Enter CHORUS

Handwritten note: "Down"

Now all the youth of England are on fire,
And silken dalliance in the wardrobe lies:
Now thrive the armourers, and honour's thought
Reigns solely in the breast of every man.
They sell the pasture now to buy the horse,   5
Following the mirror of all Christian kings,
With winged heels, as English Mercuries.
For now sits Expectation in the air,
And hides a sword from hilts unto the point
With crowns imperial, crowns and coronets,   10
Promis'd to Harry and his followers.
The French, advis'd by good intelligence

ACT II

Act II] transferred by Johnson from before the 3 Chorus.

Chorus

2. *silken dalliance . . . lies*] idle pastimes and luxurious garments are alike laid aside. Cf. *1H4* v. i. 12–13, " And made us doff our easy robes of peace, To crush our old limbs in ungentle steel ", and *Cor.* i. iv. 94.

6. *mirror . . . kings*] Probably from Hall's phrase, " mirror of Christendom " (xlix^v). Hoccleve's *Ballad to Henry V*, E.E.T.S. Extra Series LXI, *Works: Minor Poems*, 1937, p. 35 has " Mirror to Princes alle ", and elsewhere (p. 62) Henry is a " mirour of prowesse ".

6. *mirror*] pattern of perfection. The word was in common use in Shakespeare's time.

7. *winged . . . Mercuries*] In classical legend Mercury, or Hermes, was the messenger and herald of the gods. He is usually represented as wearing a winged cap and winged sandals, and as bearing a winged serpent-entwined rod. Cf. *1H4* IV. i. 104–10.

9–10. *And hides . . . coronets*] Possibly Shakespeare was thinking of the woodcut of Edward III holding a sword ringed by two crowns in the first edition of Holinshed, 1577, p. 885. On the other hand, the device of Edward III, a sword ringed by three crowns, may have been known to Shakespeare as he specifically mentions three types of crowns. Scott-Giles, *Shakespeare's Heraldry*, 1950, pp. 108–9, explains that this device was " either in allusion to the three great victories of his reign—Cressy, Neville's Cross and Poictiers —or to the kingdoms of England, France, and of the Romans, the latter crown having been offered to him by the Electors ".

9. *hilts*] Not the handle but the arms of the crosspiece guarding the hand.

12. *intelligence*] secret reports, espionage.

Of this most dreadful preparation,
Shake in their fear, and with pale policy
Seek to divert the English purposes.   15
O England! model to thy inward greatness,
Like little body with a mighty heart,
What might'st thou do, that honour would thee do,
Were all thy children kind and natural!
But see, thy fault France hath in thee found out,   20
A nest of hollow bosoms, which he fills
With treacherous crowns; and three corrupted men,
One, Richard Earl of Cambridge, and the second,
Henry Lord Scroop of Masham, and the third,
Sir Thomas Grey, knight, of Northumberland,   25
Have, for the gilt of France,—O guilt indeed!—
Confirm'd conspiracy with fearful France;
And by their hands this grace of kings must die,
If hell and treason hold their promises,
Ere he take ship for France, and in Southampton.   30
Linger your patience on; and we'll digest
Th' abuse of distance; force a play.
The sum is paid; the traitors are agreed;
The king is set from London; and the scene

---

14. *pale policy*] intrigue dictated by fear.

16. *model*] small replica. Cf. *R2* III. ii. 153-4, " that small model of the barren earth which serves as paste and cover to our bones ".

16–19. Cf. the Bastard's famous speech, *John* v. vii. 110–18, and the interesting note in Dover Wilson's New Cambridge edition of that play.

19. *kind and natural*] filial and obedient to the law of nature.

21. *hollow*] (*a*) empty, (*b*) false.

21. *bosoms*] (*a*) dresses " considered as receptacles for money or valuables " (*O.E.D.* " bosom " 3b), (*b*) seats of thoughts or feelings.

26. *gilt*] i.e. crowns.

26. *guilt*] As Dover Wilson notes " an irresistible pun to Shakespeare".

Cf. *2H4* IV. v. 127; *Mac.* II. ii. 57–8, etc.

28. *grace of kings*] Steevens compares Chapman's *Seaven Bookes of the Iliades of Homere*, 1598, Bk. I, p. 11,

" with her, the grace of kings
Wise *Ithacus* ascended too ".

31–2. *digest . . . distance*] set in order our changes of place, i.e. our breach of the unity of place. Cf. *Troil.*, Prologue 28–9,

" starting thence away
To what may be digested in a play ",
and *Ham.* II. ii. 460. There is a possible quibble on the normal meaning of " digest ".

32. *force*] compel. Dover Wilson interprets as " farce ", i.e. cram or stuff, and adds " a culinary word, following close upon ' digest ' ".

Is now transported, gentles, to Southampton   35
There is the playhouse now, there must you sit;
And thence to France shall we convey you safe,
And bring you back, charming the narrow seas
To give you gentle pass; for if we may,
We'll not offend one stomach with our play.   40
But, till the king come forth and not till then,
Unto Southampton do we shift our scene.   [*Exit.*

SCENE I.—*London.   A Street.*

Enter CORPORAL NYM *and* LIEUTENANT BARDOLPH.

Bard. Well met, Corporal Nym.

Nym. Good morrow, Lieutenant Bardolph.

Bard. What, are Ancient Pistol and you friends yet?

Nym. For my part, I care not: I say little; but when
        time shall serve there shall be smiles; but that   5
        shall be as it may.   I dare not fight; but I will
        wink and hold out mine iron.   It is a simple one;
        but what though? it will toast cheese, and it will
        endure cold as another man's sword will: and
        there's an end.   10

40. *offend one stomach*] (*a*) displease anyone, (*b*) cause anyone to be seasick.

41–2. These lines hardly agree with ll. 35–6. See Introduction, p. xxxvi.

Scene 1

For this scene and scene iii see Introduction, p. xxxvi.

2. *Lieutenant*] In III. ii. 3 Nym calls Bardolph corporal, a return to the rank he held in *2H4* III. iv. 164.

3. *Ancient*] a corruption of " ensign ", standard-bearer.

4. *I say little*] I keep my own counsel. Cf. III. ii. 37–41.

4–5. *but . . . smiles*] but when it suits my purpose I shall be friendly enough.

6–9. Nym may have had a comical stage sword.

8. *toast cheese*] Cf. *John* IV. iii. 99, " I'll so maul you and your toasting-iron ".

9. *endure cold*] Nym's sword is usually hot for its main use is the toasting of cheese, yet it will survive being drawn for its legitimate purpose. Poor quality iron has been known to snap in intense cold.

Bard. I will bestow a breakfast to make you friends,
and we'll be all three sworn brothers to France:
let 't be so, good Corporal Nym.

Nym. Faith, I will live so long as I may, that's the
certain of it; and when I cannot live any longer,   15
I will do as I may: that is my rest, that is the
rendezvous of it.

Bard. It is certain, corporal, that he is married to
Nell Quickly; and certainly she did you wrong,
for you were troth-plight to her.   20

Nym. I cannot tell; things must be as they may:
men may sleep, and they may have their throats
about them at that time; and some say knives
have edges. It must be as it may: though
patience be a tired mare, yet she will plod.   25
There must be conclusions. Well, I cannot tell.

Enter PISTOL *and Hostess.*

Bard. Here comes Ancient Pistol and his wife. Good corporal, be patient here.   How now, mine host Pistol!

Pist. Base tike, call'st thou me host?

---

13. *let it*] Rowe; *Let't* F.   25. *mare*] Q, Theobald; *name* F.
26. Hostess] Camb.; Quickly F.   28. *How . . . Pistol*] F; Nim. *How do*
you my Hoste Q.

12. *sworn brothers*] a brotherhood
of thieves. Cf. III. ii. 47, "sworn
brothers in filching".

15–16. *when . . . may*] A proverbial
expression, "He that cannot do as
he would must do as he may".
Cf. *Tit.* II. i. 106–7. (Tilley, *Elizabethan Proverb Lore*, p. 720.)

16. *rest*] last resolve. A phrase
borrowed from the game of primero,
"to set up one's rest", to stake one's
all. Cf. *Lr.* I. i. 125.

17. *rendezvous*] retreat or refuge,
last resort. Cf. v. i. 87, and *1H4*
IV. i. 57.

20. *troth-plight*] betrothed. A more
binding contract than the modern
engagement.

24–5. *though . . . plod*] to be patient

is wearisome, yet it will achieve its
object in the end.

25. *mare*] Theobald's adoption of
the Q reading implies a simple misreading on the part of the F compositor. Cf. the proverb "Patience is a
good nag, but she'll bolt" Apperson,
p. 485. The tiredness of horses was
proverbial. Cf. Tilley, *Dictionary of
Proverbs*, H. 640, 642, 662.

28. *How . . . Pistol*] The Q assigns
the corresponding speech to Nym,
and many editors follow on the
grounds that Nym is the aggressor
whereas Bardolph is the peacemaker.
It is difficult, however, to see anything offensive in this speech, and
Bardolph may well be the speaker in
his anxiety to keep the peace.

Now, by this hand I swear, I scorn the term;   30
Nor shall my Nell keep lodgers.

Host. No, by my troth, not long; for we cannot lodge
and board a dozen or fourteen gentlewomen that
live honestly by the prick of their needles, but it
will be thought we keep a bawdy-house straight.   35
O well-a-day, Lady, if he be not here now! we

    [*Nym and Pistol draw.*

shall see wilful adultery and murder committed.

Bard. Good lieutenant! good corporal! offer nothing
here.

Nym. Pish!

Pist. Pish for thee, Iceland dog! thou prick-eared cur of
Iceland!

Host. Good Corporal Nym, show thy valour and put up
your sword.

Nym. Will you shog off? I would have you solus.

(handwritten marginal note: more dog imagery)

36. Nym ... draw] added Camb. after l. 35.   39. *here*] Ed.; *here.* Knight;
hewne, F, Dover Wilson; *drawn* Hanmer.   40. Nym. *Pish*!] after *here.* l. 39 F.
41. *Iceland ... Iceland*] Steevens; *Island ... Island* F.

36. *well-a-day*] " welliday " F which
perhaps preserves a Shakespearian
spelling.

36. *here*] Most editions follow
Hanmer's emendation " drawn "
which is difficult to justify as a misreading since " h " and " d " are
totally unlike in the secretary hand.
Dover Wilson retains F reading citing
O.E.D. " hewn " 6b4 in support.
This will not do for in all the *O.E.D.*
examples " hewn " is completed by
the addition of " down " or equivalent phrase.

It is possible that the Q version of
this line, " O Lord heeres Corporall
Nims . . ." preserves in general what
happened on the stage; namely,
that the Hostess, aware of the
existing hostility between Nym and
Pistol, and of her share in it, is
startled at seeing Nym and fears a
renewal of the quarrel. It is not so
much the drawing of the sword that
alarms her, but the fact that Nym is
there at all. One may perhaps

guess that she enters triumphantly
on Pistol's arm, in the full glory of a
newly wedded wife, and, addressing
her remarks to the audience, fails at
first to see Nym.

The emendation " here " (spelt
" heere ") is put forward in the light
of the above interpretation, and on
the ground that " hewne " is a
possible misreading of " heere " in
Shakespeare's hand. For " e ":
minim errors cf. II. iii. 26; III. vii.
12; 4 Chorus 20; V. ii. 45, 77.

38. *lieutenant*] Cf. l. 27.

41. *prick-eared cur of Iceland*] pointed-
eared, long-haired lap-dog. Iceland
dogs were very hairy and inclined to
be snappish, in both presumably an
apt description of Nym.

42–3. *show . . . sword*] The Hostess
speaks more profoundly than she
intended. Valour among the " irregular humorists " was not shown
by sheathing the sword.

44. *shog off*] come along.

Pist. " Solus ", egregious dog?   O viper vile!   45
     The " solus " in thy most mervailous face;
     The " solus " in thy teeth, and in thy throat,
     And in thy hateful lungs, yea, in thy maw, perdy;
     And, which is worse, within thy nasty mouth!
     I do retort the " solus " in thy bowels;   50
     For I can take, and Pistol's cock is up,
     And flashing fire will follow.

Nym. I am not Barbason;   you cannot conjure me.
     I have an humour to knock you indifferently well.
     If you grow foul with me, Pistol, I will scour you   55
     with my rapier, as I may, in fair terms: if you
     would walk off, I would prick your guts a little,
     in good terms, as I may;   and that's the humour
     of it.

---

45. *solus*] (a) alone, (b) single, unmarried (Hotson, " Ancient Pistol ", *Yale Review*, 1948, 38, pp. 51–66).

46–50. *The solus . . . bowels*] Pistol's outburst is a parody of that part of the service of exorcism known as the " conjuratio ". The forms of exorcism varied considerably. Cf. " Signo oculos tuos, signo aures tuas signo . . . nares tuas . . . signo cor tuum " (*Malleus Maleficarum*, 1600, II. 297).

46. *mervailous*] Probably retains a Shakespearian spelling.

48. *maw*] stomach.

48. *perdy*] by God.

49. *nasty*] foul. A word of greater force in Shakespeare's time.

51. *take*] (a) cause harm or evil to befall you, curse you. Cf. *Ham.* I. i. 163, " No fairy takes ", (b) strike.

51. *cock is up*] is cocked for firing, i.e. Pistol's blood is up.

53. *Barbason*] This word occurs in *Wiv.* II. ii. 311, where it is stated to be a devil's " addition " (i.e. title). It is not given in Scot's *Discoverie of Witchcraft*, nor in the works of Wierus and Collin de Plancy's *Dic-*

tionnaire Infernal. Dover Wilson's suggestion that it is Marbas or Barbas, the fiend that appears in the form of a raging lion (see Wierus, *Pseudo monarchia*, 1583, p. 914) is probably correct. Shakespeare, however, may have confused the demon's name with that of the celebrated French knight Barbason who encountered Henry in single combat in the mines at the siege of Melun (Holinshed, III. 577).

55–6. *If . . . rapier*] If you discharge your ill-humour upon me, I will cleanse you by running my rapier through you. The barrel of a pistol was said to be foul after it had been discharged, and it was normally cleaned by a scouring-rod.

56–9. *in fair terms . . . in good terms . . . that's the humour of it*] Fashionable phrases as Moore Smith and Dover Wilson note. Cf. *2 Return from Parnassus*, ll. 1372–3, " It shal be thy task (Phantasma) to cut this gulles throate with faire tearmes " (i.e. in speech not in fact).

58–9. *that's . . . of it*] that's the mood I'm in, or that's the way things are.

Pist. O braggard vile and damned furious wight!   60
      The grave doth gape, and doting death is near;
      Therefore exhale.

Bard. Hear me, hear me what I say: he that strikes
      the first stroke, I'll run him up to the hilts, as I
      am a soldier.   [*Draws.* 65

Pist. An oath of mickle might; and fury shall abate.
      Give me thy fist, thy fore-foot to me give;
      Thy spirits are most tall.

Nym. I will cut thy throat, one time or other, in fair
      terms; that is the humour of it.   70

Pist. " Couple a gorge! "
      That is the word. I thee defy again.
      O hound of Crete, think'st thou my spouse to get?
      No; to the spital go,
      And from the powdering-tub of infamy   75
      Fetch forth the lazar kite of Cressid's kind,
      Doll Tearsheet she by name, and her espouse:
      I have, and I will hold, the quondam Quickly

---

65. Draws] added Malone.   72. *thee defy*] Q, Capell; *defie thee* F.

---

61. *gape*] opens its mouth hungrily. Cf. l. 93 and 2*H4* v. v. 58.

61. *doting death*] The idea of death loving its victims was not uncommon. Cf. *Rom.* v. iii. 103–5.

62. *exhale*] draw forth.

68. *tall*] courageous.

71. *Couple a gorge*] Typical Pistolian French.

73. *hound of Crete*] Dover Wilson quotes Golding's trans. of Ovid's *Metamorphoses*, 1565, III. 267, " And shaggie Rugge with other twaine that had a syre of Crete ".

74. *spital*] hospital.

75. *powdering-tub*] a current term for a heated tub to treat venereal diseases by sweating. Normally the powdering tub was used for salting beef.

76. *lazar kite of Cressid's kind*] leprous whore. The phrase " kite of Cressid's kind " occurs frequently (Steevens refers to Greene, *Carde of France*, 1587, IV. 132, and to Gas-

coigne, *Dan Bartholomew of Bath*, 1577, l. 69).

76. *kite*] probably a quibble (*a*) Kate or Kit, (*b*) kite, a bird of prey, (*c*) cat. The story of Troilus and Cressida, which has no classical authority, came into English with Chaucer's adaptation of it based on Boccaccio's *Filostrato*. Henryson continued Chaucer's story in his *Testament of Cresseid*, describing how Cressida was punished by Saturn and Cynthia who caused her to be afflicted with leprosy, and, cast off by Diomede, she " like a leper dwelt at the Spittail hous ". Henryson's work was published in Stowe's edition of Chaucer, 1561.

77. *Doll Tearsheet*] See 2*H4* II. iii. 165–85 and later v. iv. where she was taken to prison. Cf. also Pistol's last remark v. i. 85.

78–9. *I have and I will hold . . . for the only she*] Pistol, newly wed, has of course agreed " to have and, to hold . . . forsaking all other . . . "

For the only she; and—pauca, there's enough.
Go to.   80

Enter the Boy.

Boy. Mine host Pistol, you must come to my master,
and your hostess: he is very sick, and would to
bed. Good Bardolph, put thy face between his
sheets and do the office of a warming-pan. Faith,
he's very ill.   85

Bard. Away, you rogue!

Host. By my troth, he'll yield the crow a pudding one
of these days. The king has killed his heart.
Good husband, come home presently.

[Exeunt Hostess and Boy.

Bard. Come, shall I make you two friends? We must   90
to France together. Why the devil should we
keep knives to cut one another's throats?

Pist. Let floods o'erswell, and fiends for food howl on!

Nym. You'll pay me the eight shillings I won of you
at betting?

Pist. Base is the slave that pays.   95

Nym. That now I will have; that's the humour of it,

Pist. As manhood shall compound: push home.

[They draw.

Bard. By this sword, he that makes the first thrust,
I'll kill him; by this sword, I will.   100

79–80. *enough. Go to*] Pope; *enough to go to* F.
Hanmer.   89. Exeunt . . . Boy] Capell; Exit F.
draw] Q; Draw F.   82. *your*] F; *you*
98. *They*

79. *only she*] the one woman in the
world.

81. *my master*] i.e. Falstaff. The
Boy is Falstaff's page given him by
Prince Hal, *2H4* I. ii.

83. *thy face*] Cf. *1H4* III. iii. 27–59.

87. *he'll . . . pudding*] he (the Boy)
will become food for crows on the
gallows. A proverbial expression.

87. *pudding*] stuffed guts.

88. *killed his heart*] disheartened him
completely. Cf. *Wint.* IV. ii. 89.
Falstaff, it will be remembered, had
been rejected by Henry after the

coronation. See *2H4* v. v. 51–
77.

96. *Base . . . pays*] Steevens quotes
Heywood, *Fair Maid of the West*,
Works, 1874, II. 416, " My motto
shall be, Base is the man that pays ".
Editors have suspected that this is a
proverbial saying, but Heywood may
be echoing Pistol. It may be a
Pistolic version of " The poor man
always pays ". Cf. Clarke, *Paroemio-
logia*, 1639, p. 99.

98. *As . . . compound*] That is as
courage shall decide.

Pist. Sword is an oath, and oaths must have their course.

Bard. Corporal Nym, an thou wilt be friends, be
      friends: an thou wilt not, why then, be enemies
      with me too.   Prithee, put up.

Nym. I shall have my eight shillings I won of you at   105
      betting?

Pist. A noble shalt thou have, and present pay;
      And liquor likewise will I give to thee,
      And friendship shall combine, and brotherhood:
      I'll live by Nym, and Nym shall live by me.   110
      Is not this just? for I shall sutler be
      Unto the camp, and profits will accrue.
      Give me thy hand.

Nym. I shall have my noble?

Pist. In cash most justly paid.   115

Nym. Well then, that's the humour of't.

Re-enter Hostess.

Host. As ever you come of women, come in quickly
      to Sir John. Ah, poor heart! he is so shaked
      of a burning quotidian tertian, that it is most
      lamentable to behold.   Sweet men, come to him.   120

Nym. The king hath run bad humours on the knight;
      that's the even of it.

Pist. Nym, thou hast spoke the right;
      His heart is fracted and corroborate.

105–6. *I shall . . . betting?*] Q, added Capell.   116. *that's*] F 2; *that*
F 1.   Re-enter] Theobald;   Enter F.   117. *come of*] F 1, Dover Wilson;
came of Q, F 2.   118. *Ah*] Pope; *A* F.

101. *Sword is an oath*] Dover Wilson
compares *Ham.* I. v. 147.

105–6. *I . . . betting*] The addition
of this line from Q gives the necessary
continuity.

107. *noble*] 6s. 8d. A liberal dis-
count for cash down!

107. *present*] immediate.

110. *I'll . . . Nym*] I'll live by the
aid of a thief.   " Nim ", a thief.

111. *sutler*] seller of provisions to
the army.

112. *profits will accrue*] there will be
pickings.

119. *quotidian tertian*] The feverish

symptoms of the quotidian recur
daily while those of the tertian recur
on alternate days.   The Hostess is
thoroughly confused over the names
of the fevers.

121. *run . . . on*] vented his ill-
humour on (Moore Smith).

122. *that's . . . it*] that's the truth
of the matter.

124. *fracted and corroborate*] Editors
generally assume that Pistol is involved by his latinisms in an amusing
self-contradiction, though they tacitly
ignore the malapropism that this assumption implies.   Pistol may be

Nym. The king is a good king: but it must be as it 125
    may; he passes some humours and careers.
Pist. Let us condole the knight; for, lambkins, we will
    live.
                                                    [*Exeunt.*

SCENE II.—*Southampton. A council-chamber.*

Enter EXETER, BEDFORD, *and* WESTMORELAND.

Bed. 'Fore God, his grace is bold to trust these traitors.
Exe. They shall be apprehended by and by.

128. *Exeunt*] Not in F.

Scene II

Southampton] Pope. A council-chamber] Malone.

continuing the theme of "bad humours" mentioned by Nym, and "corroborate" may stand for "corrupted", i.e. Falstaff's grief has caused his heart to swell with ill-humours (cf. *John* IV. ii. 79–81 and *Ham.* IV. iv. 27–9); "Fracted" then would mean "abashed", "humbled", as in the medieval phrase "fractus animus".

Alternatively, the phrase may be the "broken and contrite heart" from the neck-verse psalm 51 misconstrued in Pistolic jargon.

As, however, Pistol is not guilty of a malapropism elsewhere, any possible interpretation of the phrase as it stands must be considered. The puritan Perkins, writing of repentance (*Works*, I. 378) gives a specialized meaning to the word "corroboration". "The cause why a Christian cannot quite fal away from grace, is this; after that he is sanctified he receueth from God another speciall grace which may be called Corroboration." In other words Falstaff, repentant for the last time, has humbled his "hardness of heart" ("fracted") and is receiving grace ("corroborate") ready for his translation to "Arthur's bosom".

126. *passes . . . careers*] indulges in some wild and freakish behaviour. Evans notes that "to pass a career" was a recognized phrase in horsemanship and meant to make a short gallop at full speed. He quotes Baret, *Alvearie*, 1580, for the definition, "the short turning of a nimble horse, now this way, nowe that way".

127. *condole*] with.

Scene II

An account of the plot and of the unmasking of the conspirators is given in Hall and Holinshed. Shakespeare has added the incident of the drunkard who reviled Henry and the commissions which are presented to the conspirators. He may have drawn upon Chelidonius, p. 137, who relates how a soldier was pardoned by Pyrrhus, king of Epirus, for drunkenly reviling him. Le Fèvre, I. 222–3, may also have provided an idea which Shakespeare developed. He recounts how Henry assembled his council including the conspirators and told them of a plot to seize his crown, an act of treachery

West. How smooth and even they do bear themselves!
  As if allegiance in their bosoms sat,
  Crowned with faith and constant loyalty.   5
Bed. The king hath note of all that they intend,
  By interception which they dream not of.
Exe. Nay, but the man that was his bedfellow,
  Whom he hath dull'd and cloy'd with gracious favours,
  That he should, for a foreign purse, so sell   10
  His sovereign's life to death and treachery!

  Trumpets sound.   *Enter* KING HENRY, SCROOP,
        CAMBRIDGE, GREY, *and Attendants.*

K. Hen. Now sits the wind fair, and we will aboard,
  My Lord of Cambridge, and my kind Lord of Masham,
  And you, my gentle knight, give me your thoughts:
  Think you not that the powers we bear with us   15
  Will cut their passage through the force of France,
  Doing the execution and the act
  For which we have in head assembled them?
Scroop. No doubt, my liege, if each man do his best.
K. Hen. I doubt not that; since we are well persuaded   20
  We carry not a heart with us from hence
  That grows not in a fair consent with ours;
  Nor leave not one behind that doth not wish
  Success and conquest to attend on us.
Cam. Never was monarch better fear'd and lov'd   25
  Than is your majesty: there's not, I think, a subject

---

11. Trumpets . . . Attendants] Camb.;   Sound Trumpets.   Enter the King,
Scroop, Cambridge and Gray F.   and Attendants] added Theobald.

he found it impossible to believe. If,   of March himself who informed
however, it turned out to be true, he   Henry of the plot.
asked each in turn what punishment   8. *bedfellow*] Scroop.
should be meted out to the plotters.   9. *dull'd and cloy'd*] whose appetites
The three guilty men advised a   have been satisfied and surfeited.
death so cruel that it would deter   10. *foreign purse*] So Hall and Holin-
others and thus convicted themselves.   shed, but they add that the con-
See Introduction, p. xxv.   spirators hoped to place the Earl of
  4–5. *As if . . . loyalty*] An ironic   March on the throne. Cf. ll. 155–7.
echo of 2 Chorus 21–2.   22. *grows . . . consent*] is not in
  7. *By interception*] It was the Earl   agreement.

That sits in heart-grief and uneasiness
Under the sweet shade of your government.

Grey. True: those that were your father's enemies
Have steep'd their galls in honey, and do serve you   30
With hearts create of duty and of zeal.

K. Hen. We therefore have great cause of thankfulness,
And shall forget the office of our hand,
Sooner than quittance of desert and merit
According to the weight and worthiness.   35

Scroop. So service shall with steeled sinews toil,
And labour shall refresh itself with hope,
To do your grace incessant services.

K. Hen. We judge no less. Uncle of Exeter,
Enlarge the man committed yesterday   40
That rail'd against our person: we consider
It was excess of wine that set him on;
And on his more advice we pardon him.

Scroop. That's mercy, but too much security:
Let him be punish'd, sovereign, lest example   45
Breed, by his sufferance, more of such a kind.

K. Hen. O, let us yet be merciful.

Cam. So may your highness, and yet punish too.

Grey. Sir,
You show great mercy, if you give him life,   50
After the taste of much correction.

K. Hen. Alas, your too much love and care of me
Are heavy orisons 'gainst this poor wretch!
If little faults, proceeding on distemper,

---

29. Grey] Gray F 4; Kni. F 1. | 49. *Sir*] F (l. 50).

30. *galls*] bitterness. Moore Smith quotes *Lucr.*, l. 889, " Thy honey turns to gall ".

33. *forget . . . hand*] A possible reminiscence of *Ps.* cxxxvii. Noble quotes the Genevan version, " let my right hand forget to play '.

40. *Enlarge*] set free.

40–3. Cf. Chelidonius, p. 137 and first note to this scene.

43. *on his more advice*] on his thinking better of it.

44. *security*] over-confidence. Cf.

Mac. iii. v. 32–3, " security Is mortals' chiefest enemy ".

46. *by his sufferance*] by allowing him to go unpunished.

53. *heavy orisons*] pleas that weigh heavily.

54. *proceeding on distemper*] committed while drunk.

54–7. *If . . . us*] If we may not turn a blind eye to little faults . . . how seriously must we regard premeditated capital crimes when they are brought to our notice!

Shall not be wink'd at, how shall we stretch our eye   55
When capital crimes, chew'd, swallow'd, and digested,
Appear before us?   We'll yet enlarge that man,
Though Cambridge, Scroop, and Grey, in their dear
    care
And tender preservation of our person,
Would have him punish'd.   And now to our French
    causes: 60
Who are the late commissioners?

Cam. I one, my lord:
Your highness bade me ask for it to-day.

Scroop. So did you me, my liege.

Grey. And I, my royal sovereign.   65

K. Hen. Then, Richard Earl of Cambridge, there is yours;
There yours, Lord Scroop of Masham; and, sir knight,
Grey of Northumberland, this same is yours:
Read them; and know, I know your worthiness.
My Lord of Westmoreland, and uncle Exeter,   70
We will aboard to-night.   Why, how now, gentlemen!
What see you in those papers that you lose
So much complexion?   Look ye, how they change!
Their cheeks are paper.   Why, what read you there,
That have so cowarded and chas'd your blood   75
Out of appearance?

Cam.   I do confess my fault,
And do submit me to your highness' mercy.

Grey, Scroop. To which we all appeal.

K. Hen. The mercy that was quick in us but late
By your own counsel is suppress'd and kill'd: 80
You must not dare, for shame, to talk of mercy;
For your own reasons turn into your bosoms,
As dogs upon their masters, worrying you.

58. *dear*] Dover Wilson suggests an
ironical quibble, (*a*) deeply felt, (*b*)
dire. For the latter sense cf. *R2* i. iii.
151, "dear exile".
    61. *late*] lately appointed.
    63. *it*] the written commission.
    76. *appearance*] sight.
79–81. *The mercy . . . mercy*] Cf.
Eccles. xxviii. 4, "Hee that sheweth
no mercie to a man which is like

himselfe, how dare hee aske forgive-
ness of his sinnes?"   In line with
Noble's findings, quotations are
taken from the Bishops' Bible except
where otherwise stated.
    83. *As . . . masters*] Possibly a remin-
iscence of Acteon's fate. He, having
surprised Diana bathing, was turned
by her into a stag and pursued and
killed by his own hounds.

See you, my princes and my noble peers,
These English monsters!   My Lord of Cambridge
    here,   85
You know how apt our love was to accord
To furnish him with all appertinents
Belonging to his honour; and this man
Hath, for a few light crowns, lightly conspir'd,
And sworn unto the practices of France,   90
To kill us here in Hampton: to the which
This knight, no less for bounty bound to us
Than Cambridge is, hath likewise sworn.   But O,
What shall I say to thee, Lord Scroop? thou cruel,
Ingrateful, savage and inhuman creature!   95
Thou that didst bear the key of all my counsels,
That knew'st the very bottom of my soul,
That almost might'st have coin'd me into gold
Would'st thou have practis'd on me for thy use,
May it be possible that foreign hire   100
Could out of thee extract one spark of evil
That might annoy my finger? 'tis so strange
That, though the truth of it stands off as gross
As black and white, my eye will scarcely see it.
Treason and murder ever kept together,   105
As two yoke-devils sworn to either's purpose,
Working so grossly in a natural cause

87. *him*] added F 2.   99. *use*,] Camb.; *use?* F.   107. *a natural*]
F2; *an naturall* F 1.

84. *English monsters*] unnatural creatures, abortions, of the kind displayed
to the Elizabethan public. To the
latter, monsters were invariably Afri-
can; possibly this could be traced
back to the proverb derived from
Pliny, *Historia Naturalis* II. viii. 42,
" Ex Africa semper aliquid novi ".
Henry ironically introduces the
traitors to his noblemen bitterly
emphasizing the word English. Cf.
Nashe, *Martin's Month's Mind*, Pre-
face, " These men, would I call (as
well I might) Monsters; save that in
these mischeevous daies, wherein our
Europa, is become an *Africa*, in
bringing dailie foorth newe monsters,

I can account them but ordinarie
Vermin ".
    86. *accord*] agree, consent.
    89. *light . . . lightly*] treacherous
. . . readily.
    90. *practices*] plots.
    98–9. Scroop had been Treasurer
until 1411.
    99. *Would'st . . . use*] if you had
used me for your own ends.
    100. *May*] can.
    102. *might*] could.
    102. *annoy*] hurt.
    103. *stands off as gross*] stands out
as plain.
    107–8. *Working. . . them*] working
so obviously in a cause natural to

That admiration did not hoop at them:
But thou, 'gainst all proportion, didst bring in
Wonder to wait on treason and on murder: 110
And whatsoever cunning fiend it was
That wrought upon thee so preposterously
Hath got the voice in hell for excellence:
All other devils that suggest by treasons
Do botch and bungle up damnation   115
With patches, colours, and with forms, being fetch'd
From glist'ring semblances of piety;
But he that temper'd thee bade thee stand up,
Gave thee no instance why thou should'st do treason,
Unless to dub thee with the name of traitor.   120
If that same demon that hath gull'd thee thus
Should with his lion gait walk the whole world,
He might return to vasty Tartar back,
And tell the legions: " I can never win

114. *All*] Hanmer; *And* F.

them that they aroused no outcry of
astonishment.

108. *admiration*] wonder.

108. *hoop*] whoop, outcry. Cf.
AYL. III. ii. 204.

109. *proportion*] natural order.

111–12. *And . . . preposterously*] Cf.
Pseudo-Elmham, *Vita*, p. 36, " . . .
suggestione diabolica insubversionem
Christianissimi principis . . . prodi-
torie conspirarunt ".

112. *preposterously*] unnaturally.

113. *Hath . . . voice*] has won the
vote, is acknowledged.

114. *suggest*] tempt.

115–17. *Do . . . piety*] clumsily
attempt to conceal that the treasons
will damn a man's soul by covering
them with shoddy adornments, false
pretexts, and with illusory outward
forms, mere tricks simulating the
bright outward appearances of piety.

116. *colours*] pretexts. A rhetorical term used for proofs that are
suspect. Cf. *LLL.* IV. ii. 16;
"colourable colours ". Hoccleve 5 in
his poem addressed to Oldcastle
condemns those who have perverted

him with their " sly coloured arguments " (281).

116. *fetch'd*] derived from. Probably with an echo of "fetch ", a
trick, decoy. For the construction
Moore Smith compares *1H4* I. iii.
49, " smarting with my words being
cold ".

118. *temper'd thee*] moulded you to
his will—as Falstaff Shallow. Cf.
2H4 IV. iii. 142, " I have him
already tempering between my finger
and thumb ".

118. *bade thee stand up*] ordered you
to support his cause.

120. *Unless . . . traitor*] unless it
was to confer on you the rank of
Sir Traitor.

122. *lion gait*] Cf. 1 *Pet.* v. 8,
" your adversary the devil, as a
roaring lion, walketh about, seeking
whom he may devour ".

123. *Tartar*] i.e. Tartarus, the place
of torment in classical mythology.

124. *legions*] Cf. *Mark* v. 9, Legion,
the name of the unclean spirit, " for
we are many ", and *Tw.N.* III. iv.
96–8.

A soul so easy as that Englishman's." 125
O, how hast thou with jealousy infected *quieter—hurt*
The sweetness of affiance! Show men dutiful?
Why, so didst thou: seem they grave and learned?
Why, so didst thou: come they of noble family?
brave Why, so didst thou: seem they religious? 130
Why, so didst thou: or are they spare in diet,
Free from gross passion or of mirth or anger,
Constant in spirit, not swerving with the blood,
Garnish'd and deck'd in modest complement,
Not working with the eye without the ear, 135
And but in purged judgment trusting neither?
Such and so finely bolted didst thou seem:
And thus thy fall hath left a kind of blot,
To mark the full-fraught man and best indued
With some suspicion. I will weep for thee; 140
For this revolt of thine, methinks, is like
Another fall of man. Their faults are open:
Arrest them to the answer of the law;
And God acquit them of their practices!

Exe. I arrest thee of high treason, by the name of 145
Richard Earl of Cambridge.
I arrest thee of high treason, by the name of
Henry Lord Scroop of Masham.
I arrest thee of high treason, by the name of
Thomas Grey, knight, of Northumberland. 150

Scroop. Our purposes God justly hath discover'd,
And I repent my fault more than my death;

139–40. *To . . . With*] Malone; *To make thee full fraught man, and best indued
With* F; *To mark the full-fraught man, the best endow'd, With* Capell.
148. *Henry*] Q , Theobald; *Thomas* F.   *Masham*] Rowe; *Marsham* F.

126. *jealousy*] suspicion.

127. *affiance*] trust.

134. *complement*] outward bearing
or appearance.

135. *Not . . . ear*] Not trusting the
evidence of either eye or ear alone.

137. *bolted*] sifted (like flour).
refined.

139. *To . . . indued*] It seems best
to follow Malone's emendation which
is based on that of Theobald.

" Make " for " mark " or " marke "
is a possible misreading in the secretary hand.

139. *full-fraught . . . indued*] fully
laden and endowed with the best
qualities.

143. *to . . . law*] to answer the
charges brought against them.

148. *Henry*] The F reading
" Thomas " was probably caught
from l. 150.

Which I beseech your highness to forgive,
Although my body pay the price of it.

Cam. For me, the gold of France did not seduce,   155
Although I did admit it as a motive
The sooner to effect what I intended:
But God be thanked for prevention;
Which I in sufferance heartily will rejoice,
Beseeching God and you to pardon me.   160

Grey. Never did faithful subject more rejoice
At the discovery of most dangerous treason
Than I do this hour joy o'er myself,
Prevented from a damned enterprise.
My fault, but not my body, pardon, sovereign.   165

K. Hen. God quit you in his mercy! Hear your sentence.
You have conspir'd against our royal person,
Join'd with an enemy proclaim'd, and from his coffers
Receiv'd the golden earnest of our death;
Wherein you would have sold your king to slaughter,
His princes and his peers to servitude,   171
His subjects to oppression and contempt,
And his whole kingdom into desolation.
Touching our person seek we no revenge;
But we our kingdom's safety must so tender,   175
Whose ruin you have sought, that to her laws
We do deliver you.   Get you therefore hence,
Poor miserable wretches, to your death;
The taste whereof, God of his mercy give
You patience to endure, and true repentance   180
Of all your dear offences! Bear them hence.
                    [*Exeunt Cambridge, Scroop, and Grey, guarded.*

---

159. *I*] added F 2.   176. *you have sought*] Q, Knight; *you sought*
F 1; *you three sought* F 2.   F 1; 181. Exeunt . . . guarded] Camb.;
Exit F.

155-7. Holinshed gives the details.   166-181. Close to Holinshed. See
Moore Smith notes that this plot is   Appendix, p. 161.
the beginning of the Yorkist claim to   169. *golden earnest*] advance part-
the throne, since the real motive   payment as a guarantee of further
was to place the Earl of March on   payment as the work has been
the throne.   done.
166. *quit*] acquit, absolve.   175. *tender*] cherish.
                                      181. *dear*] dire, grievous.

Now, lords, for France; the enterprise whereof
Shall be to you, as us, like glorious.
We doubt not of a fair and lucky war,
Since God so graciously hath brought to light   185
This dangerous treason lurking in our way
To hinder our beginnings.   We doubt not now
But every rub is smoothed on our way.
Then forth, dear countrymen: let us deliver
Our puissance into the hand of God,   190
Putting it straight in expedition.
Cheerly to sea; the signs of war advance:
No king of England, if not king of France.

[*Flourish.   Exeunt.*

*there's a maturing — a new
brutality and purpose & less of the puerile energy*

SCENE III.—*London.   Before a Tavern.*

Enter PISTOL, *Hostess*, NYM, BARDOLPH, *and Boy.*

Host. Prithee, honey-sweet husband, let me bring thee
  to Staines. *on road to Southampton*

Pist. No; for my manly heart doth earn.
  Bardolph, be blithe; Nym, rouse thy vaunting veins:
  Boy, bristle thy courage up; for Falstaff he is dead, 5
  And we must earn therefore. *massive void.*

193. Flourish.   Exeunt] Flourish F 1 ; Exeunt F 2.

Scene III

London . . . Tavern] Capell.   Enter . . . Boy] Capell;   enter Pistoll,
Nim, Bardolph, Boy, and Hostesse F.   3. *earn*] erne F 1 ; *yern* F 3.

183. *like*] alike, equally.
188. *rub*] obstacle. A word borrowed from the game of bowls in
which it was used to describe any
unevenness of the ground which
impeded or diverted the bowl. Cf.
John III. iv. 128–9, "Shall blow each
dust, each straw, each little rub Out
of the path ".
191. *in expedition*] in motion.
192. *the signs . . . advance*] raise
the ensigns or standards.

192. *advance*] raise. Cf. *Tp.* IV. i
178, " Advanced their eyelids ".

Scene III

See Introduction, p. xxxix.
2. *Staines*] i.e. on the road to
Southampton.
3. *earn*] grieve, mourn.
4. *vaunting veins*] brisk spirits. Cf.
IV. iii. 26.
5. *bristle*] " brissle " F. Possibly a
Shakespearian spelling.

Bard. Would I were with him, wheresome'er he is, either in heaven or in hell!

Host. Nay, sure, he's not in hell: he's in Arthur's bosom, if ever man went to Arthur's bosom. A'   10 made a finer end, and went away an it had been any christom child; a' parted ev'n just between twelve and one, ev'n at the turning o' th' tide: for after I saw him fumble with the sheets and play with flowers and smile upon his fingers' end,   15 I knew there was but one way; for his nose was as sharp as a pen, and a' babbled of green fields.

11. *a finer*] F 1, 2; *finer* F 3; *a fine* Capell.   15. *end*] F; *ends* Q, Capell.
17. *and a' babbled*] Theobald; *and a Table* F.

9-10. *Arthur's bosom*] The Hostess means Abraham's bosom. See *Luke* xvi. 19-31 for the whole parable of Dives and Lazarus. This parable and the Prodigal Son were popular with Falstaff. Cf. *1H4* III. iii. 34; IV. i. 26, etc.

11. *finer end*] i.e. than going to hell.

12. *christom child*] A child in its first month after baptism during which time it wore a white robe called a chrism-cloth (chrism, the oil then used for anointing), hence an innocent babe.

12-13. *a' parted . . . tide*] A very old belief. Cf. Pliny, *Nat. Hist.* tr. Holland, 1601, II. 98, " Hereunto addeth *Aristotle* . . . that no living creature dieth but in the refluxe and ebbe of the sea ".

14-17. *fumble . . . pen*] Shakespeare's version of a portion of the famous Hippocratic " facies " contained in the *Prognostics* where Hippocrates describes the signs of approaching death. Editions of the *Prognostics* were available in Greek, in Latin, French and possibly English translations accompanied by the commentaries of Galen and others. Christopher à Vega's Latin text (1552) has the following: " De manuum vero latione haec nosse oportet quibuscunque in acutis febribus . . . ante faciem feruntur vel venantur frustra, aut colli-

gunt festucas, aut stamina de vestibus euellunt, vel stipules de pariete carpunt, omnes malas esse atque lethales " (*Liber Prognosticon*, p. 76) and earlier, " Erit autem talis nasus gracilis in extremis " (p. 30).

Peter Lowe's translation of the latter runs, " hee shall esteeme it in perill and danger of death when the nose and the nostrils are extenuated and sharpened by the same Malady " (*The Presages of Diuine Hippocrates*, 1611, Sig. A4ᵛ.) Dover Wilson cites Lupton, *Thousand Notable Things*, 1578, Bk. IX, " . . . and his nose waxe sharpe—if he pull strawes, or the cloathes of his bedde . . . ". One wonders whether Galen's comment that the nose becomes " aquillinus " may have suggested a " quill " and thus inspired the immortal " sharp as a pen " as the Hostess' muddled version.

17. *a' babbled*] Theobald's famous emendation has received support from modern studies of the secretary handwriting. The original spelling was presumably " babld " (Note the F spelling " bable ", IV. i. 71), and the similarity between "t" and "b", " e " and " d " in that handwriting makes misreading likely (see Greg, *Principles*, pp. 129, 155, 172). Thiselton, *Notulae Criticae*, 1904, p. 14, suggested " Tatld ", his point being

"How now, Sir John?" quoth I: "what, man!
be o' good cheer." So a' cried out "God, God,
God!" three or four times: now I, to comfort him,   20
bid him a' should not think of God, I hoped there
was no need to trouble himself with any such
thoughts yet. So a' bade me lay more clothes on
his feet: I put my hand into the bed and felt
them, and they were as cold as any stone; then I   25
felt to his knees, and so upward, and upward, and
all was as cold as any stone.

Nym. They say he cried out of sack.

Host. Ay, that a' did.

Bard. And of women.   30

Host. Nay, that a' did not.

Boy. Yes, that a' did; and said they were devils
incarnate.

Host. A' could never abide carnation; 'twas a colour
he never liked.   35

Boy. A' said once, the devil would have him about
women.

Host. A' did in some sort, indeed, handle women; but

---

19. *be o' good*] Capell; *be a good* F.
Camb.; *vp-peer'd and vpward* F 1.
Rowe; Woman F.   36. *devil*] *Deule* F.

26. *upward, and upward*] Q, F 3,
32. *devils*] *Deules* F.   34. Host.]

---

that if the capital T of the F "Table"
was in the manuscript before the
compositor, a misreading of "B"
for "T" would be highly improb-
able. Bradley, *The Academy*, 21
April, 1894, and *O.E.D.* "field" 14,
sought to keep the pen image by
reading "pen on a table of green
field", interpreting "green field" in
the light of a 15th century example
as "green cloth". But "babbled
of green fields" is surely more in
character with the Falstaff who
quoted the Scriptures, who heard the
chimes at midnight, and who lost his
voice hallooing of anthems. Now he
is in the valley of the shadow, the
"green pasture" of Psalm 23 might
well be on his lips.
"Babbled" may be an unconscious

reminiscence of Fox's account of
Oldcastle's trial. Oldcastle's enemies
issued a formal repentance falsely stating that it was written by Oldcastle,
and "caused it to be blown abroad by
their feed servants, friends, and bab-
bling sir Johns". (*Acts & Monuments*
III. 338.) See further, Appendix V.
28. *of sack*] against sack.
32, 36. *devils*], *devil*] "Deules . . .
Deule" F. A Shakespearian spelling.
32–3. *devils incarnate*] This phrase,
a somewhat daring paradox, was
made, popular by Lodge, *Wits
Miserie*, 1596, Sig. B1ʳ, in which he
describes the "Devils Incarnate of
this age".
33. *incarnate*] (*a*) in the flesh, (*b*)
red.

then he was rheumatic, and talked of the whore
of Babylon.   40

Boy. Do you not remember a' saw a flea stick upon
Bardolph's nose, and a' said it was a black soul
burning in hell?

Bard. Well, the fuel is gone that maintained that fire:
that's all the riches I got in his service.   45

Nym. Shall we shog? the king will be gone from
Southampton.

Pist. Come, let's away.   My love, give me thy lips.
Look to my chattels and my moveables:
Let senses rule, the word is " Pitch and pay ";   50
Trust none;
For oaths are straws, men's faiths are wafer-cakes,
And hold-fast is the only dog, my duck:
Therefore, Caveto be thy counsellor.

---

43. *hell*] F, Q 3, Dover Wilson after Greg;   *hell fire* Q 1, 2, Capell.
50. *word*] Q 1, 3, Rowe (ed. 3); *world* F, Q 2.   54. *Caveto*] F; *cophetua* Q.

39. *rheumatic*] F spelling " rumatique" indicates the current pronunciation $[\overline{u}]$. The " o " in Rome
was also pronounced $[\overline{u}]$, cf. the
quibble on room—Rome in *Caes.*, I.
ii. 155. Here the pronunciation suggests Rome-atic in preparation for
the " whore of Babylon ".

39–40. *whore of Babylon*] (*a*) the
" scarlet woman " of *Rev.* xvii.
4–5, and hence a continuation of
the thought of " incarnate " and
" carnation ", (*b*) the Church of
Rome.   This expression was ap-
plied by Wyclif and the Lollards
to the Church of Rome whence its
use became common in Elizabethan
times.   Cf. Ocland's tract, *The
Fountain . . . of Variance . . . wherein
is declared . . . that Rome . . . is
signified . . . by name of Babylon . . . in
the Revelation of St. John*, 1589. For
the allusion to Oldcastle in these
lines, see Introduction, p. xxxix.

44. *the fuel . . . fire*] i.e. the liquor
that Falstaff provided for Bardolph.

Cf. *1H4* III. iii. 52–4, " I have maintained that salamander of yours with
fire any time this two-and-thirty
years ".

45. *all the . . . service*] Cf. *1H4* III.
iii. 88–9, " look upon his face; what
call you rich? let them coin his
nose ".

50. *Let senses rule*] keep on the
alert, or, let good sense prevail.

50. *word*] watchword.

50. *Pitch and pay*] cash down, no
credit.   *Oxford Dict. of Proverbs* quotes
Mirr. Mag. Warwick, 1559, iv, " I
vsed playnnes, ever pitch and pay ".

52. *men's faiths . . . wafer-cakes*]
men's promises are easily broken.
Cf. proverb, " Promises and pie-
crusts are made to be broken "
(Apperson, p. 513).

53. *hold-fast . . . dog*] Proverbial,
" Brag is a good dog, but Holdfast is
a better " (Apperson, p. 63).

54. *Caveto*] beware.

Go, clear thy crystals.   Yoke-fellows in arms,   55
Let us to France; like horse-leeches, my boys,
To suck, to suck, the very blood to suck!
Boy. And that's but unwholesome food, they say.
Pist. Touch her soft mouth, and march.
Bard. Farewell, hostess.   [*Kissing her.* 60
Nym. I cannot kiss, that is the humour of it; but
adieu.
Pist. Let housewifery appear; keep close, I thee com-
mand.
Host. Farewell; adieu.   [*Exeunt.*

SCENE IV.—*France.   The French King's Palace.*

Flourish.   Enter the FRENCH KING, *the* DAUPHIN, *the Dukes of*
BERRI *and* BRETAGNE, *the Constable, and Others.*
Fr. King. Thus comes the English with full power upon us;
And more than carefully it us concerns
To answer royally in our defences.
Therefore the Dukes of Berri and of Bretagne,
Of Brabant and of Orleans, shall make forth,
And you, Prince Dauphin, with all swift dispatch,   5

60. Kissing her] added Capell.

Scene IV

France] added Pope.   The French King's Palace] added Theobald.
Flourish . . . Others] Camb.   Flourish.   Enter the French King, the Dolphin,
the Dukes of Berry and Britaine F.

55. *clear thy crystals*] wipe your
eyes.   "Crystals" is occasionally
used for "eyes" during this period,
but now, however, with Pistol's
ludicrous affectation.

58. *that's . . . food*] Dover Wilson
quotes A. Boorde, *Dyetary*, 1542
(*E.E.T.S.*, Extra Series 10), p. 276,
"The blode of all beestes & fowles
is not praysed, for it is hard of
digestyon".   Opinion varied, however, and other writers specified the
blood of bulls as being particularly
unwholesome.

63. *Let . . . close*] show your virtues

as a housewife, and occupy yourself
within the house.

Scene IV

See note to III. v.   Berri does not
speak; he is referred to in l. 4; and
addressed in III. v. 4.
1. *comes*] Cf. Prologue 9.   Wright
suggests, in view of "royally" (l. 3),
that "English" stands for "English
king" and compares IV. iv. 78; v.
ii. 218.   This seems unnecessary.
2-3. *and . . . defences*] and we
should be more than usually careful
to see that our defences are fully
equipped to meet the attack.

To line and new repair our towns of war
With men of courage and with means defendant;
For England his approaches makes as fierce
As waters to the sucking of a gulf.   10
It fits us then to be as provident
As fear may teach us out of late examples
Left by the fatal and neglected English
Upon our fields.

Dau.   My most redoubted father,
It is most meet we arm us 'gainst the foe;   15
For peace itself should not so dull a kingdom,
Though war nor no known quarrel were in question,
But that defences, musters, preparations,
Should be maintain'd, assembled, and collected,
As were a war in expectation.   20
Therefore, I say 'tis meet we all go forth
To view the sick and feeble parts of France:
And let us do it with no show of fear;
No, with no more than if we heard that England
Were busied with a Whitsun morris-dance: 25
For, my good liege, she is so idly king'd
Her sceptre so fantastically borne
By a vain, giddy, shallow, humorous youth,
That fear attends her not.

Con.   O peace, Prince Dauphin!
You are too much mistaken in this king.   30
Question your grace the late ambassadors,
With what great state he heard their embassy,

7. *line*] reinforce.

10. *gulf*] whirlpool. Cf. iv. iii. 82.

12. *late examples*] i.e. Cressy, 1346, and Poitiers, 1356.

13. *fatal and neglected*] fatally underrated or despised.

19. *maintain'd . . . collected*] The verbs correspond in order to the nouns in l. 18.

25. *Whitsun morris-dance*] The morris or moorish dance was a grotesque dance in which the performers blackened their faces and wore fanciful costume with bells. The name seems to have originated from the blackened faces of the performers who were thought, incorrectly, to represent Moors. The dance was frequently performed at Whitsuntide when popular legendary characters were represented, e.g. Robin Hood and Maid Marian. Cf. *Wint.* iv. iii. 133–4 (Chambers, *Med. Stage*, I. 160–81, 195–201).

27. *Her sceptre . . . borne*] her royal power so freakishly and fancifully exercised. Cf. i. ii. 250–5.

28. *humorous*] capricious, unstable.

29. *attends*] accompanies.

How well supplied with noble counsellors,
How modest in exception, and withal
How terrible in constant resolution,
And you shall find his vanities forespent   35
Were but the outside of the Roman Brutus,
Covering discretion with a coat of folly;
As gardeners do with ordure hide those roots
That shall first spring and be most delicate.   40

Dau. Well, 'tis not so, my lord high constable;
But though we think it so, it is no matter:
In cases of defence 'tis best to weigh
The enemy more mighty than he seems:
So the proportions of defence are fill'd;   45
Which of a weak and niggardly projection
Doth, like a miser, spoil his coat with scanting
A little cloth.

Fr. King.   Think we King Harry strong;
And, princes, look you strongly arm to meet him.
The kindred of him hath been flesh'd upon us,   50
And he is bred out of that bloody strain
That haunted us in our familiar paths;
Witness our too much memorable shame
When Cressy battle fatally was struck,
And all our princes captiv'd by the hand   55
Of that black name, Edward, Black Prince of
    Wales;
Whiles that his mountain sire, on mountain standing,

---

34. *in exception*] in demurring, in raising an objection. Cf. IV. ii. 25.

37. *Brutus*] Lucius Junius Brutus, one of the first two consuls, 509 B.C. He is stated to have assumed dullness of intellect ("brutus", heavy, stupid) to preserve his life from Tarquinius Superbus, his uncle. He took part in the expulsion of the Tarquins from Rome. Cf. *Lucr.*, ll. 1807–17.

45. *so . . . fill'd*] in this way means for defence are provided in full.

46. *which . . . projection*] which, if on a small and scanty scale.

47. *scanting*] begrudging.

50. *flesh'd*] trained in war at our cost. Hounds and hawks were trained by feeding them on flesh.

51. *strain*] breed.

52. *haunted*] pursued. Cf. *1H4* v. iii. 4, "I do haunt thee in the battle thus", and *Troil.* IV. i. 9–10.

54. *when . . . struck*] Holinshed has later in the story, "King Edward the third a little before that had stricken the battle of Cressie", III. 551 (Wright).

54. *struck*] fought. The use of "strike" in this sense has persisted in the phrase "stricken field" for "battlefield".

57. *mountain*] great above all others. F reading has been retained, awkward

Up in the air, crown'd with the golden sun,
Saw his heroical seed, and smil'd to see him,
Mangle the work of nature, and deface   60
The patterns that by God and by French fathers
Had twenty years been made.   This is a stem
Of that victorious stock; and let us fear
The native mightiness and fate of him.

Enter a Messenger.

Mess. Ambassadors from Harry King of England   65
Do crave admittance to your majesty.
Fr. King. We'll give them present audience.   Go, and
    bring them.

                    [*Exeunt Messenger and certain Lords.*
You see this chase is hotly follow'd, friends.
Dau. Turn head, and stop pursuit; for coward dogs
Most spend their mouths when what they seem to
    threaten   70
Runs far before them.   Good my sovereign,
Take up the English short, and let them know
Of what a monarchy you are the head:
Self-love, my liege, is not so vile a sin
As self-neglecting.

Re-enter Lords, with EXETER *and Train.*

Fr. King.   From our brother of England?   75
Exe. From him; and thus he greets your majesty.
He wills you, in the name of God Almighty,
That you divest yourself, and lay apart

67. Exeunt . . . Lords] added Capell.   68. *follow'd*] Pope; followed F.
75. Re-enter . . . Train] Capell; Enter Exeter F.

though it is.   It seems possible
that Shakespeare originally wrote
" mighty " (cf. I. ii. 102) and that
the compositor's eye erred by attraction to the second " mountain ".
    64. *The native . . . him*] the
great destiny to which he was
born.

68–71. For imagery, cf. ll. 50–2;
I. ii. 266.
    69. *Turn head*] turn at bay.
    69. *head*] antlers. Cf. *1H6* IV. ii.
51, " Turn on the bloody hounds
with heads of steel ".
    70. *spend their mouths*] cry, give
tongue. Cf. *Ven.*, l. 695.

The borrow'd glories that by gift of heaven,
By law of nature and of nations, longs   80
To him and to his heirs; namely, the crown
And all wide-stretched honours that pertain
By custom and the ordinance of times
Unto the crown of France.   That you may know
'Tis no sinister nor no awkward claim,   85
Pick'd from the worm-holes of long-vanish'd days,
Nor from the dust of old oblivion rak'd,
He sends you this most memorable line,
In every branch truly demonstrative;
Willing you overlook this pedigree;   90
And when you find him evenly deriv'd
From his most fam'd of famous ancestors,
Edward the Third, he bids you then resign
Your crown and kingdom, indirectly held
From him the native and true challenger.   95

Fr. King. Or else what follows?

Exe. Bloody constraint; for if you hide the crown
Even in your hearts, there will he rake for it:
Therefore in fierce tempest is he coming,
In thunder and in earthquake like a Jove,   100
That, if requiring fail, he will compel;

79. *borrow'd*] Pope; *borrowed* F.

79–80. *by gift . . . nations*] i.e. by
every right, divine and human.
This conception of universal law
was inherited from the medieval
modifications of classical theory.
Controlling all things was the divine
law knowable only by revelation,
within this was the law of nature
embodying the philosophical and
scientific truths learned by the
exercise of the human reasoning
powers, and subordinate to this was
the law of nations which, although it
should be consistent with the law of
nature, was in fact frequently decided
by custom and expediency.

80. *longs*] belong. Cf. Prologue, 9
" longs " is a normal aphetic form
from O.E. " gelang ".

83. *ordinance of times*] established
practice.

85. *sinister*] irregular, out of wed-
lock. Cf. Greene, *Plays and Poems*, ed.
Churton Collins, *James IV*, v. vi.
ll. 2351–2, " thou, quite misled by
youth, Hast sought sinister loves and
foreign joys ".

85. *awkward*] not straightforward,
illegitimate.

86–7. *Pick'd . . . rak'd* "Suggesting
(*a*) selection, (*b*) search " (Dover
Wilson).

87. *dust . . . rak'd*] Cf. *Cor.* ii. iii.
126, " dust on antique time would
lie unswept ".

88. *line*] pedigree, line of descent.

91. *evenly*] directly.

94. *indirectly*] wrongfully.

95. *challenger*] claimant.

97. *constraint*] force, war. Cf.
John i. i. 18.

And bids you, in the bowels of the Lord,
Deliver up the crown, and to take mercy
On the poor souls for whom this hungry war
Opens his vasty jaws; and on your head 105
Turning the widows' tears, the orphans' cries,
The dead men's blood, the prived maidens' groans,
For husbands, fathers, and betrothed lovers,
That shall be swallow'd in this controversy.
This is his claim, his threat'ning, and my message; 110
Unless the Dauphin be in presence here,
To whom expressly I bring greeting too.

Fr. King. For us we will consider of this further:
To-morrow shall you bear our full intent
Back to our brother of England.

Dau.   For the Dauphin, 115
I stand here for him: what to him from England?

Exe. Scorn and defiance; slight regard, contempt,
And any thing that may not misbecome
The mighty sender, doth he prize you at.
Thus says my king: an if your father's highness 120
Do not, in grant of all demands at large,
Sweeten the bitter mock you sent his majesty,
He'll call you to so hot an answer of it,
That caves and womby vaultages of France

---

107. *prived*] Ed.; *priuy* F; *pining* Q, Pope.   109. *swallow'd*] Pope;
swallowed F.   112. *greeting too*] Q, F 2; *greeting to* F 1.

---

102. *in the bowels of the Lord*]
Shakespeare may be following Holinshed. The phrase, however, was
well known from *Phil.* i. 8, "in the
bowels of Jesus Christ".

106–9. *Turning . . . controversy*]
Although many descriptions of the
evils of war had been written, this
seems a clear reminiscence of Hall,
iii^v, the description of the grief of
the French after Agincourt:

"And yet the dolor was not
onely hys, for the ladyes souned for
the deathes of theyr husebandes, the
Orphalines wepte, and rent their
heares for the losse of their parentes,
the fayre damoselles defyed that

daye in which they had lost their
paramors. . . ."

107. *prived*] Editors generally have
followed Pope in adopting the
Q reading " pining ". On the other
hand " prived " (" bereft ") not
only improves the sense but is at
least as likely to be misread " privy "
or " priuie " as " pining ", by an
" e ": " d " misreading and a normalizing of " e " to " i ". *O.E.D.* quotes
Hall, p. 195: " kyng Edwardes ii
sonnes declared bastardes, & in
conclusion priued of ther liues ".

124. *womby vaultages*] hollow
caverns.

Shall chide your trespass and return your mock   125
In second accent of his ordinance.
Dau. Say, if my father render fair return,
It is against my will; for I desire
Nothing but odds with England: to that end,
As matching to his youth and vanity,   130
I did present him with the Paris-balls.
Exe. He'll make your Paris Louvre shake for it,
Were it the mistress-court of mighty Europe:
And, be assur'd, you'll find a difference,
As we his subjects have in wonder found,   135
Between the promise of his greener days
And these he masters now. Now he weighs time
Even to the utmost grain; that you shall read
In your own losses, if he stay in France.
Fr. King. To-morrow shall you know our mind at full.   140
                                    [*Flourish.*

Exe. Dispatch us with all speed, lest that our king
Come here himself to question our delay;
For he is footed in this land already.
Fr. King. You shall be soon dispatch'd with fair con-
    ditions;
A night is but small breath and little pause   145
To answer matters of this consequence.

                                    [*Exeunt.*

129. F divides after *England.*   132. *Louvre*] Pope; *Louer* Q, F 1; *Lower* F 3.
134. *difference*] Camb.; *diff'rence* F.

126. *second accent*] echo.
126. *ordinance*] ordnance.
131. *Paris-balls*] tennis-balls were so called.
132-3. Close to Holinshed. See Appendix, p. 161.
132. *Louvre*] F 1 spelling " Louer " and F3 " Lover " give the point of " mistress-court " in the next line.
136. *greener days*] Cf. I. ii. 120.
137. *masters*] possesses. Cf. Sonnet 106, 8, " Even such a beauty as you master now ".

140. Flourish] Dyce transferred this stage direction to the end of the scene. Capell's justification of its position here is surely sound: " the French king rises from his throne in this place, as dismissing the embassy . . . it shews the boldness of Exeter, who will not be so dismiss'd ".
143. *For . . . already*] Exeter's embassy took place in February, 1415. Henry did not actually land until 14 August.

ACT III

Enter CHORUS.

Thus with imagin'd wing our swift scene flies
In motion of no less celerity
Than that of thought. Suppose that you have seen
The well-appointed king at Hampton pier
Embark his royalty; and his brave fleet
With silken streamers the young Phœbus fanning:
Play with your fancies, and in them behold
Upon the hempen tackle ship-boys climbing;
Hear the shrill whistle which doth order give
To sounds confus'd; behold the threaden sails,   10
Borne with th' invisible and creeping wind,
Draw the huge bottoms through the furrow'd sea,
Breasting the lofty surge. O, do but think
You stand upon the rivage and behold
A city on th' inconstant billows dancing;   15
For so appears this fleet majestical,

ACT III

Chorus

Act III] Pope; Actus Secundus F.
4. *Hampton*] Theobald; *Dover* F.
12. *furrow'd*] Rowe; *furrowed* F.

2. F divides after *thought*.
6. *fanning*] Rowe; *fayning* F.

ACT III

Act III] See Introduction, p. xxxv

Chorus

1. *imagin'd wing*] wing of imagination. Cf. *Mer.V.* III. ii. 52, "imagin'd speed".

4. *Hampton*] Southampton.

5. *brave*] fine, gallant.

6. *the young Phoebus fanning*] waving
against the rising sun. In support
of Rowe's emendation "fanning",
cf. *Mac.* I. ii. 49,

"Where the Norweyan banners
    flout the sky
And fan our people cold",

and *Edward III* IV. iv. 19–21, where
the banners
            "cuff the aire
    And beat the windes".

The compositor may have set up
"yn" by misreading "nn" or "n"
as "in", namely three minims
instead of four or two.

9. *whistle*] i.e. blown by the master
of the ship. Cf. *Tp.* I. i. 6.

12. *bottoms*] vessels.

14. *rivage*] shore.

56

Holding due course to Harfleur.   Follow, follow!
Grapple your minds to sternage of this navy,
And leave your England, as dead midnight still,
Guarded with grandsires, babies, and old women,   20
Either past or not arriv'd to pith and puissance:
For who is he, whose chin is but enrich'd
With one appearing hair, that will not follow
These cull'd and choice-drawn cavaliers to France?
Work, work your thoughts, and therein see a siege; 25
Behold the ordnance on their carriages,
With fatal mouths gaping on girded Harfleur.
Suppose th' ambassador from the French comes back;
Tells Harry that the king doth offer him
Katharine his daughter; and with her, to dowry,   30
Some petty and unprofitable dukedoms:
The offer likes not: and the nimble gunner
With linstock now the devilish cannon touches,
                    [*Alarum, and chambers go off.*
And down goes all before them.   Still be kind,
And eke out our performance with your mind.   35
                                    [*Exit.*

17. *Harfleur*] *Harflew* F and elsewhere.   26. *ordnance*] Camb.;   *Ordenance*
F 1.   35. *eke*] *eech* F 1.

18. *Grapple . . . navy*] Follow with
your minds in the wake of these
ships.
19. *as . . . still*] i.e. still as silent
midnight.
21. *pith*] strength.
26. *ordinance*] ordnance. See II.
iv. 126.
27. *girded*] surrounded, besieged.
28–31. *Suppose . . . dukedoms*]
Actually these offers were made at
Winchester in June about two
months before Henry landed.
32. *nimble gunner*] Garrard, *Art of*

Warre, 1591, p. 5, recommends the
effectiveness of a "nimble discharge".
33. *linstock*] a stick pointed at one
end for thrusting in the ground and
forked at the other end for holding
the gunner's match.   From " lunt "
a slow-match and " stock " a stick.
33. *touches*] touches off, fires.
S.D. *chambers*] small guns without carriages used for ceremonial
salutes.
35. *eke*] F " eech " preserves the
current pronunciation.

SCENE I.—*France.   Before Harfleur.*

Alarum.   Enter KING HENRY, EXETER, BEDFORD,
    GLOUCESTER, *and Soldiers with scaling-ladders.*

K. Hen. Once more unto the breach, dear friends, once more,
    Or close the wall up with our English dead.
    In peace there's nothing so becomes a man
    As modest stillness and humility:
    But when the blast of war blows in our ears,   5
    Then imitate the action of the tiger;
    Stiffen the sinews, conjure up the blood,
    Disguise fair nature with hard-favour'd rage;
    Then lend the eye a terrible aspect;
    Let it pry through the portage of the head   10
    Like the brass cannon; let the brow o'erwhelm it
    As fearfully as doth a galled rock
    O'erhang and jutty his confounded base,
    Swill'd with the wild and wasteful ocean.
    Now set the teeth and stretch the nostril wide,   15
    Hold hard the breath, and bend up every spirit

Scene 1

France . . . Harfleur] added Rowe.   Enter . . . ladders] Camb.;
Enter the King, Exeter, Bedford, and Gloucester.   Alarum: Scaling Ladders
at Harflew] F.   7. *conjure*] Ed.; *commune* F; *summon* Rowe.

Scene 1

7. *conjure*] It is almost heresy to
suggest emending any word in this
speech, but it is difficult to see how
Rowe's emendation "summon" for
F "commune", which all editors
hitherto have accepted, can possibly
be justified. Initial "s" and "c"
are not likely to be confused, and
"summune" is not a likely spelling
for "summon". "Conjure", however, spelt "coniure", is almost
identical with "commune" (spelt
"comune" or "comune" as Brooks
points out). It also offers a satisfactory meaning in view of the current
Galenist doctrines of vital spirits
contained in the blood. Cf. V. ii.
307, "conjure up the spirit of love".
There and in V. ii. 310, 311 F

spelling is "coniure". Cf. also
MND. iii. ii. 158–9.
    8. *Disguise . . . rage*] conceal your
natural kindly looks with grim-faced
rage.
    10. *portage*] portholes.
    11–14. *let . . . ocean*] let the brow,
frowning in anger overhang the eyes
as threateningly as a worn rock
overhangs its base which is washed
and undermined by wild and destructive waves.
    12. *galled*] fretted, washed away.
    13. *confounded*] demolished, ruined.
    14. *Swill'd*] greedily swallowed.
Cf. *R3* v. ii. 7–9,
    " The . . . usurping boar
Swills your warm blood like wash ".
    16. *bend up*] strain to the utmost. A
metaphor that is derived from drawing a bow. Cf. *Mac.* i. vii. 78–80,

Unto the breach (dear friends)
phenomenally powerful
yet desperate

To his full height! On, on, you noblest English!
Whose blood is fet from fathers of war-proof;
Fathers that, like so many Alexanders,
Have in these parts from morn till even fought,   20
And sheath'd their swords for lack of argument.
Dishonour not your mothers; now attest
That those whom you call'd fathers did beget you.
Be copy now to men of grosser blood,   24
And teach them how to war.   And you, good yeomen,
Whose limbs were made in England, show us here
The mettle of your pasture; let us swear
That you are worth your breeding; which I doubt not;
For there is none of you so mean and base
That hath not noble lustre in your eyes.   30
I see you stand like greyhounds in the slips,
Straining upon the start.   The game's afoot:
Follow your spirit; and upon this charge
Cry, " God for Harry, England, and Saint George! "

[Exeunt. Alarum, and chambers go off.

17. noblest] F 2; *Noblish* F 1.
32. *Straining*] Rowe; *Straying* F.
34. Exeunt] added Camb.

" bend up
Each corporal agent to this terrible
feat ".

17-21. *you . . . argument*] Cf. Hall,
Henry's speech before Agincourt,
xlix^r,
" Frenche men, whome youre noble
auncestoures have so often overcome
and vanquished ".

18. *fet*] derived.

18. *of war-proof*] proved in war.

19-21. *Alexanders . . . argument*]
Cf. Juvenal, *Satires* X,
" Unus Pellaeo inveni non sufficit
orbis;
aestuat infelix angusto limite mundi."

21. *argument*] i.e. opponents. Cf.
IV. i. 146; IV. ii. 23.

22-5. Contrast the Dauphin's reference to " Norman bastards ", III.
v. 5-10, 26-31.

24. *men*] The F compositor may
have misread " men " as " mee "
(cf. note II. i. 36). Alternatively,
Brooks suggests that he may have
failed to read a title, or that the

title had been obliterated, or even
that Shakespeare had omitted it.

27. *mettle of your pasture*] " the
fine quality of your rearing " (Moore
Smith).

31. *slips*] leashes.

32. *Straining upon the start*] straining
to start.   Cf. " strain at the leash '.
Rowe's emendation of the F " straying " is generally accepted.   See
note to 3 Chorus 6.

33. *Follow your spirit*] Cf. I. ii. 128-
30.

33. *upon this charge*] as you charge.

33, 34. *charge*] *George*] note the
rhyme.   Henry makes no appeal to
St. George at this siege in either
Hall or Holinshed, though the latter
records that one of Henry's first acts
as king was to cause Convocation to
celebrate St. George's day as a
double feast.   In the *Famous Victories*
the appeal comes before Agincourt.
The *Liber Metricus*, however, has
an appeal " Sancte George! "
l. 517, and a further reference
ll. 575-80.

Immediate undercut — completely immediate — this is the real people fighting

SCENE II.—*The Same.*

Enter NYM, BARDOLPH, PISTOL, *and Boy.*

Bard. On, on, on, on, on! to the breach, to the
breach!

Nym. Pray thee, corporal, stay; the knocks are too hot;
and for mine own part, I have not a case of lives:
the humour of it is too hot, that is the very plain-   5
song of it.

Pist. The plain-song is most just, for humours do abound:

> Knocks go and come, God's vassals drop and die;
>   And sword and shield,
>   In bloody field,   10
>   Doth win immortal fame.

Boy. Would I were in an alehouse in London! I would
give all my fame for a pot of ale, and safety.

Pist. And I:

> If wishes would prevail with me,   15
> My purpose should not fail with me,
>   But thither would I hie.

Boy.   As duly,
>   But not as truly,
> As bird doth sing on bough.   20

Enter FLUELLEN.

Flu. Up to the breach, you dogs! avaunt, you cullions!
                         [*Driving them forward.*

Scene II

8–11, 15–20. Capell's arrangement. Prose F.   21. Driving them
forward] added Camb.

Scene II

See Introduction, p. xxxvii.
3. *corporal*] Cf. II. i. 2.
4. *case*] set. A case of pistols was
a pair.
5–6. *plain-song*] the simple air without variations (Evans), the plain
truth.

8–11, 15–20. Possibly fragments of
old songs.

11. *Doth*] Cf. Prologue 9.

19. *truly*] (*a*) honourably, (*b*) in
tune (Dover Wilson).

21. *cullions*] vile creatures.

Pist. Be merciful, great duke, to men of mould!
    Abate thy rage, abate thy manly rage;
    Abate thy rage, great duke!   24
    Good bawcock, bate thy rage; use lenity, sweet chuck!
Nym. These be good humours! your honour wins bad
    humours.   [*Exeunt all but Boy.*
Boy. As young as I am, I have observed these three
    swashers. I am boy to them all three, but all
    they three, though they would serve me, could   30
    not be man to me; for indeed three such antics
    do not amount to a man. For Bardolph, he
    is white-livered and red-faced; by the means
    whereof a' faces it out, but fights not. For
    Pistol, he hath a killing tongue and a quiet   35
    sword; by the means whereof a' breaks words,
    and keeps whole weapons. For Nym, he hath
    heard that men of few words are the best men;
    and therefore he scorns to say his prayers, lest a'

22–5. Pope's arrangement. Prose F.   27. Exeunt . . . Boy] added
Camb.; Exit F.   31. antics] Camb.; *Antiques* F.

22. *great duke*] See Introduction, p. xxxvii.

22. *men of mould*] men of earth, mere mortals. Dyce quotes from the ballad *True Thomas*, Jamieson's *Popular Ballads*, II. 16, "Man of Molde, thou wilt me marre".

25. *Good bawcock . . . sweet chuck*] ingratiating colloquial familiarities.

25. *bawcock*] fine fellow (Fr. *beau coq*).

26. *These . . . humours*] Nym is ironical.

28–57. Note the quibbles and antitheses throughout the Boy's speech.

29. *swashers*] swaggerers.

29. *I . . . all three*] (*a*) servant to them, (*b*) boy as compared with them.

31. *be . . . me*] (*a*) less of a man than I am, (*b*) be my servant.

31. *antics*] freaks, buffoons.

33. *white-livered*] cowardly, i.e. no blood in his liver. Cf. *Tw.N.* III. ii. 69–70, " if he were opened, and

you find so much blood in his liver as will clog the foot of a flea . . .", and *Mer.V.* III. ii. 86–7.

33. *red-faced*] courageous. Cf. *1H4* II. iv. 240, 315–21.

35–6. *a killing . . . sword*] Cf. *2H4* II. iv. 184 for Pistol's "bitter words", and II. iv. 105 for Falstaff's description of him as a " tame cheater ".

36. *breaks words*] (*a*) breaks his word, (*b*) exchanges words (and not blows). *O.E.D.* quotes *Err.* III. i. 75, " A man may break a word with you, sir, and words are but wind ".

38. *men of few . . . men*] Cf. *Eccles.* v. i, " therefore let thy wordes be few "; and *Wiv.* I. i. 134–5, where Nym pretends to want few words only lest a fight with Slender be delayed, " Slice, I say! pauca pauca; slice! that's my humour ". The saying was, of course, proverbial, usually in the form in which it occurs in *LLL.* IV. ii. 82–3, " vir sapit qui pauca loquitur ".

should be thought a coward: but his few bad   40
words are matched with as few good deeds; for
a' never broke any man's head but his own, and
that was against a post when he was drunk.
They will steal any thing and call it purchase.
Bardolph stole a lute-case, bore it twelve leagues,   45
and sold it for three half-pence. Nym and Bardolph are sworn brothers in filching, and in Calais
they stole a fire-shovel; I knew by that piece of
service the men would carry coals. They would
have me as familiar with men's pockets as their   50
gloves or their handkerchers: which makes much
against my manhood if I should take from
another's pocket to put into mine; for it is plain
pocketing up of wrongs. I must leave them and
seek some better service: their villany goes   55
against my weak stomach, and therefore I must
cast it up.   [Exit.

Re-enter FLUELLEN, GOWER *following.*

Gow. Captain Fluellen, you must come presently to
the mines; the Duke of Gloucester would speak
with you.   60
Flu. To the mines! tell you the duke it is not so good
to come to the mines. For look you, the mines is

---

47. *Calais*] Pope; *Callice* F.   57. Re-enter . . . following] Steevens;
Enter Gower F.

40–1. *few bad . . . good deeds*] The old   49. *service*] Ironical.
saying, "Deeds not words", is not   49. *carry coals*] (*a*) do degrading
true of Nym even though he believes   service, (*b*) show cowardice. Cf.
in brevity of speech.   *Rom.* I. i. 1.

44. *purchase*] euphemism for   54. *pocketing . . . wrongs*] (*a*) putting
"swag", stolen goods.   up with insults, (*b*) receiving stolen
                                      goods.
47. *sworn brothers*] Cf. II. i. 12.   56. *against . . . stomach*] (*a*) against
                                      my inclination, (*b*) makes me ill.
47. *Calais*] "How Nym and Bard.   57. *cast it up*] (*a*) throw up their
had come from Calais, towards which   service, (*b*) be sick.
they would soon be marching we are   S.D. See Introduction, p. xxxvii.
not told. Perhaps Sh.'s inadver-   58–68. According to Holinshed,
tence" (Dover Wilson). Brooks links   III. 550 the "countermining some-
this error with the "Dover" error   what disappointed the Englishmen".
in 3 Chorus 4.

not according to the disciplines of the war; the
concavities of it is not sufficient; for, look you, th'
athversary, you may discuss unto the duke, look 65
you, is digt himself four yard under the countermines. By Cheshu, I think a' will plow up all
if there is not better directions.

Gow. The Duke of Gloucester, to whom the order of
the siege is given, is altogether directed by an 70
Irishman, a very valiant gentleman, i' faith.

Flu. It is Captain Macmorris, is it not?

Gow. I think it be.

Flu. By Cheshu, he is an ass, as in the world: I will
verify as much in his beard: he has no more 75
directions in the true disciplines of the wars, look
you, of the Roman disciplines, than is a puppy-dog.

Enter Captain MACMORRIS *and Captain* JAMY.

Gow. Here a' comes; and the Scots captain, Captain
Jamy, with him.

Flu. Captain Jamy is a marvellous falorous gentleman, 80
that is certain; and of great expedition and
knowledge in th' aunchiant wars, upon my particular knowledge of his directions: by Cheshu,

72. Flu.] Rowe; Welch F (and so to the end of the scene).
77. Enter . . . Jamy] Camb.; enter Makmorrice, and Captaine Jamy F.

63. *disciplines . . . war*] conventions
and practice of warfare. See note to
l. 77.

65. *discuss*] inform.

66–7. *is digt . . . countermines*] " has
digged himself countermines four
yards under the mines " (Johnson).

67. *plow*] blow. For Fluellen's
"p's" and "b's" see Introduction,
p. xxxvii

74–5. *I will . . . beard*] I will prove
it to his face.

77. *Roman disciplines*] Military tac-
tics were the subject of vigorous controversy in the closing years of the
century. See Introduction, p. xxx.
Fluellen sides with those who be-

lieved that the introduction of gunpowder had made no essential
difference to military practice. Cf.
Digges, *Foure Paradoxes*, 1604, p. 41:
" I therefore to the contrarie averre:
That neither the furie of Ordinance
. . . hath or can worke any such
alteration: But that the auncient
discipline of the *Romane* and Martiall
Græcian States (euen for our time)
are rare and singular *Præcedents*."

81. *expedition*] readiness, having a
ready knowledge of (a rhetorical
term).

82. *aunchiant*] Possibly a Shakespearian spelling though it might be
an indication of Fluellen's pronunciation.

he will maintain his argument as well as any
military man in the world, in the disciplines of 85
the pristine wars of the Romans.

Jamy. I say gud day, Captain Fluellen.

Flu. God-den to your worship, good Captain James.

Gow. How now, Captain Macmorris! have you quit
the mines? have the pioners given o'er?   90

Mac. By Chrish, la! tish ill done: the work ish give
over, the trompet sound the retreat. By my hand,
I swear, and my father's soul, the work ish ill
done; it ish give over: I would have blowed up
the town, so Chrish save me, la! in an hour: O, 95
tish ill done, tish ill done; by my hand, tish ill done!

Flu. Captain Macmorris, I beseech you now, will you
voutsafe me, look you, a few disputations with you
as partly touching or concerning the disciplines of
the war, the Roman wars, in the way of argument, 100
look you, and friendly communication; partly to
satisfy my opinion, and partly for the satisfaction,
look you, of my mind, as touching the direction
of the military discipline: that is the point.

Jamy. It sall be vary gud, gud feith, gud captains 105
bath: and I sall quit you with gud leve, as I
may pick occasion; that sall I, marry.

Mac. It is no time to discourse, so Chrish save me:
the day is hot, and the weather, and the wars, and
the king, and the dukes: it is no time to discourse. 110
The town is beseeched, and the trumpet call us
to the breach; and we talk, and, be Chrish, do
nothing: 'tis shame for us all; so God sa' me, 'tis
shame to stand still; it is shame, by my hand; and
there is throats to be cut, and works to be done; 115
and there ish nothing done, so Chrish sa' me, la!

---

87. Jamy] Rowe; Scot F (and so to the end of the scene).   91. Mac.]
Rowe; Irish F (and so to the end of the scene).   91, 95, 116. *la*]
Capell; *law* F. 116 Chrish] Christ F.

90. *pioners*] pioneers; i.e. sappers,
miners.
101. *communication*] A rhetorical
figure in which either the opposing
speaker or the judges were taken
into consultation. See Quintilian,
Institutiones, 1580, p. 499, hence the
aptness of the epithet " friendly ".
106. *quit*] requite, answer.
111. *beseeched*] besieged.

Jamy. By the mess, ere theise eyes of mine take themselves to slomber ay'll de gud service, or I'll lig
i' th' grund for it; ay, or go to death; and I'll
pay 't as valorously as I may, that sall I suerly 120
do, that is the breff and the long.　Marry, I wad
full fain hear some question 'tween you tway.

Flu. Captain Macmorris, I think, look you, under your
correction, there is not many of your nation—

Mac. Of my nation!　What ish my nation?　Ish a 125
villain, and a bastard, and a knave, and a rascal—
What ish my nation?　Who talks of my nation?

Flu. Look you, if you take the matter otherwise than
is meant, Captain Macmorris, peradventure I shall
think you do not use me with that affability as in 130
discretion you ought to use me, look you; being
as good a man as yourself, both in the disciplines
of war, and in the derivation of my birth, and in
other particularities.

Mac. I do not know you so good a man as myself: 135
so Chrish save me, I will cut off your head.

Gow. Gentlemen both, you will mistake each other.

Jamy. A! that's a foul fault.　　　　　*[A parley sounded.*

Gow. The town sounds a parley.

Flu. Captain Macmorris, when there is more better 140
opportunity to be required, look you, I will be so
bold as to tell you I know the disciplines of
war; and there is an end.　　　　　*[Exeunt.*

---

122. *hear*] Camb.; *heard* F.　　138. A. . . . *sounded*] Rowe; A Parley
F.　　　　143. Exeunt] Rowe; Exit F.

122. *hear*] The F "heard" is probably an "e"; "d" misreading of
"heare".

125. *Of my nation!*] Macmorris is
enraged the moment Fluellen appears
to be about to criticize his nation:
"What are you going to say agin
my country now?　I suppose you'll
be after calling me a villain and a
bastard?" (Craig quoted Evans).
Strict martial laws were enforced to

prevent quarrelling of this kind.　Cf.
Garrard, *Art of Warre*, p. 40, Law
30, "there shal no souldiers or other
men, procure or stir up any quarrell
with any stranger, that is of any other
nation and such as serue under one
head and Lord with them".

137. *you will mistake*] you persist in
mistaking.

141. *to be required*] presents itself.

SCENE III.—*The Same.*

Some Citizens on the walls above the gates.   Enter KING HENRY
and all his Train before the gates.

K. Hen. How yet resolves the governor of the town?
This is the latest parle we will admit:
Therefore to our best mercy give yourselves;
Or like to men proud of destruction
Defy us to our worst: for, as I am a soldier,   5
A name that in my thoughts becomes me best,
If I begin the batt'ry once again,
I will not leave the half-achiev'd Harfleur
Till in her ashes she lie buried.
The gates of mercy shall be all shut up,   10

Scene III

The same . . . gates] Ed.; The Same. Before the Gates. The Governor
and some Citizens on the walls; the English Forces below.   Enter King Henry
and his Train Camb.; Enter the King and all his Traine before the Gates
F.

Scene III

1–43. A description of the horrors
accompanying the sacking of a city
was a frequent theme of contemporary
writers.   Such sackings did occur in
Shakespeare's time in the Nether-
lands, and he may have had in mind
such an appalling affair as the sack
of Bovaigne (see Barwick, *A Breefe
Discourse,* 1594, pp. 9–10).

Henry's conduct of the siege is in
accordance with military law.   As
Gentili explains (*De Iure Belli,* 1612,
ed. Rolfe, II. 216–30) there is a
point of time in a siege after which
no surrender is possible, and whether
the defenders lay down their arms or
not makes no difference, the city falls
by assault and is sacked (e.g. " if
bombards are brought up to weak
places, no room seems to be left for
surrender "). Henry announces to
the Governor that this point of time
has now been reached.   An interesting contemporary parallel was

Stanley's surrender of Deventer to
the Spaniards in 1587 strictly in
accordance with the law, a surrender
that aroused considerable controversy.

Deut. xx. may be the source of this
law, but Dover Wilson's claims that
Henry's speech is " merely an elabora-
tion of *Deut.* xx. 10–14 " and the
whole incident " clearly based on
Gesta " which at this point asserts
Henry's compliance with the law of
Deuteronomy, are both unconvincing.
Shakespeare could have found the
reference to *Deut.* xx on the previous
page of Hall, in a letter written to
Charles by Henry at Southampton,
or for that matter frequently in
writers on military discipline.

4. *proud of destruction*] glorying in
their deaths.

10. *gates of mercy*] The phrase is
not in the *Bible.*   Its familiarity may
be due to Gray's *Elegy,* l. 68. Cf.
3H6 I. iv. 177, " Open thy gate of
mercy, gracious God ! "

And the flesh'd soldier, rough and hard of heart,
In liberty of bloody hand shall range
With conscience wide as hell, mowing like grass
Your fresh-fair virgins and your flow'ring infants.
What is it then to me, if impious war, 15
Array'd in flames like to the prince of fiends,
Do, with his smirch'd complexion, all fell feats
Enlink'd to waste and desolation?
What is't to me, when you yourselves are cause,
If your pure maidens fall into the hand 20
Of hot and forcing violation?
What rein can hold licentious wickedness
When down the hill he holds his fierce career?
We may as bootless spend our vain command
Upon th' enraged soldiers in their spoil 25
As send precepts to the leviathan
To come ashore. Therefore, you men of Harfleur,
Take pity of your town and of your people,
Whiles yet my soldiers are in my command;
Whiles yet the cool and temperate wind of grace 30
O'er blows the filthy and contagious clouds
Of heady murder, spoil, and villainy.
If not, why, in a moment look to see
The blind and bloody soldier with foul hand

26. F. divides after *ashore*.

32. *heady*] F 3; *headly* F 1; *headdy* F 2.

11. *flesh'd*] trained or initiated in slaughter. Cf. II. iv. 50.

11–13. *the flesh'd soldier . . . hell*] the soldier inured to blood . . . with a free hand to indulge in slaughter, shall be turned loose with a conscience stretched wide enough to sanction hellish deeds.

15. *impious war*] " bellum impium " in Latin writers means " civil war ". Cf. *Georgics* Bk. I. 511. Henry asserts that they are disloyally fighting against their lawful sovereign (see l. 43), and therefore he has no responsibility for the ills that befall them.

15–18. *What . . . desolation*] what is it to me then, if the evils of civil war which you have brought about,

fiery and hellish in their nature, bring with them their black foulness all the horrible deeds that accompany the razing and sacking of cities? Dover Wilson compares *Ham.* II. ii. 481–95.

23. *career*] uncontrollable gallop.

26–7. *As . . . ashore*] Cf. *Job* xli. 1–4.

26. *precepts*] summons in writing. Note the stress on the second syllable.

32. *heady*] F reading " headly " has some support from Wyclif who uses " hedly " in the sense of " deadly " (*O.E.D.*). Brooks, however, suggests that Wyclif's " hedly " means " capital ".

34. *blind*] reckless, heedless.

Defile the locks of your shrill-shrieking daughters;   35
Your fathers taken by the silver beards,
And their most reverend heads dash'd to the walls;
Your naked infants spitted upon pikes,
Whiles the mad mothers with their howls confus'd
Do break the clouds, as did the wives of Jewry   40
At Herod's bloody-hunting slaughtermen.
What say you? will you yield, and this avoid?
Or, guilty in defence, be thus destroy'd?

Enter GOVERNOR *and Attendants.*

Gov. Our expectation hath this day an end.
The Dauphin, whom of succours we entreated,   45
Returns us that his powers are yet not ready
To raise so great a siege.   Therefore, great king,
We yield our town and lives to thy soft mercy.
Enter our gates; dispose of us and ours;
For we no longer are defensible.   50
K. Hen. Open your gates! Come, uncle Exeter,
Go you and enter Harfleur; there remain,
And fortify it strongly 'gainst the French:
Use mercy to them all.   For us, dear uncle,

---

35. *Defile*] Rowe (ed.3); *Desire* F.   43. Enter . . . Attendants] Ed.;
Enter Governour F.   54. *all. For*] Pope; *all for* F.

40-1. *wives . . . slaughtermen*] See
Matt. ii. 16-18, " In Rama was there
a voice heard, lamentation, and
weeping and great mourning, Rachel
weeping for her children, and would
not be comforted, because they are
not ".

43. *guilty in defence*] (*a*) to blame
for holding out (see note to ll. 1-43),
(*b*) disloyal in withholding the town
from its rightful king.

43. Enter . . . Attendants] Editors
have omitted the F stage direction.
What happens is surely that the
Governor comes through the wicket
accompanied by a few attendants
and, offering the keys of the town to
Henry, makes his submission. There

is no need for the Governor to be on
the walls in person, though he could
of course move down during Henry's
speech.

45-7. Cf. Holinshed, see Appendix,
p. 161.

50. *defensible*] capable of offering
defence.

52-3. Exeter placed Sir John
Fastolf in charge. On the muster
roll of 14 June 1428 at Honfleur
where Sir John Fastolf was in charge
appears the name of Johan Bardolf,
a mounted man-at-arms (*M.L.N.*
XLVIII, 1933, pp. 436-7).

54. *Use mercy*] Not according to
Holinshed.

The winter coming on and sickness growing   55
Upon our soldiers, we will retire to Calais.
To-night in Harfleur will we be your guest;
To-morrow for the march are we addrest.

[*Flourish.   The King and his Train enter the town.*

SCENE IV.—*Rouen.   A Room in the Palace.*

Enter PRINCESS KATHARINE *and* ALICE, *an old Gentlewoman.*

Kath. Alice, tu as été en Angleterre, et tu parles
bien le langage.
Alice. Un peu, madame.
Kath. Je te ptie, m'enseignez; il faut que j'apprenne
à parler.   Comment appellez-vous la main en   5
Anglais?

58. Flourish . . . town] Camb.; Flourish and enter the Towne F.

Scene IV

Rouen . . . Palace] Malone.   Princess . . . Gentlewoman] Dover Wilson.
Enter Katherine and an old Gentlewoman F.   1. *été*] *este* F.   1–2. *parles
bien*] *bien parlas* F.

55–6. *sickness . . . Calais*] Apparently
dysentery and fevers.   So Hall and
Holinshed.
58. *addrest*] ready, prepared.

Scene IV

Some editors consider that Shakespeare did not write this scene, but
their arguments are singularly unconvincing.
The French of F has been corrected
and modernized by various editors.
Dover Wilson notes: " If we allow
for Sh.'s handwriting, for the F
compositor's ignorance of Fr., for
phonetic spellings to help the boy
players, and for the occurrence of
early mod. Fr. forms, it is doubtful
whether there was orig. very much

wrong with Sh.'s Fr. except the
genders."
A selection of F readings is given
by way of illustration.
M. L. Radoff, " Influence of
French Farce in *Henry V* and the
Merry Wives", *M.L.N.* XLVIII,
1933, pp. 427–35, suggests that
Shakespeare is here indebted to
French farces because no other
Elizabethan play makes use of a
language lesson, because the patterns
are the same, and because this lesson
and three French farces in particular
end with the same obscene word.
Language lessons of a kind, however,
do occur in other plays, notably
Wager's *The Longer Thou Livest* and
Redford's *Wit and Science*, otherwise
Radoff's third parallel is sufficiently
striking to carry weight.

Alice. La main? elle est appellée de hand.

Kath. De hand. Et les doigts?

Alice. Les doigts? ma foi, j'oublie les doigts, mais
je me souviendrai. Les doigts? je pense qu'ils   10
sont appellés de fingres; ou, de fingres.

Kath. La main, de hand; les doigts, de fingres. Je
pense que je suis le bon écolier. J'ai gagné
deux mots d'Anglais vitement. Comment
appellez-vous les ongles?   15

Alice. Les ongles? nous les appellons de nails.

Kath. De nails. Ecoutez; dites moi si je parle
bien: de hand, de fingres, et de nails.

Alice. C'est bien dit, madame; il est fort bon
Anglais.   20

Kath. Dites moi l'Anglais pour le bras.

Alice. De arm, madame.

Kath. Et le coude?

Alice. D' elbow.

Kath. D' elbow. Je m'en fais la répétition de tous   25
les mots que vous m'avez appris dés à présent.

Alice. Il est trop difficile, madame, comme je pense.

Kath. Excusez-moi, Alice; écoutez: d' hand, **de
fingre**, de nails, d' arma, de bilbow.

Alice. D' elbow, madame.   30

Kath. O Seigneur Dieu! je m'en oublie; d' elbow.
Comment appellez-vous le col?

Alice. De nick, madame.

Kath. De nick. Et le menton?

Alice. De chin.   35

Kath. De sin. Le col, de nick; le menton, de sin.

Alice. Oui. Sauf votre honneur, en vérité, vous
prononcez les mots aussi droit que les natifs
d'Angleterre.

9–13. Theobald's rearrangement.   F assigns *Et les doigts* to Alice, ll. 9–11
to Katharine, and *La main . . . écolier* to Alice.   10. *souviendrai*] *souemeray* F.
16. *nous*] added Camb.   *nails*] *Nayles* F.

16. *nails*] Duthie suggests that the   29. *de bilbow*] A bilbo was a sword,
F spelling "Nayles" denotes a   but perhaps a glance at "bilboes",
disyllabic pronunciation. Cf.   fetters, was intended.
"mails", l. 45 (F "Maylees").

Kath. Je ne doute point d'apprendre par la grace de   40
  Dieu, et en peu de temps.
Alice. N'avez vous pas déjà oublié ce que je vous ai
  enseigné?
Kath. Non, je réciterai à vous promptement. D'
  hand, de fingre, de mails,—   45
Alice. De nails, madame.
Kath. De nails, de arm, de ilbow.
Alice. Sauf votre honneur, d'elbow.
Kath. Ainsi dis-je; d'elbow, de nick, et de sin. Com-
  ment appellez-vous le pied et la robe?   50
Alice. Le foot, madame; et le count.
Kath. Le foot, et le count? O Seigneur Dieu! ils
  sont les mots de son mauvais, corruptible, gros,
  et impudique, et non pour les dames d'honneur
  d'user. Je ne voudrais prononcer ces mots devant 55
  les seigneurs de France, pour tout le monde.
  Foh! le foot et le count! Néanmoins je reciterai
  une autre fois ma leçon ensemble: d'hand, de
  fingre, de nails, d'arm, d'elbow, de nick, de sin, de
  foot, le count.   60
Alice. Excellent, madame!
Kath. C'est assez pour une fois: allons-nous à dîner.

[*Exeunt.*

42. *déjà*] *desia* F.   45. *mails*] *Maylees* F.   48. *Sauf*] *Sans* F.
62. *Exeunt*] F 2; Exit F 1.

50. *la robe*] *de roba* F, a loose
woman. Cf. *2H4* III. ii. 26, " bona
robas ".

Again the imagery of hand
 - but this time in play
 - in the peaceful, silly
   learning of the enemy's
   hand and way.

SCENE V.—*The Same.*

Enter the KING OF FRANCE, *the* DAUPHIN, *the Duke of*
BRETAGNE, *the Constable of France, and others.*

Fr. King. 'Tis certain he hath pass'd the river Somme.
Con. And if he be not fought withal, my lord,
    Let us not live in France; let us quit all,
    And give our vineyards to a barbarous people.
Dau. O Dieu vivant! shall a few sprays of us,   5
    The emptying of our fathers' luxury,
    Our scions, put in wild and savage stock,
    Spirt up so suddenly into the clouds,
    And overlook their grafters?
Bret. Normans, but bastard Normans, Norman bastards! 10
    Mort Dieu! ma vie! if they march along
    Unfought withal, but I will sell my dukedom,
    To buy a slobb'ry and a dirty farm
    In that nook-shotten isle of Albion.

Scene v

Enter ... others] Enter the King of France, the Dolphin, the Constable of
France and others F.   10. Bret.], Ed.; Brit. F, Dover Wilson; Bour.
Theobald, Camb.   11. Dieu!] Dover Wilson after Greg; *du* F 1; *de* F 2,
Camb.

Scene v

Most editors add Q " Bourbon " to
the entry notice and assign the speeches
at pp. 10, 32 to him in place of F
" Brit ".   They also substitute him
for F " Britaine " in the entry notice
to II. iv.   The characters in Q, however, have been greatly reduced to
fit a smaller cast, and Bourbon takes
a much larger part including that of
the Dauphin in III. vii.   He is not
mentioned by Hall or Holinshed at
this point, while both Berri and
" Britain " are.

    1. *pass'd ... Somme*] on his retreat
to Calais.   See III. iii. 56.

    5. *sprays*] offshoots, bastards.

    6. *emptying ... luxury*] outpouring
or dregs of our ancestors' lust.

    6. *luxury*] lust.   Cf. *Troil.* v. ii. 53;
Wiv. v. v. 100–2.

    7. *Our scions ... stock*] The offspring
of intermarriage between Normans
and Saxons.

    7. *scions*] shoots (for grafting).

    7. *savage*] uncultivated, wild.

    7. *stock*] the rooted stem of a tree,
usually of a wild tree, into which a
shoot is grafted.   Cf. *Wint.* IV. iii.
92–3

    " You see, sweet maid, we marry
A gentler scion to the wildest stock ".

    8. *spirt*] sprout, shoot up.

    9. *grafters*] original trees from
which the scion was taken.

    11. *vie*] Two syllables.

    12. *but*] if ... not.   The word is
dependent on the oath " Mort
Dieu! ma vie! " If I do not sell, etc.

    13. *slobbery*] wet, sloppy.

    14. *nook-shotten*] running into cor-
ners, indented.   Here used con-
temptuously.

Con. Dieu de batailles! where have they this mettle?   15
      Is not their climate foggy, raw and dull,
      On whom, as in despite, the sun looks pale,
      Killing their fruit with frowns? Can sodden water,
      A drench for sur-rein'd jades, their barley broth,
      Decoct their cold blood to such valiant heat?   20
      And shall our quick blood, spirited with wine,
      Seem frosty? O, for honour of our land,
      Let us not hang like roping icicles
      Upon our houses' thatch, whiles a more frosty people
      Sweat drops of gallant youth in our rich fields!—   25
      Poor we may call them in their native lords.
Dau. By faith and honour,
      Our madams mock at us, and plainly say
      Our mettle is bred out; and they will give
      Their bodies to the lust of English youth   30
      To new-store France with bastard warriors.
Bret. They bid us to the English dancing-schools,
      And teach lavoltas high and swift corantos;

[handwritten marginal note: couplant both to the roping image and the image of Catherine.]

26. *may*] added F 2.   32. Bret.] Ed.; Brit. F, Dover Wilson;
Bour. Theobald, Camb.

18. *sodden*] boiled.
19. *drench*] a medicinal draught given to horses. Cf. Pliny, *Nat. Hist.* (tr. Holland), 1601, II. 144, "Poure this drench with an horne downe the throat of labouring jades".
19. *sur-rein'd*] over-ridden.
19. *barley broth*] i.e. ale. English farriers used ale for horse drenches whereas those on the Continent used wine. Cf. Pliny's remedies with those of Markham, *Maister-Peece*, 1615, p. 39, etc.
20. *Decoct*] warm, or perhaps infuse.
21. *quick*] lively.
21. *spirited with wine*] The Constable assumes that wine is essential to both courage and culture. Cf. l. 4.
23. *roping*] congealing, lit. capable of being drawn out into a thread. Cf. Ovid, *Metamorphoses*, tr. Golding, 1565, I, 2*b*, "Then isycles hung roping down", and iv. ii. 48.

25–6. *rich . . . lords*] rich fields!— rather should we call them poor because they have bred such poor spirited masters. Cf. iii. i. 25–7 and l. 29 below, "mettle is bred out".
29. *bred out*] degenerate, exhausted. Cf. *Tim.* i. i. 259–6,
      "The strain of man's bred out
      Into baboon and monkey".
32. *They . . . dancing schools*] They bid us become mere dancing-masters to the English.
33. *lavoltas high*] The lavolta was a dance in three-four time consisting of a body turn in two steps followed by a high leap. It seems to have originated in Italy as the name "volta", a leap or whirl, implies. Cf. *Troil.* iv. iv. 85–6,
            "I cannot sing
      Nor heel the high lavolt".
33. *swift corantos*] The coranto was a dance in two-four time something

Saying our grace is only in our heels,
And that we are most lofty runaways.   35
Fr. King. Where is Montjoy the herald? speed him hence:
Let him greet England with our sharp defiance.
Up, princes! and, with spirit of honour edg'd
More sharper than your swords, hie to the field:
Charles Delabreth, high constable of France;   40
You Dukes of Orleans, Bourbon, and of Berri,
Alençon, Brabant, Bar, and Burgundy;
Jacques Chatillon, Rambures, Vaudemont,
Beaumont, Grandprè, Roussi, and Faulconbridge,
Foix, Lestrale, Bouciqualt, and Charolois;   45
High dukes, great princes, barons, lords, and knights,
For your great seats now quit you of great shames,
Bar Harry England, that sweeps through our land
With pennons painted in the blood of Harfleur:
Rush on his host, as doth the melted snow   50
Upon the valleys, whose low vassal seat
The Alps doth spit and void his rheum upon:
Go down upon him, you have power enough,

---

43. *Vaudemont*] F 2; Vandemont F 1.   44. *Faulconbridge*] F; *Fauconberg*
Capell.   45. *Foix*] Capell; *Loys* F.   *Lestrale*] F, Camb.; *Lestrake*
Dover Wilson.   *Bouciqualt*] Theobald; *Bouciquall* F.   *Charolois*] Capell;
Charaloyes F.   46. *knights*] Pope (ed. 2) from Theobald's conjecture;
Kings F.

---

like the Victorian Gallop. Its distinguishing feature was its running step similar to that used in country dances.

34. *grace*]? saving grace.

34. *in our heels*] (*a*) in taking to our heels, (*b*) in dancing.

35. *lofty runaways*] accomplished cowards. The phrase neatly summarizes the essential character of both dances.

40–5. These names, with the exception of Charolois and Berri, are taken from Holinshed's list of those slain or taken prisoner at Agincourt.

44. *Faulconbridge*] Although Holinshed has " Fauconberg " in this list, he uses the form "Fauconbridge" on the previous page (Dover Wilson).

45. *Foix*] Capell's reading after Holinshed's " Fois ".

45. *Lestrale*] Holinshed has " Lestrake ".

47. *For . . . seats*] for the sake of the great positions you occupy.

52. *The Alps . . . upon*] Shakespeare probably owes this image to Quintilian's condemnation of Furius' line, " Iuppiter hybernas cana niue conspuit Alps " as harsh and strained. Horace also, as Steevens noted, ridicules the line (*Satires*, II. 5, 41). Shakespeare who adapts the figure in his own way, with full knowledge of its rhetorical significance, puts this far-fetched and vicious metaphor into the mouth of the grandiloquent French king (Baldwin, II. 212–13).

And in a captive chariot into Rouen
Bring him our prisoner.

Con.   This becomes the great. 55
Sorry am I his numbers are so few,
His soldiers sick and famish'd in their march,
For I am sure when he shall see our army
He'll drop his heart into the sink of fear,
And for achievement offer us his ransom. 60

Fr. King. Therefore, lord constable, haste on Montjoy,
And let him say to England that we send
To know what willing ransom he will give.
Prince Dauphin, you shall stay with us in Rouen.

Dau. Not so, I do beseech your majesty. 65

Fr. King. Be patient, for you shall remain with us.
Now forth, lord constable and princes all,
And quickly bring us word of England's fall.

[*Exeunt.*

SCENE VI.—*The English Camp in Picardy.*

Enter the English and Welsh Captains, GOWER *and* FLUELLEN.

Gow. How now, Captain Fluellen! come you from the
bridge?

Flu. I assure you there is very excellent services
committed at the bridge.

54, 64. *Rouen*] Malone; *Roan* F.

Scene VI

The . . . Picardy] added Malone.   Enter . . . Fluellen] Ed.; Enter
Captaines, English and Welch, Gower and Fluellen F.

54. *captive chariot*] Drawn from
Holinshed.

56. See note to IV. ii. 16–24.

59. *sink*] pit.

60. *for achievement*] (*a*) to conclude
the business, (*b*) instead of an honourable encounter.

64. *Prince . . . Rouen*] This is in
accordance with Hall and Holinshed.

Scene VI
1. *the bridge*] Henry sent a detach-
ment ahead of his main forces to
seize the bridge over the Ternoise at
Blangy. After a skirmish with French
forces guarding the bridge, the
Englishmen captured the bridge on
23 October, and Henry's main
forces crossed over on 24 October,
the night before Agincourt.

3. *services*] deeds of arms, exploits.

Gow. Is the Duke of Exeter safe?　　　　　　　　　5

Flu. The Duke of Exeter is as magnanimous as Agamemnon; and a man that I love and honour with my soul, and my heart, and my duty, and my life, and my living, and my uttermost power: he is not,—God be praised and blessed!—any 10 hurt in the world, but keeps the bridge most valiantly, with excellent discipline. There is an aunchient lieutenant there at the pridge; I think in my very conscience he is as valiant a man as Mark Antony; and he is a man of no estimation in 15 the world; but I did see him do as gallant service.

Gow. What do you call him?

Flu. He is called Aunchient Pistol.

Gow. I know him not.

Enter PISTOL.

Flu. Here is the man.　　　　　　　　　　　　20

Pist. Captain, I thee beseech to do me favours:
　　　The Duke of Exeter doth love thee well.

Flu. Ay, I praise God; and I have merited some love at his hands.

Pist. Bardolph, a soldier firm and sound of heart, 25
　　　And of buxom valour, hath, by cruel fate
　　　And giddy Fortune's ~~furious fickle~~ wheel,

---

9. *life*] Q, Rowe; *live* F.　　　21-2, 25-9, 40-50. Capell's arrangement.
Prose F.

5. *Exeter*] According to Hall and Holinshed Exeter was not present at the capture of the bridge.

9. *life*] The F " live " is probably an anticipation of " living ".

13. *aunchient lieutenant*] possibly sub-lieutenant or first lieutenant.

14-16. This is not consistent with Pistol's character elsewhere. Perhaps the French, like their compatriot M. le Fer later on, were overawed by Pistol's " killing tongue ".

15. *Mark Antony*] " the garland of the war . . . the soldier's pole " of *Ant.* IV. xv. 64-5.

26. *buxom*] brisk, sturdy.

27-39. For a detailed discussion of the medieval and renaissance treatment of the Roman goddess Fortuna see H. R. Patch, *The Goddess Fortuna in Mediaeval Literature*, 1927. Fortune was the common theme of medieval and renaissance poets, artists and emblem writers. The painter in *Tim.* claims to show " A thousand moral paintings . . . That shall demonstrate these quick blows of Fortune's ". It is not clear that Fluellen had any particular painter or poet in mind, although Greene, *Farewell to Folly* (*Works*, ed. Grosart, IX. 264), refers specifically to a

That goddess blind,
That stands upon the rolling restless stone—
Flu. By your patience, Aunchient Pistol. Fortune is   30
painted blind, with a muffler afore her eyes, to signify
to you that Fortune is blind: and she is painted
also with a wheel, to signify to you, which is the
moral of it, that she is turning, and inconstant, and
mutability, and variation: and her foot, look you, is   35
fixed upon a spherical stone, which rolls, and rolls,
and rolls: in good truth, the poet makes a most excellent description of it: Fortune is an excellent moral.
Pist. Fortune is Bardolph's foe, and frowns on him;   40
For he hath stol'n a pax, and hanged must a' be.

29. *stone* —] Rowe; *stone* F.   31. *her*] Q, Capell; *his* F, Dover Wilson.

painting by Zeuxes. Indeed, as J. H. P. Pafford has indicated privately, Shakespeare may have drawn on Greene's frequent references to the Fortune emblem. See S. L. Wolff, *Greek Romances in Elizabethan Prose Fiction*, 1912, pp. 381–92. Baldwin, II. 73–6, however, urges that Fluellen's description is a parallel parody of some lines of Pacuvius which are quoted in *Ad Herennium* as an illustration of faulty reasoning. Moreover, he claims that Shakespeare was using the particular version of these lines contained in Lambinus' *Ciceronis Opera Omnia*, 1573, I. 37:

"Fortunam insanam esse & caecam & brutam perhibent philosophi,
Saxoque illam instare globoso praedicant volubili.
Ideo, quo saxu impulerit fors, cadere eo fortuna autumat.
Caecam ob eam rem esse iterant, quia nihil cernat, quo sese applicet.
Insanam autem aiunt, quia atrox, incerta, instabilisq; sit.
Brutam, quia dignu, atq; indignum nequeat internoscere."

He adds that the "learned grammarians" in the audience should have recognized his stock illustration of faulty reasoning, and perhaps should have remembered its sequel in which the existence of Fortune is denied and men's misfortunes are attributed to their own rashness. In other words Bardolph had only his own rashness to blame for his misfortune—an excellent moral indeed!

27. *furious*] cruel.

40. *Fortune . . . foe*] Usually taken to refer to the ballad,
" Fortune, my foe! why dost thou frown on me? "
The phrase may have been proverbial long before. Cf. Chaucer, *Troil.* I. 837, " Wel fynde I that Fortune is my fo ". Pistol implies that Fortune punishes sacrilege, an interesting function for a pagan goddess.

41. *he . . . a' be*] Holinshed narrates the theft of a pyx, not a pax, and its punishment. See Appendix, p. 162. Henry had previously issued orders on this matter: "yf Any . . . of our hooste presume to take Awaye frome Any churche . . . Any of theyr goodes, that ys, to saye vestments, chalices, bookes, Iuwells, or Any Relyques . . . they be forthwyth hanged therefore . . . no man vnder payne of dethe be so bolde As to touche onreuerently the sacrament of the Auter, or the pyxe, or Any other boxe wherein yt ys conteynyd " (Upton, *De Studio Militari*, tr. Blount, ed. Dudden, p. 34).

A damned death!
Let gallows gape for dog, let man go free,
And let not hemp his wind-pipe suffocate.
But Exeter hath given the doom of death   45
For pax of little price.
Therefore, go speak; the duke will hear thy voice;
And let not Bardolph's vital thread be cut
With edge of penny cord and vile reproach:
Speak, captain, for his life, and I will thee requite.   50

Flu. Aunchient Pistol, I do partly understand your
meaning.

Pist. Why then, rejoice therefore.

Flu. Certainly, aunchient, it is not a thing to rejoice
at; for if, look you, he were my brother, I would   55
desire the duke to use his good pleasure and put
him to execution; for discipline ought to be used.

Pist. Die and be damn'd; and figo for thy friendship!

Flu. It is well.

Pist. The fig of Spain!   [*Exit.*   60

Flu. Very good.

Gow. Why, this is an arrant counterfeit rascal: I
remember him now; a bawd, a cut-purse.

Flu. I'll assure you a' uttered as prave words at the
pridge as you shall see in a summer's day. But   65

As Dover Wilson notes " the agreement of F and Q (" packs ") proves that ' pax ' was spoken on the stage ".

The pyx is the box in which the consecrated wafers are kept; the pax is a small metal plate with a crucifix impressed on it. In the celebration of mass in the early Christian Church a kiss of peace was given to the communicants by the priest. In the thirteenth century a metal plate or tablet was kissed by the priest instead and then passed to the congregation to kiss in turn. Shakespeare, who surely must have known the difference, may have substituted " pax " for some reason not now clear.

45. *doom*] judgment.

46. *of little price*] Dover Wilson sees in this a direct link with the *Gesta*, p. 41, " pixidam de cupro deaurato, quam forte credebet auream . . . rapuisset ". The excuse, however, is a natural one under the circumstances.

53. *Why . . . therefore*]. Cf. *2H4* v. iii. 110, *Pistol*, " Why then, lament therefore ".

58, 60. *figo*], *fig of Spain*] An expression of contempt accompanied by a coarse gesture in which the thumb was thrust between the fingers or into the mouth. " Fig of Spain " seems to have been more emphatic than " figo ".

62. *arrant*] A form of " errant ", vagabond, used as an intensive, Here means " out - and - out ". " thorough ", " absolute ", etc.

it is very well; what he has spoke to me, that is 65
well, I warrant you, when time is serve.

Gow. Why, 'tis a gull, a fool, a rogue, that now and
then goes to the wars to grace himself at his return into London under the form of a soldier.   And
such fellows are perfect in the great commanders'   70
names, and they will learn you by rote where services were done; at such and such a sconce, at
such a breach, at such a convoy; who came off
bravely, who was shot, who disgraced, what terms
the enemy stood on; and this they con perfectly   75
in the phrase of war, which they trick up with
new-tuned oaths: and what a beard of the general's cut and a horrid suit of the camp will do
among foaming bottles and ale-washed wits, is
wonderful to be thought on.   But you must learn   80
to know such slanders of the age, or else you may
be marvellously mistook.

Flu. I tell you what, Captain Gower; I do perceive he
is not the man that he would gladly make show
to the world he is: if I find a hole in his coat I   85
will tell him my mind.   [*Drum heard.*
Hark you, the king is coming, and I must speak
with him from the pridge.

Drum and Colours.   Enter KING HENRY, GLOUCESTER, *and
his poor soldiers.*

Flu. God pless your majesty!

86. Drum heard] added Capell.   88. Enter ... soldiers] Dover
Wilson.   Enter the King and his poore Souldiers F.

67. *gull*] stupid fellow.

71–2. *services*] Cf. l. 3.

72. *sconce*] fort, earthwork.

73. *came off*] acquitted himself.

74–5. *what terms ... stood on*] what
was the condition of the enemy.

76–7. *phrase of war ... new-tuned
oaths*] Cf. *Oth.* i. i. 14, " Horribly
stuff'd with epithets of war. "

77. *new-tuned*] newly coined.

77–8. *beard ... cut*].   Trimmed to
the same fashion as that favoured by
the General.

78. *horrid ... camp*] fearsome battle-
dress.

81. *slanders of the age*] those who
bring shame on their times.

85. *find ... coat*] have the chance to
expose him.

K. Hen. How now, Fluellen! cam'st thou from the
    bridge?   90

Flu. Ay, so please your majesty. The Duke of Exeter
    has very gallantly maintained the pridge: the
    French is gone off, look you, and there is gallant
    and most prave passages. Marry, th' athversary
    was have possession of the pridge, but he is en-   95
    forced to retire, and the Duke of Exeter is master
    of the pridge. I can tell your majesty the duke
    is a prave man.

K. Hen. What men have you lost, Fluellen?

Flu. The perdition of th' athversary hath been very 100
    great, reasonable great: marry, for my part, I
    think the duke hath lost never a man but one
    that is like to be executed for robbing a church;
    one Bardolph, if your majesty know the man: his
    face is all bubukles, and whelks, and knobs, and 105
    flames o' fire; and his lips blows at his nose, and
    it is like a coal of fire, sometimes plue and some-
    times red; but his nose is executed, and his fire's
    out.

K. Hen. We would have all such offenders so cut off: 110
    and we give express charge that in our marches
    through the country there be nothing compelled
    from the villages, nothing taken but paid for, none
    of the French upbraided or abused in disdainful
    language; for when lenity and cruelty play for a 115
    kingdom, the gentler gamester is the soonest
    winner.

                Tucket. Enter MONTJOY

106. *o'*] Dyce; *a* F.   115. *lenity*] Q, Rowe; *Leuitie* F.

94. *passages*] i.e. of arms.

105. *bubukles*] A confusion of Latin
" bubo ", an abscess, with carbuncle
in its M.E. form " charbucle ".

105. *whelks*] pimples. Craig (quoted
Evans) suggests that Shakespeare
may have had Chaucer's Somnour in
mind with his " fyr-reed cherubinnes
face ", and his " whelkes whyte ".
Cf. *Prol. to Cant. Tales*, ll. 624–33.

108. *executed*] " slit as he stood in
the pillory, before being hanged "
(Dover Wilson).

108. *his fire's*] its fire's.

111–15. *we give . . . language*] So
Hall and Holinshed.

117. Tucket] a trumpet call.

Montjoy] The title of the chief
Herald of France, not his name.

Mont. You know me by my habit.

K. Hen. Well then I know thee: what shall I know of
　　thee?

Mont. My master's mind.　　　　　　　　　　　　　　120

K. Hen. Unfold it.

Mont. Thus says my king: Say thou to Harry of
　　England: Though we seemed dead, we did but
　　sleep: advantage is a better soldier than rashness.
　　Tell him we could have rebuked him at Harfleur, 125
　　but that we thought not good to bruise an injury till
　　it were full ripe: now we speak upon our cue, and
　　our voice is imperial: England shall repent his
　　folly, see his weakness, and admire our sufferance.
　　Bid him therefore consider of his ransom, which 130
　　must proportion the losses we have borne, the sub-
　　jects we have lost, the disgrace we have digested;
　　which in weight to re-answer, his pettiness would
　　bow under. For our losses, his exchequer is too
　　poor; for th' effusion of our blood, the muster of his 135
　　kingdom too faint a number; and for our disgrace,
　　his own person, kneeling at our feet, but a weak
　　and worthless satisfaction. To this add defiance:
　　and tell him, for conclusion, he hath betrayed
　　his followers, whose condemnation is pronounced. 140
　　So far my king and master, so much my office.

K. Hen. What is thy name? I know thy quality.

Mont. Montjoy.

---

127. *our cue,*] Rowe; *our Q. F.*

---

118. *You ... habit*] A particularly
insolent greeting.

118. *habit*] i.e. herald's sleeveless
coat (a tabard) bearing his coat-of-
arms upon it.

124. *advantage*] a timely seizing of
opportunity.

126. *bruise*] crush, squeeze.

126-7. *injury ... full ripe*] an image
from a boil.

127. *now ... cue*] now the time has
come for us to speak in this drama.

128. *England*] i.e. Henry.

129. *admire our sufferance*] wonder at
our patience.

133-4. *which ... under*] to make
full reparation for which is beyond
his slender means.

143. *Montjoy*] See note to S.D.
above.

K. Hen. Thou dost thy office fairly. Turn thee back,
    And tell thy king I do not seek him now, 145
    But could be willing to march on to Calais
    Without impeachment; for, to say the sooth,
    Though 'tis no wisdom to confess so much
    Unto an enemy of craft and vantage,
    My people are with sickness much enfeebled, 150
    My numbers lessen'd, and those few I have
    Almost no better than so many French;
    Who when they were in health, I tell thee, herald,
    I thought upon one pair of English legs
    Did march three Frenchmen. Yet, forgive me, God, 155
    That I do brag thus! this your air of France
    Hath blown that vice in me; I must repent.
    Go therefore, tell thy master here I am;
    My ransom is this frail and worthless trunk,
    My army but a weak and sickly guard; 160
    Yet, God before, tell him we will come on,
    Though France himself and such another neighbour
    Stand in our way. There's for thy labour, Montjoy.
    Go, bid thy master well advise himself:
    If we may pass, we will; if we be hinder'd, 165
    We shall your tawny ground with your red blood
    Discolour: and so, Montjoy, fare you well.
    The sum of all our answer is but this:
    We would not seek a battle as we are;
    Nor, as we are, we say we will not shun it: 170
    So tell your master.

Mont. I shall deliver so. Thanks to your highness. [*Exit.*

Glou. I hope they will not come upon us now.

K. Hen. We are in God's hand, brother, not in theirs.
    March to the bridge; it now draws toward night: 175
    Beyond the river we'll encamp ourselves,
    And on to-morrow bid them march away. [*Exeunt.*

---

172. Exit] added Rowe.

145–67. In his speech ll. 146–8, 162–8 are close to Holinshed. See Appendix, p. 162.

147. *impeachment*] hindrance.
149. *of craft and vantage*] who has the advantage of power and initiative.

SCENE VII.—*The French Camp, near Agincourt.*

Enter, the Constable of France, the LORD RAMBURES,
ORLEANS, DAUPHIN, *with others.*

Con. Tut! I have the best armour of the world.
Would it were day!

Orl. You have an excellent armour; but let my horse
have his due.

Con. It is the best horse of Europe.

Orl. Will it never be morning?   5

Dau. My lord of Orleans, and my lord high constable, you talk of horse and armour?

Orl. You are as well provided of both as any prince
in the world.   10

Dau. What a long night is this. I will not change my
horse with any that treads but on four pasterns.
Ça, ha! He bounds from the earth as if his entrails

Scene VII

The . . . Agincourt] Theobald.
13. *Ça, ha,*] Theobald; *ch' ha* F.

12. *pasterns*] F 2; *postures* F 1.

Scene VII

Dauphin] The Dauphin's presence
at Agincourt is unhistorical. See
III. v. 64–6. Q gives The Dauphin's
part to Bourbon.

3. *an . . . armour*] a suit of armour.
Cf. *2H4* IV. v. 29, " a rich armour ".

12. *pasterns*] hoofs. Actually that
part of the leg between the fetlock
and the hoof.

11–42. *I will . . . nature*] The
Dauphin himself illustrates how to
" vary deserved praise " in composing a " theme ". A " theme " was
a term in rhetoric for a literary com-
position, prose or verse, arranged in
strictly observed parts. One of the
standard authorities on the writing
of themes was Aphthonius' *Progymnasmata*, 1580, in which (p. 110) is
described the type of theme for
praising some object. To " vary " a

theme was to enlarge it by adding
verse quotations. illustrations, allu-
sions, or by the invention of new
matter. Here the theme has an
obvious relationship to the war horse
of *Job* xxxix. 19–25.

13. *Ça ha!*] Perhaps a reminiscence of *Job* xxxix. 25, " He saith
among the trumpets, Ha, ha ".

13–14. *He bounds . . . hairs*] i.e. as
if he were a tennis ball. Tennis balls
were stuffed with hair. Cf. *Ado*, III. ii.
45–7, " the barber's man hath been
seen with him; and the old ornament
of his cheek hath already stuffed
tennis-balls ". With this picture of
the frivolous Dauphin extolling his
palfrey (a lady's horse) and its
parlour tricks, one may contrast
Henry, the " feather'd Mercury " of
1H4, who fully armed could leap on
to his horse.

were hairs; le cheval volant, the Pegasus, chez
les narines de feu! When I bestride him, I soar,　15
I am a hawk: he trots the air; the earth sings when
he touches it; the basest horn of his hoof is more
musical than the pipe of Hermes.

Orl. He's of the colour of the nutmeg.

Dau. And of the heat of the ginger. It is a beast　20
for Perseus: he is pure air and fire; and the dull
elements of earth and water never appear in him,
but only in patient stillness while his rider
mounts him: he is indeed a horse: and all other
jades you may call beasts.　25

Con. Indeed, my lord, it is a most absolute and
excellent horse.

Dau. It is the prince of palfreys; his neigh is like the
bidding of a monarch, and his countenance
enforces homage.　30

14. *chez*] Theobald; *ches* F; *qui a* Capell.

14. *Pegasus*] The winged horse
which sprang from the blood of the
gorgon Medusa when Perseus cut off
her head. According to Ovid,
Metam. IV. 662, Perseus was mounted
on Pegasus when he rescued Andro-
meda from the dragon. Earlier
stories narrate that Bellerophon alone
was the rider of Pegasus. (For a full
discussion of this see Baldwin,
" Perseus Purloins Pegasus ", *P.Q.*
XX, July, 1941) Cf. *Troil.* I. iii. 42;
IV. v. 186.

15. *les narines de feu*] Cf. *Job* xxxix.
20, " The glory of his nostrils is
terrible ".

16–18. *the earth . . . Hermes*]
Pegasus struck Mt. Helicon with his
hoof, and the fountain of the Muses,
Hippocrene, sprang forth. In Renaissance story Pegasus was regarded
as the horse of the Muses and the
symbol of poetry.

18. *pipe of Hermes*] Probably derived from Ovid, *Metam.* I. 677,
where Hermes charms asleep the
monster Argus by the strains of his
pipe. Hermes, a Greek god, was
identified by the Romans with
Mercury.

19, 21. *colour of the nutmeg . . .
pure air and fire*] Cf. Blundeville,
Arte of Ridynge, I. fol. 1: " A horse
for the most part is coloured
according as he is complexioned. . . .
Again he is complexioned according
as he doth participat more or lesse
of any of the iiii Elementes. . . .
If of the aire, then he is a sanguine,
and therfore pleasant, nimble, and of
colour is most commonlye a baye.
And if of the fier, then he is cholorique
and therefore lighte, whote, and
fiery, a sterer, and seldome of anye
great strength, and is wont to be of
Colour a bright sorel."

28. *prince of palfreys*] i.e. the
effeminate Dauphin is riding a lady's
horse. Cf. *Edward III*, IV. iv. 90,
where the Duke of Normandy
(Dauphin) insults the Black Prince
by sending him a " nimble ioynted
iennet ".

Orl. No more, cousin.

Dau. Nay, the man hath no wit that cannot, from the
rising of the lark, to the lodging of the lamb,
vary deserved praise on my palfrey: it is a
theme as fluent as the sea; turn the sands into   35
eloquent tongues, and my horse is argument
for them all. 'Tis a subject for a sovereign to
reason on; and for a sovereign's sovereign to
ride on; and for the world, familiar to us and
unknown, to lay apart their particular functions   40
and wonder at him. I once writ a sonnet in his
praise and began thus: " Wonder of nature,"—

Orl. I have heard a sonnet begin so to one's mistress.

Dau. Then did they imitate that which I composed
to my courser; for my horse is my mistress.

Orl. Your mistress bears well.   45

Dau. Me well; which is the prescript praise and
perfection of a good and particular mistress.

Con. Nay, for methought yesterday your mistress
shrewdly shook your back.   50

Dau. So perhaps did yours.

Con. Mine was not bridled.

Dau. O, then, belike she was old and gentle, and you
rode, like a kern of Ireland, your French hose
off, and in your strait strossers.   55

Con. You have good judgment in horsemanship.

Dau. Be warned by me, then: they that ride so, and

32–3. *from . . . lamb*] Proverbial.
Cf. Breton, *Courtier and Countryman*
II. 6, " We rise with the lark and
go to bed with the lamb ".

37–8. *a sovereign to reason on*] A
possible quibble on " sovereign
reason ", a current phrase. Cf.
Ham. I. iv. 73, " sovereignty of
reason "; III. i. 166, " that noble and
most sovereign reason ".

38. *reason*] discourse.

47. *prescript*] prescribed, appropriate.

48. *particular*] having one lover
only.

50. *shrewdly*] severely, cursedly.

52. *bridled*] as (*a*) horse, (*b*) a
shrewish woman compelled to wear
a bridle, with a glance at " shrewdly "
l. 50.

54. *kern*] light-armed Irish soldiers.

54. *French hose*] loose, wide
breeches.

55. *strait strossers*] tight trousers, i.e.
bare-legged.

56. *You . . . horsemanship*] Ironical.
In view of the Dauphin's reply
" horsemanship " is possibly equivo-
cal.

ride not warily, fall into foul bogs. I had rather
have my horse to my mistress.

Con. I had as lief have my mistress a jade.   60

Dau. I tell thee, constable, my mistress wears his own
hair.

Con. I could make as true a boast as that if I had a
sow to my mistress.

Dau. Le chien est retourné à son propre vomissement,   65
et la truie lavée au bourbier: thou makest use of
any thing.

Con. Yet do I not use my horse for my mistress; or
any such proverb so little kin to the purpose.

Ram. My lord constable, the armour that I saw   70
in your tent to-night, are those stars or suns
upon it?

Con. Stars, my lord.

Dau. Some of them will fall to-morrow, I hope.

Con. And yet my sky shall not want.   75

Dau. That may be, for you bear a many superfluously,
and 'twere more honour some were away.

Con. Ev'n as your horse bears your praises; who
would trot as well were some of your brags dis-
mounted.   80

Dau. Would I were able to load him with his desert!
Will it never be day? I will trot to-morrow a
mile, and my way shall be paved with English
faces.

60. *lief*] Capell; *liue* F.   66. *et*] Rowe; *est* F.   *truie*] Rowe; *leuye* F.

60. *jade*] (*a*) a horse, (*b*) a loose
woman.

65–70, 113–25. There is a proverb-
capping contest in Grange, *Golden
Aphroditis*, 1577, Sig. D4ᵛ.

65–6. *Le chien . . . bourbier*] 2 *Peter*
ii. 22. Noble notes that the version
is that of de Tournes' *Testament*,
Lyons, 1551. It is not impossible
that Shakespeare translated the
English version directly into French.
Cf. *2H4* I. iii. 97–9.

71. *stars*] Apparently some form of

ornamentation without any heraldic
significance (Giles, p. 116).

74–5. *Some . . . want*] The Constable
replies that his honour will be in no
way diminished. "Sky" here may
be Falstaff's "clear sky of fame"
(*2H4* IV. iii. 56). There may be a
proverbial expression behind these
lines. J. Grange, *Golden Aphroditis*,
1577, Sig. A4ʳ, states that unkind
critics of his work "say behinde my
backe, 'A blasing starre will shoote',"
implying that such splendour is
transitory and contemptible.

Con. I will not say so for fear I should be faced out   85
    of my way.   But I would it were morning, for I
    would fain be about the ears of the English.

Ram. Who will go to hazard with me for twenty
    prisoners?

Con. You must first go yourself to hazard, ere you   90
    have them.

Dau. 'Tis midnight; I'll go arm myself.   [*Exit.*

Orl. The Dauphin longs for morning.

Ram. He longs to eat the English.

Con. I think he will eat all he kills.   95

Orl. By the white hand of my lady, he's a gallant
    prince.

Con. Swear by her foot, that she may tread out the oath.

Orl. He is simply the most active gentleman of France.

Con. Doing is activity, and he will still be doing.   100

Orl. He never did harm, that I heard of.

Con. Nor will do none to-morrow: he will keep that
    good name still.

Orl. I know him to be valiant.

Con. I was told that by one that knows him better   105
    than you.

Orl. What's he?

Con. Marry, he told me so himself; and he said he
    cared not who knew it.

Orl. He needs not; it is no hidden virtue in him.   110

Con. By my faith, sir, but it is; never any body saw it
    but his lackey: 'tis a hooded valour; and when
    it appears, it will bate.

Orl. Ill will never said well.

85–6. *faced . . . way*] (*a*) put out of countenance, shamed, (*b*) driven off.

88. *go to hazard*] take a wager.   Cf. 4 Chorus 17–19.

95. *I . . . kills*] Cf. *Ado* I. i. 42–5.

98. *tread out*] spurn, treat with contempt.

112. *but his lackey*] i.e. his lackey is the only one who has felt the valour of his blows.

112–13. *hooded . . . bate*] valour concealed as a hawk is masked by its hood, and, like a hawk unhooded in the presence of game, gives a little flutter.

113. *bate*] (*a*) flutter, (*b*) dwindle. For the association of courage and a hawk's flight cf. *R2* I. i. 109, "how high a pitch his resolution soars", and *John* II. i. 82.

Con. I will cap that proverb with " There is flattery in 115
    friendship ".

Orl. And I will take up that with " Give the devil his
    due".

Con. Well placed: there stands your friend for the
    devil: have at the very eye of that proverb with 120
    " A pox of the devil".

Orl. You are the better at proverbs, by how much
    " A fool's bolt is soon shot ".

Con. You have shot over.

Orl. 'Tis not the first time you were overshot. *parleying with witticisms* 125

Enter a Messenger

Mess. My lord high constable, the English lie within
    fifteen hundred paces of your tents.

Con. Who hath measured the ground?

Mess. The Lord Grandpré.

Con. A valiant and most expert gentleman. Would 130
    it were day! Alas! poor Harry of England, he
    longs not for the dawning as we do.

Orl. What a wretched and peevish fellow is this king
    of England, to mope with his fat-brained followers
    so far out of his knowledge! 135

Con. If the English had any apprehension, they would
    run away.

Orl. That they lack; for if their heads had any in-
    tellectual armour, they could never wear such
    heavy head-pieces. 140

Ram. That island of England breeds very valiant crea-
    tures; their mastiffs are of unmatchable courage.

115–16. *flattery in friendship*] Proverbial (Tilley, *Elizabethan Proverb
Lore*, p. 268). Cf. *Tw.N.* v. i. 13–22.

  122. *how much*] as much as.

  124. *shot over*] i.e. over the mark.

  125. *overshot*] outshot, beaten in
shooting.

  127. *fifteen hundred paces*] Considerably farther than Holinshed's " two
hundred and fiftie pases ".

133. *peevish*] thoughtless, foolish.

134–5. *to mope . . . knowledge*] to
wander aimlessly with his stupid
followers leaving his common sense
so far behind him.

136. *apprehension*] (*a*) common
sense, intelligence, (*b*) fear.

142. *mastiffs*] The English mastiff
had a high reputation for courage.

Orl. Foolish curs! that run winking into the mouth of
  a Russian bear and have their heads crushed like
  rotten apples.   You may as well say that's a valiant 145
  flea that dare eat his breakfast on the lip of a lion.

Con. Just, just; and the men do sympathize with the
  mastiffs in robustious and rough coming on, leaving
  their wits with their wives: and then give them
  great meals of beef and iron and steel, they will 150
  eat like wolves and fight like devils.

Orl. Ay, but these English are shrewdly out of beef.

Con. Then shall we find to-morrow they have only
  stomachs to eat and none to fight.   Now is it
  time to arm; come, shall we about it?   155

Orl. It is now two o'clock: but, let me see, by ten
  We shall have each a hundred Englishmen.   [*Exeunt.*

*Really no apprehension as
to the meaning of individual
death at all*

156. *o*'] Theobald (ed. 2); *a* F.

147. *sympathize with*] resemble.

150–4. *great meals . . . to fight*] This
may have been prompted by Hall,
xlvii^v–xlviii^r: " keepe an Englishman one moneth from his warme bed,
fat befe and stale drynke, and let him
that season tast colde and suffre
hunger, you then shall se his courage
abated."   The idea, however, was
common.   *Famous Victories*, Sig. E4^r

follows Hall very closely, but does not
mention beef.   Moore Smith quotes
Edward III III. iii. 159.
" but scant them of their chines of
      beefe
And take awaie their downie fether
      bedes,
And presently they are as resty stiffe
As twere a many ouer ridden iades ".
    154. *stomachs*] inclinations.

*The
Hu*

*The English —
all become
demoralised.*

ACT IV

Enter CHORUS.

Now entertain conjecture of a time
When creeping murmur and the poring dark
Fills the wide vessel of the universe.
From camp to camp through the foul womb of night
The hum of either army stilly sounds,   5
That the fix'd sentinels almost receive
The secret whispers of each other's watch:
Fire answers fire, and through their paly flames
Each battle sees the other's umber'd face;
Steed threatens steed, in high and boastful neighs   10
Piercing the night's dull ear; and from the tents
The armourers, accomplishing the knights,
With busy hammers closing rivets up,

ACT IV

Chorus

Act IV] Pope: Actus Tertius F.   Enter] added Rowe.

ACT IV

Chorus

1. *entertain conjecture*] imagine.

2. *poring*] eye-straining.

3. *wide vessel*] hollow vault. Cf. "foul womb of night", l. 4.

8. *paly*] (*a*) pale, (*b*) divided by vertical lines with alternate tinctures (in heraldry).

9. *battle*] army.

9. *umber'd*] Three interpretations have been put forward: (*a*) wearing a visor or umbrer, (*b*) shadowed, or stained as with umber, (*c*) outlined (in heraldry). The first seems premature in spite of the activities of the armourers (ll. 12–13), unless the phrase "umber'd face" is used figuratively for armed appearance or array. The second is favoured by most editors. The third was suggested by M. Holmes, *N.Q.* 5 August, 1952, p. 333. He interprets "umber'd" as a variant of "umbrated" or "in ombre", a heraldic term meaning "depicted in outline only, the colour or colours of the field showing through". The term, he claims, was familiar to armorists in the fifteenth and sixteenth centuries, This third interpretation would suit well with the heraldic "paly", l. 8, and with the context, but further evidence of the use of "umder'd" would be desirable to make it acceptable.

12. *accomplishing*] completing the armouring of.

13. *hammers closing rivets up*] The helmet was riveted to the cuirass while the latter was being worn.

90

Give dreadful note of preparation.
The country cocks do crow, the clocks do toll,   15
And the third hour of drowsy morning name.
Proud of their numbers, and secure in soul,
The confident and over-lusty French
Do the low-rated English play at dice;
And chide the cripple tardy-gaited night   20
Who, like a foul and ugly witch, doth limp
So tediously away.   The poor condemned English,
Like sacrifices, by their watchful fires
Sit patiently, and inly ruminate
The morning's danger, and their gesture sad   25
Investing lank-lean cheeks and war-worn coats
Presenteth them unto the gazing moon
So many horrid ghosts. O, now, who will be-
    hold
The royal captain of this ruin'd band
Walking from watch to watch, from tent to tent,   30
Let him cry, "Praise and glory on his head!"
For forth he goes and visits all his host,
Bids them good-morrow with a modest smile,
And calls them brothers, friends and countrymen.
Upon his royal face there is no note   35
How dread an army hath enrounded him;
Nor doth he dedicate one jot of colour

---

16. *name*] Steevens (1778) after Tyrwhitt; *nam'd* F.   20. *cripple tardy-gaited*] Capell; *creeple-tardy-gated* F.   27. *Presenteth*] Hanmer; *Presented* F.

14. *note*] (*a*) sound, (*b*) warning.

17. *secure*] careless, over-confident.

18. *over-lusty*] over-merry.

19. *low-rated*] Cf. II. iv. 13, "neglected".

19. *play*] play for.   Cf. III. vii. 88–9. So Hall and Holinshed.

20–1. *night ... witch*] Cf. IV. i. 277.

23. *Like sacrifices*] i.e. to Bellona or Mars. Cf. *1H4* IV. i. 113–17.

28. *horrid*] fearful.

28–47. There is no mention in Hall or Holinshed that Henry visited and cheered his soldiers on the eve of Agincourt. While there were precedents, classical and other

(cf. *R3*, v. iii. 69–71) Shakespeare may have drawn on the description of the siege of Harfleur in *The First English Life of Henry V* (ed. Kingsford), p. 381. There Henry "daylie and nightlie in his owne person visited and searched the watches, orders, and stacions of euerie part of his hoast, and whome he found dilligent he praised and thanked, and the negligent he corrected and chastened".

36. *enrounded*] surrounded.

37–8. *Nor ... night*] Nor have his cheeks given up any of their flesh colour because of a sleepless night.

Unto the weary and all-watched night;
But freshly looks and overbears attaint
With cheerful semblance and sweet majesty;   40
That every wretch, pining and pale before,
Beholding him, plucks comfort from his looks.
~~A largess universal like the sun~~
His liberal eye doth give to every one,
Thawing cold fear, that mean and gentle all,   45
Behold, as may unworthiness define,
A little touch of Harry in the night.
And so our scene must to the battle fly;
Where, O for pity! we shall much disgrace
With four or five most vile and ragged foils,   50
Right ill-dispos'd in brawl ridiculous,
The name of Agincourt. Yet sit and see;
Minding true things by what their mock'ries be.

                                                    [*Exit.*

39. *overbears attaint*] overcomes any
sign of exhaustion. Cf. *Ven.* 741–2,
" The marrow-eating sickness, whose
    attaint
Disorder breeds by heating of the
    blood ".
43–4. *A largess . . . one*] Baldwin II.
197–8, compares Quintilian, *Institutio*,
1580, p. 16, " Non enim vox illa
praeceptionis, vt coena, minus pluri-
bus sufficit: sed vt sol, vniuersis idem
lucis calorisq; largitur ". While
" largess universal " may owe something to Quintilian, the shining of
the sun on all alike was proverbial.
Cf. *Tw.N.* III. i. 45 and *Wint.* IV. iii.
457–8.

46. *as . . . define*] as far as our
unworthy selves can present it.
47. *touch*] description, account.
Moore Smith quotes H*8* v. i. 12–13,
            " Give your friend
Some touch of your late business ".
50. *four . . . foils*] Cf. Jonson's
sneer in *Every Man In His Humour*,
Prologue 9–11,
" Or, with three rusty swords,
And help of some few foot and half-
    foot words,
Fight over York and Lancaster's long
    jars ".
50. *foils*] rapiers.
53. *Minding*] Calling to mind.

SCENE I.—*The English Camp at Agincourt.*

Enter KING HENRY, BEDFORD, *and* GLOUCESTER.

K. Hen. Gloucester,'tis true that we are in great danger;
    The greater therefore should our courage be.
    Good morrow, brother Bedford.   God Almighty!
    There is some soul of goodness in things evil,
    Would men observingly distil it out;   5
    For our bad neighbour makes us early stirrers,
    Which is both healthful and good husbandry:
    Besides, they are our outward consciences,
    And preachers to us all; admonishing
    That we should dress us fairly for our end.   10
    Thus may we gather honey from the weed,
    And make a moral of the devil himself.

Enter ERPINGHAM.

    Good morrow, old Sir Thomas Erpingham:
    A good soft pillow for that good white head
    Were better than a churlish turf of France.   15
Erp. Not so, my liege: this lodging likes me better,
    Since I may say, " Now lie I like a king ".
K. Hen. 'Tis good for men to love their present pains
    Upon example; so the spirit is eased:

Scene I

The . . . Agincourt] Theobald.   King Henry] Rowe; the King F.
3. *Good*] Rowe; *God* F.

Scene I

3–12. Cf. the moralizing of Duke
Senior, *AYL.* II. i. 1–18.

6–7. *For . . . husbandry*] Cf. *Troil.* I.
ii. 6–8,
" And, like as there were husbandry
in war,
Before the sun rose he was harness'd
light,
And to the field he goes ".

7. *husbandry*] thrift, economy,
stewardship.

10. *dress us*] prepare ourselves.

19. *example*] A rhetorical term. A
species of simile, particularly an
illustrative incident used for the
purpose of encouraging or discourag-
ing (see Susenbrotus, *Epitome*, 1565,
p. 108).
Cf. *LLL.*I.ii.67–122, where Armado
asks for precedents to comfort him
in love. He proposes to rewrite the
King and the Beggar [Maid] " that
I may example my digression by
some mighty precedent " (see Baldwin
II. 166–71).
19–23. Two thoughts are involved
in these lines, (*a*) the reviving of a

And when the mind is quicken'd, out of doubt,   20
The organs, though defunct and dead before,
Break up their drowsy grave, and newly move
With casted slough and fresh legerity.
Lend me thy cloak, Sir Thomas.   Brothers both,
Commend me to the princes in our camp;   25
Do my good-morrow to them; and anon
Desire them all to my pavilion.

Glou. We shall, my liege.

Erp. Shall I attend your grace?

K. Hen.   No, my good knight;
Go with my brothers to my lords of England: 30
I and my bosom must debate awhile,
And then I would no other company.

Erp. The Lord in heaven bless thee, noble Harry!

                    [*Exeunt all but King.*

K. Hen. God-a-mercy, old heart! thou speak'st cheerfully.

Enter PISTOL.

Pist. Qui va là?   35
K. Hen. A friend.

---

33. Exeunt . . . King] Camb.; Exeunt F.   35. *Qui va là?*] Rowe; *Che vous la?* F.

mind heavy and dull with care, linked with the snake-image in "casted slough", and (*b*) the awakening of the faculties after sleep, linked with the death image in "drowsy grave".

In Galen's doctrines the "vital spirits" (spirit), generated in the chambers of the brain, carried thence the commands of the mind to the bodily members. When the vital spirits were exhausted by care or tiredness, the mind, no longer receiving and sending the flow of vital spirits relapsed into dullness or sleep, and the body likewise was diminished in function or slept until recalled into activity by the command of the mind.

20–2. *And when . . . grave*] Cf. the association of sleep, vacant mind and torpid body in ll. 284–5.

22. *drowsy grave*] The resemblance between sleep and death is a commonplace in Shakespeare's plays. Cf. *Mac.* II. iii. 81; "sleep, death's counterfeit", and the tag from *Sententiae Pueriles*, "somnus mortis imago". Cf. also Troil. III. iii. 201, "thoughts unveil in their dumb cradles".

23. *With casted slough*] A snake is sluggish and listless for a time immediately preceding the shedding of its skin.

23. *legerity*] nimbleness, briskness.

31–2. *I . . . company*] Dover Wilson notes that this "seems to lead up to a prayer, which we get at ll. 295–311. See Introduction, p. xxxviii.

Pist. Discuss unto me; art thou officer?

　Or art thou base, common and popular?

K. Hen. I am a gentleman of a company.

Pist. Trailest thou the puissant pike?   40

K. Hen. Even so.　What are you?

Pist. As good a gentleman as the emperor.

K. Hen. Then you are a better than the king.

Pist. The king's a bawcock, and a heart of gold,

　　A lad of life, an imp of fame;   45

　　Of parents good, of fist most valiant:

　　I kiss his dirty shoe, and from heart-string

　　I love the lovely bully.　What is thy name?

K. Hen. Harry le Roy.

Pist. Le Roy! a Cornish name: art thou of Cornish crew? 50

K. Hen. No, I am a Welshman.

Pist. Knowest thou Fluellen?

K. Hen. Yes.

Pist. Tell him, I'll knock his leek about his pate

　　Upon Saint Davy's day.   55

K. Hen. Do not you wear your dagger in your cap

　　that day, lest he knock that about yours.

Pist. Art thou his friend?

K. Hen. And his kinsman too.

Pist. The figo for thee then!   60

K. Hen. I thank you.　God be with you!

Pist. My name is Pistol called.　　　　　　　　[*Exit.*

37–8, 44–8, 54–5. Pope's arrangement.　Prose F.　　　62. Exit] F.
Manet King] F at 63.

38. *popular*] i.e. of the people, common.

39. *gentleman of a company*] gentleman volunteer.

40. *Trail'st . . . pike?*] are you an infantryman?　To trail the pike was to hold it just below the head allowing the butt to trail on the ground behind. This was the normal method of carrying the pike. Fortescue, *Shakespeare's England* I. 115, writes, " gentlemen volunteers worked their way up from the ranks, and more than one peer trailed a pike in the regiments of Maurice Nassau".

44. *bawcock*] fine fellow.　See III. ii. 25.

44. *heart of gold*] i.e. perfect man, as gold was the perfect proportion of elements.　Greensleeves, too, was " my heart of gold ".

45. *imp. of fame*] child of fame. Pistol uses the same expression in *2H4* v. v. 47.

48. *bully*] fine fellow.

50. *Cornish*] Probably a glance at the old play *Harry of Cornwall*.　See Henslowe, *Diary*, ed. Greg, II. 151. It may also be a glance at Sir Walter Ralegh, whose name was variously spelt: Rolye, Rauly, Rawlee, etc.

55. *Saint Davy's day*] 1st March.

Enter FLUELLEN *and* GOWER.

K. Hen.   It sorts well with your fierceness.

Gow.   Captain Fluellen!

Flu.   So! in the name of Jesu Christ, speak fewer.   65
It is the greatest admiration in the universal
world, when the true and aunchient prerogatifes
and laws of the wars is not kept. If you would
take the pains but to examine the wars of Pompey
the Great, you shall find, I warrant you, that   70
there is no tiddle taddle nor pibble babble in
Pompey's camp; I warrant you, you shall find
the ceremonies of the wars, and the cares of it,
and the forms of it, and the sobriety of it, and
the modesty of it, to be otherwise.   75

Gow.   Why, the enemy is loud; you hear him all night.

Flu.   If the enemy is an ass and a fool and a prating
coxcomb, is it meet, think you, that we should
also, look you, be an ass and a fool and a prating
coxcomb? in your own conscience now?   80

Gow.   I will speak lower.

Flu.   I pray you and beseech you that you will.

Exeunt Gower and Fluellen.

---

65. *So!*] Capell; 'So F.   *fewer*] F;   *lower* Q 3, Malone; *lewer* Q 1, 2.
71. *babble*] *bable* F.   82. Exeunt . . . Fluellen] Capell; Exit F.

---

63. *sorts*] agrees. Cf. " sort ", company.

65. *speak fewer*] Malone emended " fewer " to " lower " which is the reading of Q 3. Fluellen probably has in mind the tag, "pauca verba", though oddly enough it is Fluellen who does all the talking, not Gower. Holinshed records that orders were given " that no noise or clamor should be made ". Hall does not mention it.

66–8. *It is . . . kept*] i.e. it astonishes everyone that you do not observe the ancient principles of warfare.

66–84. The French chronicler Le Fèvre approved of Henry's discipline: " Et bien entretenoit la discipline de

chevalrie comme jadis faisoient les Romains " (Wylie, III. 425, n. 2).

67. *prerogatifes*] " faculties by which a thing is specially or advantageously distinguished above others " (*O.E.D.*), superior principles.

71. *tiddle taddle . . . pibble babble*] tittle tattle . . . bibble babble.

74. *sobriety*] orderliness.

75. *modesty*] correctness of conduct, propriety (Lat. modestia).

76. *the enemy is loud*] Dover Wilson compares *Gesta Henrici Quinti*, p. 48, " audivimus adversariam hospitatam, et unumquemque, ut moris est, vociferantem ". Both Hall and Holinshed record that " they made great cheare and were verie merie ".

K. Hen. Though it appear a little out of fashion,
    There is much care and valour in this Welshman.

Enter three soldiers, JOHN BATES, ALEXANDER COURT, *and*
    MICHAEL WILLIAMS.

Court. Brother John Bates, is not that the morning   85
    which breaks yonder?
Bates. I think it be; but we have no great cause to
    desire the approach of day.
Will. We see yonder the beginning of the day, but I
    think we shall never see the end of it. Who   90
    goes there?
K. Hen. A friend.
Will. Under what captain serve you?
K. Hen. Under Sir Thomas Erpingham.
Will. A good old commander and a most kind gentle-   95
    man: I pray you, what thinks he of our estate?
K. Hen. Even as men wracked upon a sand, that look
    to be washed off the next tide.
Bates. He hath not told his thought to the king?
K. Hen. No; nor it is not meet he should. For,   100
    though I speak it to you, I think the king is but
    a man, as I am: the violet smells to him as it
    doth to me; the element shows to him as it doth

94. *Thomas*] Pope (ed. 2) after Theobald; *John* F.

83. *out of fashion*] quaint.
87–8. Cf. III. vii. 131–2.
94. *Thomas*] The F reading "John"
is probably an erroneous expansion
by the compositor of " Tho.", the
usual abbreviation of Thomas, which
he took to be " Iho ", the abbreviation for Jhon or John.
101–6. The common, human attri-
butes of kings are referred to elsewhere in Shakespeare. Cf. IV. i.
244–5; *R2* III. ii. 175–7,
" I live with bread like you, feel
    want,
Taste grief, heed friends—subjected
    Thus,

How can you say to me, I am a
    king? "
There is an interesting parallel in
Montaigne, *Essays,* tr. Florio, 1893,
p. 309: " All the true commodities
that Princes have, are common unto
them, with men of meane fortune.
It is for Gods to mount winged horses
and to feed on Ambrosia. They have
no other sleep nor no other appetite
than ours. Their steele is of no
better temper than that wherewith
we arme ourselves " (see *Revue
Anglo-Américaine,* 1931–32, p. 120).
103. *element shows*] sky appears.

to me; all his senses have but human conditions:
his ceremonies laid by, in his nakedness he   105
appears but a man; and though his affections
are higher mounted than ours, yet when they
stoop, they stoop with the like wing.   Therefore
when he sees reason of fears, as we do, his fears,
out of doubt, be of the same relish as ours are: 110
yet, in reason, no man should possess him with
any appearance of fear, lest he, by showing it,
should dishearten his army.

Bates. He may show what outward courage he will,
but I believe, as cold a night as 'tis, he could   115
wish himself in Thames up to the neck, and so I
would he were, and I by him, at all adventures,
so we were quit here.

K. Hen. By my troth, I will speak my conscience of
the king: I think he would not wish himself any   120
where but where he is.

Bates. Then I would he were here alone; so should he
be sure to be ransomed, and a many poor men's
lives saved.

K. Hen. I dare say you love him not so ill to wish him   125
here alone, howsoever you speak this to feel other
men's minds: methinks I could not die any where
so contented as in the king's company, his cause
being just and his quarrel honourable.

Will. That's more than we know.   130

Bates. Ay, or more than we should seek after; for we

---

104. *conditions*] dispositions, qualities.

105. *ceremonies*] accompaniments of
royalty.

106. *affections*] emotions, desires.

107. *are higher mounted*] soar higher.
An expression from falconry.

108. *stoop*] descend. Another word
from falconry used to describe a
hawk plunging down on its prey.

109–12. *when . . . appearance of fear*]
when he sees reason for fear . . . yet
he sees reason for not showing any
signs of fear. . . . The two "reasons"
are balanced against each other.

111–12. *should possess . . . fear*] Cf.
IV. i. 296.

111. *possess him*] take possession of
him.

117. *at all adventures*] at all costs,
whatever the risks.

118. *so . . . here*] as long as we were
out of this.

119. *my conscience*] what I inwardly
believe to be true.

119–21, 127–9, etc.   Note the dramatic irony.

131. *Bates*] Capell proposed to
assign this speech to Court on the
grounds that Bates is a grumbler.

know enough if we know we are the king's subjects. If his cause be wrong, our obedience to
the king wipes the crime of it out of us.

Will. But if the cause be not good, the king him- 135
self hath a heavy reckoning to make; when
all those legs and arms and heads, chopped off
in a battle, shall join together at the latter
day, and cry all, "We died at such a place";
some swearing, some crying for a surgeon, some 140
upon their wives left poor behind them, some
upon the debts they owe, some upon their
children rawly left.   I am afeard there are
few die well that die in a battle; for how can
they charitably dispose of any thing when 145
blood is their argument?   Now, if these men
do not die well, it will be a black matter for
the king that led them to it, who to disobey
were against all proportion of subjection.

K. Hen. So, if a son that is by his father sent about 150
merchandise do sinfully miscarry upon the sea,
the imputation of his wickedness, by your rule,
should be imposed upon his father that sent him:
or if a servant, under his master's command
transporting a sum of money, be assailed by 155
robbers and die in many irreconciled iniquities,
you may call the business of the master the
author of the servant's damnation. But this is
not so: the king is not bound to answer the

148. *who*] *whom* F 2.

138–9. *at the latter day*] at the Day of
Judgement. Cf. *Job* xix. 25, "I
know that my redeemer liveth, and
that he shall stand at the latter day
upon the earth".
143. *rawly*] abruptly. Cf. *Mac.*
IV. iii. 26–8,
  "Why in that rawness left you
      wife and child . . .
  Without leave-taking?"
144. *die well*] i.e. die a Christian
death.
145. *charitably   dispose . . . thing*]

settle any thing "in love and
charity" with their neighbour.
146. *blood is their argument*] they
are engaged in shedding blood.
149. *proportion of subjection*] the
rightful duties of a subject.
151. *sinfully miscarry*] die in his
sins.
152. *imputation of*] responsibility
for.
156. *irreconciled*] unabsolved, un-
atoned.
159. *answer*] answer for.

particular endings of his soldiers, the father of his 160
son, nor the master of his servant; for they
purpose not their death when they purpose their
services. Besides there is no king, be his cause
never so spotless, if it come to the arbitrement of
swords, can try it out with all unspotted soldiers. 165
Some, peradventure, have on them the guilt of
premeditated and contrived murder; some, of
beguiling virgins with the broken seals of perjury, some, making the wars their bulwark, that
have before gored the gentle bosom of peace 170
with pillage and robbery. Now, if these men
have defeated the law and outrun native punishment, though they can outstrip men, they have
no wings to fly from God: war is his beadle, war
is his vengeance; so that here men are punished 175
for before-breach of the king's laws in now the
king's quarrel: where they feared the death they
have borne life away, and where they would be
safe they perish. Then, if they die unprovided,
no more is the king guilty of their damnation 180
than he was before guilty of those impieties for
the which they are now visited. Every subject's
duty is the king's; but every subject's soul is his
own. Therefore should every soldier in the wars
do as every sick man in his bed, wash every 185

164–5. *arbitrement of swords*] decision
by battle. Cf. *Cym.* I. iv. 55–6.

168–9. *broken seals of perjury*] Cf.
Meas. IV. i. 6, "Seals of love, but
seal'd in vain ".

169–71. *making . . . robbery*] fleeing
from retribution to the shelter of the
wars after committing crimes during
peace time.

172. *native*] in their native land.

173–5. *though . . . vengeance*] Cf.
Amos. ix. 2–4, where God's vengeance
is to be wreaked on those who seek
to escape " though they go into captivity before their enemies, thence
will I command the sword, and it

shall slay them ". Again, in a
famous passage in *Ps.* cxxxix. 9 the
fugitive in vain takes the " wings of
the morning ".

174. *beadle*] an officer who whipped
criminals.

176–9. Note the antitheses " before
. . . now", "death . . . life", "safe
. . . perish".

177–9. *where . . . perish*] Cf. *Matt.*
xvi. 25, etc.

179. *unprovided*] unprepared; i.e.
without reconciling their souls to
God.

182. *visited*] punished.

mote out of his conscience; and dying so, death
is to him advantage; or not dying, the time was
blessedly lost wherein such preparation was
gained: and in him that escapes, it were not sin
to think that, making God so free an offer, he   190
let him outlive that day to see his greatness, and
to teach others how they should prepare.

Will. 'Tis certain, every man that dies ill, the ill upon
his own head; the king is not to answer it.

Bates. I do not desire he should answer for me; and   195
yet I determine to fight lustily for him.

K. Hen. I myself heard the king say he would not be
ransomed.   — would not accept unacceptable condition

Will. Ay, he said so, to make us fight cheerfully; but
when our throats are cut, he may be ransomed,   200   ie will
and we ne'er the wiser.   keep to the
stated
cause.

K. Hen. If I live to see it, I will never trust his word after.

Will. You pay him, then! That's a perilous shot out
of an elder-gun, that a poor and a private displeasure can do against a monarch. You may as   205
well go about to turn the sun to ice with fanning
in his face with a peacock's feather. You'll never
trust his word after! come, 'tis a foolish saying.

K. Hen. Your reproof is something too round: I should
be angry with you if the time were convenient.   210

Will. Let it be a quarrel between us, if you live.   — even anger is
to be looked forward
K. Hen. I embrace it.   to —so long as there is
Will. How shall I know thee again?   life.
K. Hen. Give me any gage of thine, and I will wear
it in my bonnet: then, if ever thou darest ac-   215
knowledge it, I will make it my quarrel.

186. *mote*] Malone; *Moth* F.

186. *mote*] The F reading " Moth "
is a Shakespearian spelling but is
used by other writers.

186-7. *death . . . advantage*] Cf.
Phil. i. 21, " For Christ [is] to me
life, and death is to me advantage ".

197-8. *I . . . ransomed*] So Hall and
Holinshed.

203. *pay him*] pay him out.

203-4. *That's . . . elder-gun*] that's
as much as to expect a deadly bullet
from a pop-gun. Pop-guns used to
be made out of elder-wood from
which the pith had been removed.

204-5. *a poor . . . displeasure*] the
displeasure of a poor, common
man.

209. *round*] blunt.

Will. Here's my glove: give me another of thine.

K. Hen. There.

Will. This will I also wear in my cap: if ever thou
come to me and say after to-morrow, " This is 220
my glove ", by this hand I will take thee a box
on the ear.

K. Hen. If ever I live to see it, I will challenge it.

Will. Thou darest as well be hanged.

K. Hen. Well, I will do it, though I take thee in the 225
king's company.

Will. Keep thy word: fare thee well.

Bates. Be friends, you English fools, be friends: we
have French quarrels enow, if you could tell how
to reckon.   230

K. Hen. Indeed, the French may lay twenty French
crowns to one, they will beat us; for they bear
them on their shoulders: but it is no English
treason to cut French crowns, and to-morrow the
king himself will be a clipper.   [*Exeunt Soldiers.* 235
Upon the king! let us our lives, our souls,
Our debts, our careful wives,
Our children, and our sins lay on the king!
We must bear all.   O hard condition!
Twin-born with greatness, subject to the breath   240
Of every fool, whose sense no more can feel
But his own wringing.   What infinite heart's ease
Must kings neglect that private men enjoy!
And what have kings that privates have not too,

235. Exeunt Soldiers] Johnson; Exit Souldiers F at 230.
239–42. Camb. arrangement.   F divides after *all, Greatnesse, sence, wringing,
neglect.*

221. *take*] strike.
231. *lay*] (*a*) bet, (*b*) match.
232. *crowns*] (*a*) heads, (*b*) gold
coins (écus) worth about 6s. each.
234. *treason*] The clippers of coins
were punished under the law against
treason.
236 ff. For variations on the theme
of the cares of kingship cf. *R2* III. ii.
144–77; *2H4* III. i. 4–31; IV. v. 21–
31, etc.

237. *careful*] anxious.
240. *breath*] utterance, speech.
242. *wringing*] stomach-ache.
244–55. Grether, *Das Verhältnis von
Shakespeares Heinrich V zu Sir T.
Elyot's Governor*, 1938, notes a parallel:
Governor, ed. Croft, 1880, II. 206–7:
"Thy dignitie or autorita, wherein thou onely differest from
other, is (as it were) but a
weighty or hevy cloke, fresshely

Save ceremony, save general ceremony?   245
And what art thou, thou idol ceremony?
What kind of god art thou, that suffer'st more
Of mortal griefs than do thy worshippers?
What are thy rents? what are thy comings-in?
O ceremony, show me but thy worth!   250
What is thy soul of adoration?
Art thou aught else but place, degree, and form,
Creating awe and fear in other men?
Wherein thou art less happy, being fear'd,
Than they in fearing.   255
What drink'st thou oft, instead of homage sweet,
But poison'd flattery? O be sick, great greatness,
And bid thy ceremony give thee cure!
Think'st thou the fiery fever will go out
With titles blown from adulation?   260
Will it give place to flexure and low-bending?
Canst thou, when thou command'st the beggar's knee,
Command the health of it? No, thou proud dream,

---

251. *What . . . adoration*] Knight.   *What? is thy Soule of Odoration* F 1 ; *What?*
is thy Soule of Adoration F 2.   *is thy Soule of Adoration* F 2.
                                        259. *Think'st*] Rowe; *Thinks* F.

gliteringe in the eyen of them
that be pore blynde, where unto
the it is paynefull, if thou weare
hym in his right facion, and as
it shal best become thee."
II. 209: " . . . autoritie, beinge
well and diligently used, is but
a token of superioritie, but in
very dede it is a burden and losse
of libertie."
  251. *thy soul of adoration*] real
nature of the worship offered thee.
For the construction, cf. *Caes.* II. i.
256, " your cause of grief ".
  259. *Think'st*] Rowe's emendation.
The form of the second person
singular without the " t " is found
elsewhere in Shakespeare.
  259–60. *Think'st . . . adulation*] Do
you think that the fires of fever will
be extinguished by the empty
breath of flatterers? Cf. *Pericles* I.
ii. 38–41,

" They do abuse the king that
     flatter him;
 For flattery is the bellows blows
     up sin
 The thing the which is flatter'd,
     but a spark,
 To which that blast gives heat
     and stronger glowing."
  261. *flexure*] bowing.
  263–90. The cares of kingship that
deprive kings of sleep compared with
the untroubled sleep of labouring
men is also the theme of *2H4* III. i.
4–31. Henry IV, though his sleep-
lessness is caused by guilt, generalizes
the theme into "uneasy lies the head
that wears a crown ", and Prince
Henry takes up the theme later
IV. v. 20–30. Baldwin, II. 322–4,
505–7, shows that the origin of
Henry's speech is an example of a
theme of Priscian printed in Aphthonius, *Progymnasmata*, 1580, pp.

That play'st so subtly with a king's repose;
I am a king that find thee; and I know   265
'Tis not the balm, the sceptre and the ball,
The sword, the mace, the crown imperial,
The intertissued robe of gold and pearl,
The farced title running 'fore the king,
The throne he sits on, nor the tide of pomp   270
That beats upon the high shore of this world,
No, not all these, thrice-gorgeous ceremony,
Not at all these, laid in bed majestical,
Can sleep so soundly as the wretched slave,
Who with a body fill'd and vacant mind   275
Gets him to rest, cramm'd with distressful bread;
Never sees horrid night, the child of hell,
But, like a lackey, from the rise to set

56ᵛ–57ᵛ, to which Shakespeare has added some details from Horace, Bk. III, Ode I. 17–24. Here Shakespeare follows the general structure of Priscian's theme, but, as in *2H4*, changes its basic thought that princes ought not to sleep all night to " uneasy lies the head . . . ".

263. *proud dream*] For the association of a dream with flattery, cf. Sonnet 87,

" Thus have I had thee, as a dream doth flatter
In sleep a king, but waking, no such matter."

265. *find*] expose, find out.

266. *balm*] consecrated oil used to anoint a king at his coronation. Cf. *3H6* III. i. 18.

269. *farced title*] the lengthy, flattering titles by which a king is addressed. See Introduction, p. xvi.

269. *farced*] stuffed.

270–1. *nor the tide . . . world*] Perhaps the " sea of glory " in which Wolsey foundered. See *H8* III. ii. 359–66. Dover Wilson refers to Sonnet 64 for the imagery of the sea,

" When I have seen the hungry ocean gain
Advantage on the kingdom of the shore ".

But Erasmus has both:
" Ea littora solemus diligentissime communire, quae vehementissimam fluctuum vim excipiunt. Sunt autem innumerae res, quae possint Principum animos a recto dimovere . . . super omnia vero adulatio " (*Institutio, Opera*, IV. 564 c.).

274–6. Cf. *Eccles.* v. 2,
" A labouring man sleepeth sweetely ";
Horace, Bk. III, Ode I. 21–3,
        " somnus agrestium
lenis virorum non humilis domos fastidit."
and *Meas.* IV. ii. 69–70.

276. *distressful*] earned by the sweat of the brow. Cf. *Gen.* iii. 19.

277. *horrid . . . hell*] Probably Hecate whom Shakespeare elsewhere seems to identify with night (Root, *Classical Mythology*, 1903, pp. 53–6). Baldwin, II. 440, quotes:

" Cumque illis Hecate properans horrenda cucurrit,
Cui trinum caput est, genuit quam Tartarus olim."

Cf. *Lucr.*, l. 764,
" O comfort-killing Night, image of hell! "

278. *lackey*] a footman who ran by the coach of his master.

Sweats in the eye of Phœbus, and all night
Sleeps in Elysium; next day after dawn,   280
Doth rise and help Hyperion to his horse,
And follows so the ever-running year
With profitable labour to his grave:
And, but for ceremony, such a wretch,
Winding up days with toil and nights with sleep,   285
Had the fore-hand and vantage of a king.
The slave, a member of the country's peace,
Enjoys it; but in gross brain little wots
What watch the king keeps to maintain the peace,
Whose hours the peasant best advantages.   290

Enter ERPINGHAM.

Erp. My lord, your nobles, jealous of your absence,
    Seek through your camp to find you.
K. Hen.   Good old knight,
    Collect them altogether at my tent:
    I'll be before thee.
Erp.   I shall do't, my lord.   [*Exit.*
K. Hen. O God of battles! steel my soldiers' hearts;   295
    Possess them not with fear; take from them now

---

281. *Hyperion*] F 2, Camb.; Hiperio F 1.   292–3. F divides after
together, thee.

---

279. *Phoebus*] the sun-god.
280. *Elysium*] classical abode of the
virtuous dead on an island in the
western ocean. Vergil later placed
it in Hades. Here it is used loosely
for " paradise ".
281. *Hyperion*] Son of Uranus and
father of the sun-god, Helios, with
whom he is often confused. The
labourer helps the sun god to harness
his horses to his chariot. For the F
reading cf. note III. i. 24.
285. *Winding up*] completely occu-
pying (lit. " enwrapping ").
286. *had . . . vantage*] would be
more favourably and advantageously
situated.

287. *member*] sharer. Cf. *Oth.* III.
iv. 112, " a member of his love ".
290. *Whose . . . advantages*] whose
hours are most profitable to the
peasant. Evans compares *R3* IV.
iv. 324, " Advantaging their loan
with interest ".
291. *jealous*] anxious, worried.
295–6. *steel . . . fear*] Cf. *2H6* III. i.
331, " Now York, or never, steel thy
fearful thoughts ".
295–8. *steel . . . them*] Cf. Hall
xlix^r, " Therefore puttynge your
onely truste in hym, let not their
multytude feare youre heartes, nor
their great noumbre abate your
courages ".

The sense of reck'ning, if th' opposed numbers
Pluck their hearts from them.   Not to-day, O Lord!
O not to-day, think not upon the fault
My father made in compassing the crown!   300
I Richard's body have interred new,
And on it have bestow'd more contrite tears
Than from it issued forced drops of blood.
Five hundred poor I have in yearly pay,
Who twice a day their wither'd hands hold up   305
Toward heaven, to pardon blood; and I have built
Two chantries, where the sad and solemn priests
Sing still for Richard's soul.   More will I do;
Though all that I can do is nothing worth,
Since that my penitence comes after all,   310
Imploring pardon.

Enter GLOUCESTER.

Glou. My liege!
K. Hen.   My brother Gloucester's voice!   Ay;
I know thy errand, I will go with thee:
The day, my friends, and all things stay for me.
                                                    [*Exeunt.*

297-8. *reckoning . . . Pluck*] Steevens (1778) after Tyrwhitt; *reckning of th'
opposed numbers: Pluck* F; *reck'ning; lest th' opposed numbers Pluck* Theobald.
306-8. Pope's arrangement.   F divides after *blood, Chantries, still, doe.*   314.
friends] Q, Theobald; *friend* F.

297. *if*] Tyrwhitt's conjecture "if"
for the F "o" is graphically much
more likely than Moore Smith's conjecture "or" (before) and has therefore been retained.
  300. *compassing*] obtaining.
  301. *I Richard's . . . new*] So Holinshed.   Richard II treated Henry very
kindly during his father's banishment, and a real friendship sprang
up between them.   This reburial
may have been a mark of this friendship (Jacob, p. 24).

  307. *Two chantries*] Henry built two
religious houses, one at Sheen for
the Carthusian monks and the other
at Sion, Twickenham, for the Augus-
tinian order.   Shakespeare's information is apparently drawn from
Fabyan's *Chronicle*, 1516, p. 589, and
not from Hall or Holinshed.   Aldis
Wright notes that the charters of
foundation do not suggest that Henry
established the houses so that masses
might be sung for Richard's soul.

SCENE II.—*The French Camp.*

Enter the DAUPHIN, ORLEANS, RAMBURES, *and* BEAUMONT.

Orl. The sun doth gild our armour; up, my lords!
Dau. Montez à cheval!   My horse! varlet! lacquais! ha!
Orl. O brave spirit!
Dau. Via! les eaux et la terre!
Orl. Rien puis? l'air et le feu!   5
Dau. Ciel! cousin Orleans.

Enter Constable.

Now, my lord constable!
Con. Hark, how our steeds for present service neigh!
Dau. Mount them, and make incision in their hides,
  That their hot blood may spin in English eyes,   10
  And dout them with superfluous courage, ha!
Ram. What, will you have them weep our horses' blood?
  How shall we then behold their natural tears?

Enter Messenger.

Mess. The English are embattail'd, you French peers.
Con. To horse, you gallant princes! straight to horse!   15
  Do but behold yond poor and starved band,

Scene II

and Beaumont] F. and others Capell.   2. *Montez à*] Steevens after Capell; *Monte* F.   *varlet*] Dyce; *Verlot* F; *valet* F 2.   4. *les eaux*] Theobald; *les ewes* F.   *la terre*] Rowe; *terre* F.   5. *le feu*] Rowe; *feu* F. 6. *Ciel!*] Theobald; *Cein,* F.   11. *dout*] Rowe; *doubt* F.

Scene II

Beaumont does not speak; he is addressed at III. v. 44 and is listed among the dead at IV. iii. 102.

1–6. Various editors have tried to improve the French of these lines. The consensus of opinion is that the Dauphin, still thinking of his palfrey in terms of his previous description, says, " Away, over water and land ". At this Orleans mockingly asks, " What, nothing more? not air and fire too? " And the Dauphin replies, " Yes, Heaven itself ".

9. *make incision*] i.e. with spurs.

10. *spin*] spray.

11. *dout*] extinguish, contr. of do out

11. *superfluous courage*] i.e. overflowing blood.

16–24. *Do . . . them*] Cf. III. v. 56–9. The germ of this is in the Constable's speech in Hall, xlviiᵛ, "And on the otherside is a small handfull of pore Englishmen . . . which by reason that their vitaill is consumed & spent, are by daily famyn sore wekened, consumed & almost without

And your fair show shall suck away their souls,
Leaving them but the shales and husks of men.
There is not work enough for all our hands;
Scarce blood enough in all their sickly veins   20
To give each naked curtle-axe a stain,
That our French gallants shall to-day draw out,
And sheathe for lack of sport: let us but blow on them,
The vapour of our valour will o'erturn them.
'Tis positive 'gainst all exceptions, lords,   25
That our superfluous lackeys and our peasants,
Who in unnecessary action swarm
About our squares of battle, were enow
To purge this field of such a hilding foe,
Though we upon this mountain's basis by   30
Took stand for idle speculation:
But that our honours must not.   What's to say?
A very little let us do,
And all is done.   Then let the trumpets sound
The tucket sonance and the note to mount: 35
For our approach shall so much dare the field
That England shall couch down in fear, and yield.

Enter GRANDPRÉ.

25. *'gainst*] F 2; *against* F 1.   35. *sonance*] Johnson; *Sonuance* F.

spirites: for their force is clerly
abated and their strength vtterly
decaied, so y^t or the battailes shall
ioyne they shalbe for very feblenes
vaquished & ouercom, & instede of
men ye shal fight with shadowes. . . .
Therefore nowe, it is no mastery to
vanquishe and overthrowe them,
beyng both wery & weake, for by
reason of feblenes and faintnes their
weapons shall fall out of their handes
when they profer to strike."

18. *shales*] shells.
21. *curtle-axe*] cutlass.
23. *sheathe . . . sport*] Cf. III. i. 21.
25. *exceptions*] objections.
29. *hilding*] sorry, worthless. Cf. 2H4 I. i. 57, "some hilding fellow".
30. *mountain's basis*] A hill in Holinshed.

31. *for idle speculation*] as idle onlookers.
33–4. *A very . . . done*] Cf. Hall, xlviii^r, " . . . whiche pray is surely yours if every man strike but one stroke. . . . Therefore good felowes take courage to you, the victory is yours, the gaine is yours & the honor is yours without greate laboure or much losse."
35. *tucket sonance*] sound of the trumpet. Cf. III. vi. 118. *O.E.D.* has only one contemporary example of "sonance", from Heywood, *Lucrece*, 1608 (pr. 1638).
36. *dare*] terrify, paralyse with fright (a word used in fowling and akin to " daze"). Cf. *H8* III. ii. 282, "And dare us with his cap like larks".
37. *couch*] crouch.

Grand. Why do you stay so long, my lords of France?
 Yon island carrions, desperate of their bones,
 Ill-favouredly become the morning field: 40
 Their ragged curtains poorly are let loose,
 And our air shakes them passing scornfully:
 Big Mars seems bankrupt in their beggar'd host,
 And faintly through a rusty beaver peeps:
 The horsemen sit like fixed candlesticks,   45
 With torch-staves in their hand; and their poor
  jades
 Lob down their heads, dropping the hides and hips,
 The gum down-roping from their pale-dead eyes,
 And in their pale dull mouths the gimmal'd bit
 Lies foul with chaw'd grass, still and motionless; 50
 And their executors, the knavish crows,
 Fly o'er them all, impatient for their hour.
 Description cannot suit itself in words
 To demonstrate the life of such a battle
 In life so lifeless as it shows itself.   55
Con. They have said their prayers, and they stay for death.
Dau. Shall we go send them dinners and fresh suits,
 And give their fasting horses provender,
 And after fight with them?

---

49. *gimmal'd*] Delius; *Iymold* F; *gimmal* Johnson.   52. *them all,*] F;
them, all Rowe.   55. *lifeless*] Capell: *liueless* F.

39. *carrions*] skeletons, living carcases.

39. *desperate of*] in despair of saving.

41. *curtains*] banners.

42. *passing*] exceeding.

43-4. *Big . . . peeps*] i.e. the spirit of war, almost absent from their army, shows but faint-heartedly.

44. *beaver*] visor.

45-6. *The . . . hand*] Steevens quotes Webster, *White Devil*, ed. Dyce, 1857, p. 19 : " I saw him at last tilting : he showed like a pewter candlestick, fashioned like a man in armour, holding a tilting-staff in his hand, little bigger than a candle of twelve i' the pound." Apparently candlesticks were made in this form.

47. *Lob*] droop, hang down.

48. *down-roping*] trickling down. Cf. III. v. 23.

49. *gimmal'd bit*] i.e. twin bits, consisting of two similar parts hinged together. Cf. interleaved armour mentioned in *Edward III*, I. ii. 26–9, " Iacks of Gymould mayle ".

51. *executors*] those who dispose of what the dead leave behind. Evans quotes Topsell, *History of Four-footed Beasts*, ed. 1673, p. 177, " He destroyeth them . . . and so maketh himself executor to their heeps of honey ".

52. *them all*] Rowe's reading "them, all" gives better sense, but as F reading gives a sound meaning it has been retained.

54. *the life of*] to the life.

Con. I stay but for my guard.   On to the field!   60
I will the banner from a trumpet take,
And use it for my haste.   Come, come, away!
The sun is high, and we outwear the day.   [*Exeunt.*

SCENE III.—*The English Camp.*

Enter GLOUCESTER, BEDFORD, EXETER, ERPINGHAM, *with
all his host*; SALISBURY, *and* WESTMORELAND.

Glou. Where is the king?
Bed. The king himself is rode to view their battle.
West. Of fighting men they have full threescore thousand.
Exe. There's five to one; besides, they all are fresh.
Sal. God's arm strike with us! 'tis a fearful odds.   5
God bye you, princes all; I'll to my charge:
If we no more meet till we meet in heaven,
Then, joyfully, my noble Lord of Bedford,
My dear Lord Gloucester, and my good Lord Exeter,
And my kind kinsman, warriors all, adieu!   10
Bed. Farewell, good Salisbury; and good luck go with thee!

60. *guard. On*] F; *guidon* Rann.

Scene III

The English Camp] Theobald. Rowe.

60. *guard.   On*] Many editors emend this to " guidon ", a pennon, a word not found elsewhere in Shakespeare, referring to ll. 60-1 for support. The emendation seems unnecessary as Holinshed makes both points : (*a*) that some of the French nobles left their followers behind, and, (*b*) that " the Duke of Brabant, when his standard was not come, caused a baner to be taken from a trumpet and fastened to a speare ".

61. *trumpet*] trumpeter.

6. *bye*] Moore Smith; *buy'* F; *be wi'*

Scene III

2. *battle*] army.
3. *threescore thousand*] So Holinshed.
4. *five to one*] Holinshed and Hall give six to one.   See note to l. 76.
5. *odds*] Singular. Cf. *Oth.* II. iii. 187, " this peevish odds ".
6. *God bye you.*] God be with you. The transformations are God be with you > God be wi you > God buy (cf. Goodbye) > God buy ye.
10. *my kind kinsman*] Westmoreland's younger son had married Salisbury's daughter.

Exe. Farewell, kind lord.   Fight valiantly to-day:
       And yet I do thee wrong to mind thee of it,
       For thou art fram'd of the firm truth of valour.

                                        [*Exit Salisbury.*

~~*Bed.* He is as full of valour as of kindness;~~   15
       ~~Princely in both.~~

                    Enter KING HENRY.

West.   O that we now had here
       But one ten thousand of those men in England
       That do no work to-day!

K. Hen.   ~~dearest   Cousin York~~   What's he that wishes so?
       My ~~cousin Westmoreland?~~   No, my fair cousin:
       If we are mark'd to die, we are enow   20
       To do our country loss; and if to live,
       The fewer men, the greater share of honour.
       God's will!   I pray thee, wish not one man more.
       By Jove, I am not covetous for gold,
       Nor care I who doth feed upon my cost;   25
       It earns me not if men my garments wear;
       Such outward things dwell not in my desires:

13–14. *And . . . valour*] transposed by Theobald after Thirlby; after l. 11 in F.
14. Exit Salisbury] added Rowe.   26. *earns*] Dover Wilson; F *yernes*.

13–14. In the Folio these lines follow l. 11. Thirlby's transposition is supported by Q although the speaker is Clarence and the passage is shortened. Greg suggests (*Principles*, p. 169) that these two lines were a marginal addition wrongly placed by the compositor. Perhaps they were an afterthought.   It will be noted that l. 15 follows naturally after l. 11 as well as after l. 14. Dover Wilson's suggestion that the compositor skipped l. 12 and then inserted it in the wrong place is less likely, involving as it does two distinct errors by the compositor.

16–18. *O . . . to-day*] Holinshed records the wish but not the speaker who, according to the *Gesta* was Walter Hungerford. The *Gesta* also seems to be the authority for the figure ten thousand (p. 47): " quidam dominus Walterus Hungyrford miles impraecabatur ad faciem regis quod habuisset ad illam paucam familiam quam ibi habuit decem milia de melioribus sagitariis Angliae, qui secum desiderarent esse ".

18 ff. Cf. Holinshed. See Appendix, p. 162.

23. *not one man more*] One of Henry's standards in this battle bore the motto " une sanz plus " (Giles, p. 108).

23, 24. *God's will . . . By Jove*] Johnson comments, "The King prays like a Christian and swears like a heathen". " Jove ", however, was probably substituted for some such word as " God " to avoid contravening the Act of 1605 against profanity on the stage (Evans).

But if it be a sin to covet honour,
I am the most offending soul alive.
No, faith, my coz, wish not a man from England: 30
God's peace!   I would not lose so great an honour
As one man more, methinks, would share from me,
For the best hope I have.   O do not wish one more!
Rather proclaim it, Westmoreland, through my host,
That he which hath no stomach to this fight,   35
Let him depart; his passport shall be made,
And crowns for convoy put into his purse:
We would not die in that man's company
That fears his fellowship to die with us.
This day is call'd the feast of Crispian: 40
He that outlives this day, and comes safe home,
Will stand a tip-toe when this day is nam'd,
And rouse him at the name of Crispian.
He that shall see this day, and live old age,
Will yearly on the vigil feast his neighbours,   45
And say, " To-morrow is Saint Crispian ":
Then will he strip his sleeve and show his scars,
And say, " These wounds I had on Crispin's day ".

38. *die*] *live* Hudson after Coleridge.   44. *Shall see . . . live*] F, Dover
Wilson after Greg; *shall live . . . see* Pope; *shall see . . . live t'old* Keightley.
48. *And . . . day*] added Q, Malone.

28-9. *But . . . alive*] Henry's desire
for honour may have come from
Hall xlix[r], " for this day by famous
death or glorious victory I wyl
wynne honor and obtaine fame ".
Cf. *1H4* III. ii. 138-52. Dover
Wilson contrasts Hotspur's depreca-
tion of any one " sharing in his
honour " with Henry's gay encouragement to " his troops to rejoice in
their luck " referring to *1H4* I. iii.
201-8.

39. *die with*] Coleridge's conjecture " live with " is unnecessary, the
existing reading makes good sense :
We would not wish to die in the
company of any man who fears to
keep us company in death. Cf. IV.
viii. 103, " a royal fellowship of
death ".

40. *the feast of Crispian*] 25th
October. Crispinus and Crispianus
(l. 57) his brother, the patron saints
of shoemakers, fled from Rome to
Soissons in the time of Diocletian.
They supported themselves by shoe-
making, and suffered martyrdom in
A.D. 287.

44. Most editions follow Pope's
arrangement. Greg, *Principles*, pp.
70-1, thinks that " such a transposition is by no means a likely
error " and prefers Keightley's reading, " He that shall see this day, and
live t'old age ". This is possible
but not convincing, and it seems
better to follow Dover Wilson and
leave the Folio reading unchanged.

48. Malone added this line from
Q. There is no real justification for

Old men forget; yet all shall be forgot,
But he'll remember with advantages   50
What feats he did that day.   Then shall our names,
Familiar in his mouth as household words,
Harry the king, Bedford and Exeter,
Warwick and Talbot, Salisbury and Gloucester,
Be in their flowing cups freshly remember'd.   55
This story shall the good man teach his son;
And Crispin Crispian shall ne'er go by,
From this day to the ending of the world,
But we in it shall be remembered;
We few, we happy few, we band of brothers;   60
For he to-day that sheds his blood with me
Shall be my brother; be he ne'er so vile
This day shall gentle his condition:
And gentlemen in England now a-bed
Shall think themselves accurs'd they were not here,   65
And hold their manhoods cheap whiles any speaks
That fought with us upon Saint Crispin's day.

Re-enter SALISBURY.

Sal. My sovereign lord, bestow yourself with speed:
The French are bravely in their battles set,
And will with all expedience charge on us.   70
K. Hen. All things are ready, if our minds be so.
West. Perish the man whose mind is backward now!
K. Hen. Thou dost not wish more help from England, coz?

49–50. *be forgot, But*] Q, Malone; *be forgot: But* F.   59. *remembered*]
remembered F.   67. *Re-enter*] Capell; Enter F.

its inclusion, but editors include it probably because as Greg notes, " it has a thoroughly genuine ring ", and because F omitted II. i. 105 also preserved by Q.

50. *with advantages*] with pardonable exaggerations.

60. See Introduction, p. xxvii.

62. *vile*] lowly, of humble birth.

63. *gentle his condition*] ennoble his rank.   In 1418 Henry issued instructions to the Sheriff of Southampton restricting the right to assume coats of arms, but adding, " those excepted who bare arms with us at the battle of Agincourt " (Rymer, *Foedera*, IX. 457 ; Scott Giles, p. 121).

64–5. *And . . . here*] Cf. " qui secum desiderarent esse " in the note to ll. 16–18 (Dover Wilson).

69. *bravely . . . set*] making a brave show arrayed for battle.   Cf. IV. ii. 17.

70. *expedience*] expedition, speed.

West. God's will! my liege, would you and I alone,
  Without more help, could fight this royal battle!   75
K. Hen. Why, now thou hast unwish'd five thousand men;
  Which likes me better than to wish us one.
  You know your places: God be with you all!

Tucket.   Enter MONTJOY.

Mont. Once more I come to know of thee, King Harry,
  If for thy ransom thou wilt now compound,   80
  Before thy most assured overthrow:
  For certainly thou art so near the gulf
  Thou needs must be englutted.   Besides, in mercy,
  The constable desires thee thou wilt mind
  Thy followers of repentance; that their souls   85
  May make a peaceful and a sweet retire
  From off these fields, where, wretches, their poor
    bodies
  Must lie and fester.
K. Hen.   Who hath sent thee now?
Mont. The Constable of France.
K. Hen. I pray thee, bear my former answer back: 90
  Bid them achieve me and then sell my bones.
  Good God! why should they mock poor fellows thus?
  The man that once did sell the lion's skin

76. *five thousand*] According to ll.
3, 4 the English army numbered
12,000. Holinshed gives 15,000, the
Gesta " sex milia . . . non excessit ".
Wylie, II. 141–2, considers that the
English army was a little more than
6000.

80. *compound*] come to terms. Cf.
II. i. 98.

91–4. *Bid . . . him*] Probably suggested by Hall's comment on the
" phantasticall braggynge " of the
Frenchmen immediately before the
arrival of the herald to enquire what
ransom Henry would offer (xlix^v).
" Of thys doynge you may gether,
that it is as muche madnes to make
a determinate judgement of thinges
to come . . . ".

91. *achieve me*] overcome me, capture me.

93–4. *The man . . . hunting him*]
The proverb comes from Aesop's fable
of the Hunter and the Countryman.
Shakespeare, however, substitutes a
lion for a bear, possibly deliberately
to preserve the symbol of royalty.
Baldwin, I. 629, shows that Shakespeare was drawing on the version of
the story in Camerarius' *Fabellae
Aesopicae*, 1573, pp. 75–6. A countryman paid a hunter for a bear's skin
before the latter had caught a bear.
Later, the over-confident hunter,
surprised by the ferocity of the bear,
managed to save his life by falling
prostrate and shamming dead, what
time the countryman took refuge in a
tree. The bear, after sniffing at the

While the beast liv'd, was kill'd with hunting him.
A many of our bodies shall no doubt   95
Find native graves; upon the which, I trust,
Shall witness live in brass of this day's work;
And those that leave their valiant bones in France,
Dying like men, though buried in your dunghills,
They shall be fam'd; for there the sun shall greet
    them,   100
And draw their honours reeking up to heaven,
Leaving their earthly parts to choke your clime,
The smell whereof shall breed a plague in France.
Mark then abounding valour in our English,
That being dead, like to the bullet's crasing,   105
Break out into a second course of mischief,
Killing in relapse of mortality.
Let me speak proudly: tell the constable

---

104. *abounding*] F; *a bounding* Theobald.   105. *crasing*] F, Q, Dover
Wilson; *grasing* F2; *grazing* Theobald (ed. 2).

---

hunter's mouth and ears, departed. The countryman descended from the tree and, misunderstanding the bear's actions, enquired what the bear had whispered in his companion's ears. The hunter replied that the bear had earnestly warned him not to think of selling a bear's skin in the future until the beast had been captured and slain. Then Camerarius adds : " Fabula hoc, quod Graecum proverbium : Non esse ante victoriam exultandum, admonet, ne securitate & temerarijs animis dubia pro certis habeamus."

96. *native*] in their own country.

100–1. Cf. Drayton, *Battle of Agincourt*, ll. 30–2.

"Battles so bravely won
Have ever to the sun
By fame been raised ".

100–2. *for there ... clime*] "Honour" being immortal and the product of the element fire in man is drawn up by the fiery sun to the highest heaven

(cf. Prologue 1), just as the sun draws up vapours from a dunghill, leaving the dead bodies to infect the air.

104. *abounding*] (*a*) abundant, (*b*) rebounding. Cf. IV. ii. 11, " superfluous courage ".

105. *crasing*] A variant form of " grazing ", rebounding. *O.E.D.* quotes Fuller, *Holy and Profane State*, v. i. 358, " Those bullets which do graze on the ground do most mischief to an army ".

107. *relapse of mortality*] Most editors follow Steevens' interpretation " deadly rebound ". " Rebound ", however, is not recorded by *O.E.D.* as a meaning of " relapse ". Evans suggested " decomposition " for the whole phrase. This is consistent with " earthly parts " (l. 102) and " bodies Must lie and fester " (ll. 87–8), and it points a kind of paradox: killing while they themselves were falling back in death to the earth from which they came.

We are but warriors for the working-day;
Our gayness and our gilt are all besmirch'd   110
With rainy marching in the painful field;
There's not a piece of feather in our host—
Good argument, I hope, we will not fly—
And time hath worn us into slovenry:
But, by the mass, our hearts are in the trim;   115
And my poor soldiers tell me, yet ere night
They'll be in fresher robes, or they will pluck
The gay new coats o'er the French soldiers' heads,
And turn them out of service.   If they do this,
As, if God please, they shall, my ransom then   120
Will soon be levied.   Herald, save thou thy labour;
Come thou no more for ransom, gentle herald:
They shall have none, I swear, but these my joints;
Which if they have as I will leave 'em them,
Shall yield them little, tell the constable.   125
Mont. I shall, King Harry.   And so fare thee well:
Thou never shalt hear herald any more.   [*Exit.*
K. Hen. I fear thou wilt once more come again for a ransom.

Enter YORK.

York. My lord, most humbly on my knee I beg
The leading of the vaward.   130

121. *Will . . . labour*] F divides after *levied*.   124. *'em*] Rowe; *vm* F.
128. *thou wilt . . . for a ransom*] F; *thou'lt . . . for ransom* Theobald.

109. *for the working-day*] i.e. who
mean business, not on holiday.
111. *With rainy marching*] Both
Hall and Holinshed record that it
rained by day and froze by night
while Henry's troops were on the
march. The *Gesta* (p. 48) and *Liber
Metricus*, p. 119, refer to rain on the
eve of Agincourt.
111. *painful*] arduous.
113. *we . . . fly*] an echo of the
Constable's phrase in Hall, xlviii^r,
" fly they cannot ".
115. *in the trim*] (*a*) in fine fettle,
(*b*) fashionably attired. Cf. *1H4* IV.
i. 113, " They come like sacrifices in
their trim ".

117. *in fresher robes*] i.e. in heavenly
robes—a grim jest. Dover Wilson
refers to *Rev.* vii. 9. Cf. also *Rev.* vi. 11.
119. *turn them out of service*] strip
their liveried coats from them, and
by so doing dismiss them from their
master's service. The Elizabethan
servant wore his master's livery which
was taken from him when he left his
master's service.
128. *fear . . . ransom*] The repetition
in " once more come again " may be
evidence of " foul papers ", although
" once more . . . again " occurs in
IV. v. 11 (Brooks).
129–30. So Hall and Holinshed.
130. *vaward*] vanguard.

K. Hen. Take it, brave York. Now, soldiers, march away:
   And how thou pleasest, God, dispose the day!

                                                            [*Exeunt.*

SCENE IV.—*The Field of Battle.*

Alarum. Excursions. Enter PISTOL, *French Soldier,
and Boy.*

Pist. Yield, cur!

Fr. Sold. Je pense que vous êtes le gentilhomme de
   bonne qualité.

Pist. Qualtitie calmie custure me! Art thou a gentleman?
   What is thy name? discuss.   5

Fr. Sold. O Seigneur Dieu!

Pist. O, Signieur Dew should be a gentleman:
   Perpend my words, O Signieur Dew, and mark:
   O Signieur Dew, thou diest on point of fox,
   Except, O signieur, thou do give to me   10
   Egregious ransom.

Fr. Sold. O, prenez miséricorde! ayez pitié de moi!

Scene IV

The . . . Battle] Theobald.   and Boy] Rowe; Boy F.   7–11. Pope's
arrangement. Prose F.

Scene IV

In Q scene v precedes this scene
and with justification since, as it
stands here, it is the opening battle
scene. Pistol's capture of the French-
man was surely at the "latter end of
a fight". This may have happened
following the alterations. See Introduction, p. xxxiv.

4. *Qualtitie calmie custure me*] Malone
suggests that Pistol is quoting the
refrain of a song, "Calen o custure
me", which occurs in Robinson's
Handful of Pleasant Delights, 1584, ed.
Arber, p. 33. The words are probably a corruption of an Irish phrase,
"cailin ôg a' stor", "young girl,
my darling". Pistol, unable to
understand French, echoes the last

word spoken and adds this untrans-
latable jumble by way of jocular
comment.

Warburton and others have sought
to interpret it as "Qualtitie, call you
me, construe me!" or perhaps,
"Qualtitie, cullion, construe me!"
Malone's suggestion is preferable.

5–9. *What is . . . fox*] If Pistol is
content with Signieur Dew as the
name of his prisoner why should he
again ask for his name in ll. 23–4?
See Introduction, p. xxxiv.

9. *fox*] sword. The name is apparently derived from the maker's
mark on Passau swords, originally a
wolf, but in later times more like a
fox.

11. *Egregious*] extraordinary. Cf.
II. i. 45.

Pist. Moy shall not serve; I will have forty moys;
    Or I will fetch thy rim out at thy throat
    In drops of crimson blood.   15
Fr. Sold. Est-il impossible d'échapper la force de ton
    bras?
Pist. Brass, cur!
    Thou damned and luxurious mountain goat,
    Offer'st me brass?   20
Fr. Sold. O pardonnez-moi!
Pist. Say'st thou me so? is that a ton of moys?
    Come hither, boy: ask me this slave in French
    What is his name.
Boy. Écoutez: comment êtes-vous appellé?   25
Fr. Sold. Monsieur le Fer.
Boy. He says his name is Master Fer.
Pist. Master Fer! I'll fer him, and firk him, and
    ferret him. Discuss the same in French unto him.
Boy. I do not know the French for fer, and ferret, and 30
    firk.
Pist. Bid him prepare, for I will cut his throat.
Fr. Sold. Que dit-il, monsieur?
Boy. Il me commande à vous dire que vous faites vous
    prêt; car ce soldat ici est disposé tout à cette 35
    heure de couper votre gorge.
Pist. Owy, cuppele gorge, permafoy,

13–15. Johnson's arrangement. Prose F.   14. *Or*] Hanmer after
Theobald; *for* F.   18–20. Johnson's arrangement. Prose F.
22–4. Pope's arrangement. Prose F.   27, 28. *Master*] Capell; *M.* F.
35–6. *à cette heure*] Theobald; *asture* F.   36. *couper*] F 2; *couppes* F 1.
37–9. Camb. arrangement. Prose F.

13. *Moy*] "It seems unnecessary to
suppose that there is an allusion to
any genuine name of a coin"
(*O.E.D.*). However, "moy" was a
measure in English (about a bushel)
and in French, and Pistol may have
had this in mind. For the pronunciation cf. the rhyme "pardonnez-
moi", "destroy". *R2* v. iii. 119–20.
    14. *rim*] diaphragm.
    17, 18. *bras, Brass*] Anders, *Shake-
speare's Books*, p. 50, points out that
his quibble is legitimate since final
"s" was still sounded in French

before a pause in Shakespeare's time.
He refers for support to Thurot, *De
la Prononciation Française depuis le
Commencement du XVIe Siecle*, 1881–3.
    19. *luxurious*] lecherous.
    28. *I'll fer him*] For a similar repeti-
tion cf. *Wiv.* IV. ii. 193 and *Cor.* II. i.
146.
    28. *firk*] whip, beat.
    29. *ferret*] worry like a ferret. Cf.
Dekker, *Northward Ho* (*Works*, ed.
1873, III. 64), "weele ferret them
and firk them, in faith".
    37. *cuppele gorge*] Cf. II. i. 71.

Peasant, unless thou give me crowns, brave crowns;
Or mangled shalt thou be by this my sword.

Fr. Sold. O je vous supplie pour l'amour de Dieu,   40
me pardonner! Je suis le gentilhomme de bonne
maison: gardez ma vie, et je vous donnerai deux
cents écus.

Pist. What are his words?

Boy. He prays you to save his life: he is a gentleman   45
of a good house; and for his ransom he will give
you two hundred crowns.

Pist. Tell him my fury shall abate, and I
The crowns will take.

Fr. Sold. Petit monsieur, que dit-il?   50

Boy. Encore qu'il est contre son jurement de pardonner
aucun prisonnier; néanmoins, pour les écus que
vous l'avez promis, il est content à vous donner la
liberté, le franchisement.

Fr. Sold. Sur mes genoux je vous donne mille remer-   55
cîments; et je m'estime heureux que je suis tombé
entre les mains d'un chevalier, je pense, le plus
brave, vaillant, et très distingué seigneur d'Angleterre.

Pist. Expound unto me, boy.   60

Boy. He gives you, upon his knees, a thousand thanks;
and he esteems himself happy that he hath fallen
into the hands of one, as he thinks, the most
brave, valorous, and thrice-worthy signieur of
England.   65

Pist. As I suck blood, I will some mercy show.
Follow me!

Boy. Suivez-vous le grand capitaine.

[*Exeunt Pistol and French Soldier.*
I did never know so full a voice issue from so
empty a heart: but the saying is true, " The   70

48–9. Johnson's arrangement. Prose F.   53. *l'avez promis*] Malone:
layt a promets F.   55–6. *remercîments*] F 2; *remercious* F 1.   56. *suis
tombé*] Rowe; *intombe* F.   58. *distingué*] Capell; *distinie* F.
68. *Suivez*] Rowe; *Saaue* F.   Exeunt . . . Soldier] added Pope.

48. *fury shall abate*] Cf. II. i. 66;   69–70. *so . . . heart*] such boastful
III. ii. 23.   speech uttered by so cowardly a
66. *As . . . blood*] Cf. II. iii. 56.   man.

empty vessel makes the greatest sound". Bardolph and Nym had ten times more valour than this roaring devil i' th' old play, that every one may pare his nails with a wooden dagger; and they are both hanged; and so would this be if 75 he durst steal any thing adventurously. I must stay with the lackeys, with the luggage of our camp: the French might have a good prey of us if he knew of it; for there is none to guard it but boys.   [*Exit.* 80

SCENE V.—*Another Part of the Field.*

Enter CONSTABLE, ORLEANS, BOURBON, DAUPHIN, *and* RAMBURES.

Con. O diable!
Orl. O Seigneur! le jour est perdu! tout est perdu!
Dau. Mort Dieu! ma vie! all is confounded, all!
    Reproach and everlasting shame
    Sits mocking in our plumes.   O méchante fortune! 5
    Do not run away.   [*A short alarum.*

Scene v

Another . . . Field] added Theobald.
perdia . . . perdie F.   2. *perdu . . . perdu*] Rowe;
F; *Mort de* Rowe.   3. *Mort Dieu!*] Dover Wilson after Greg; *Mor Dieu*
     5. F divides after *plumes.*

70–1. *The empty . . . sound*] Cf. 2H4 I. iii. 74–5.
73–4. *this roaring . . . dagger*]. In the Morality plays the Devil was beaten with a wooden dagger and driven from the stage. Cf. Harsnet, *Declaration of . . . Popish Imposture,* 1603, pp. 114–5 : " It was a pretty part in the old Church-playes, when the nimble Vice would . . . ride the devil a course, and belabour him with his woodden dagger, til he made him roare." According to Malone the final indignity was to trim the Devil's nails for him. Cf. *Tw.N.* IV. ii. 138–45.

73. *this . . . that*] this fellow who is a mere . . . so that (Abbott).
75. *both hanged*] This is the last we hear of Nym.
78–80. *the French . . . boys*] A grim premonition. Cf. IV. vii. 5, where Gower reports, " 'Tis certain there's not a boy left alive ".

Scene v

5. *Sits*] Cf. Prologue 9.
5. *in our plumes*] Dover Wilson notes that the notion of disdaining them from above is common in Shakespeare, and compares *R2,* III. i. 160–3.

Con.   Why, all our ranks are broke.
Dau. O perdurable shame! let's stab ourselves.
     Be these the wretches that we play'd at dice for?
Orl. Is this the king we sent to for his ransom?
Bour. Shame, and eternal shame, nothing but shame!   10
     Let us die in arms: once more back again;
     And he that will not follow Bourbon now,
     Let him go hence, and with his cap in hand,
     Like a base pandar, hold the chamber-door
     Whilst by a slave, no gentler than my dog,   15
     His fairest daughter is contaminated.
Con. Disorder, that hath spoil'd us, friend us now!
     Let us on heaps go offer up our lives.
Orl. We are enow yet living in the field
     To smother up the English in our throngs,   20
     If any order might be thought upon.
Bour. The devil take order now! I'll to the throng:
     Let life be short, else shame will be too long.   [*Exeunt.*

11. *die in arms*] Ed. after Mason; *dye* in F; *die in honour* Knight; *die in harness*
Dover Wilson.   15. *by a slave*] Q, Pope; *a base slave* F 1; *by a base slave* F 2.
23. Exeunt] Rowe; Exit F.

11. *in arms*] The F reading has
clearly omitted something. Most
editors follow Knight in adding
" honour " which occurs in the last
line of the scene in *Q*,
     " Let's dye with honour, our shame
          doth last too long ".
" In honour ", as Greg points out
(*Principles*, p. 170), is not so natural
a phrase as " with honour ", and is
hardly consistent with " eternal
shame " in the preceding line.
Wilson reads " harness " noting *Mac.*
v. v. 52. But the phrase in Macbeth
is " with harness "—though, of course,
the situation is similar—and the expression " die in harness " is recent (see
O.E.D.). There is no such objection
to the present reading " in arms ".
Although " arms " leaves the line
metrically short, the strong caesura
may perhaps compensate for this.
11–23. Note the disorder of the
distracted French nobles in contrast
with the orderly control of Henry's
army. Did Shakespeare remember

a similar situation in *Aeneid*, II. 314–
17?   There Aeneas, awakened by
the confused fighting in Troy, seizes
his arms distractedly, not with any
particular plan in taking arms (" nec
sat rationis in armis "), and he longs
to gather a troop of men to rush to
the defence of the citadel. In his
reckless fury he thinks it would be
glorious to die in arms (" pulchrum-
que mori succurrit in armis ").
     15. *by a slave*] The F reading " a
base slave " has obviously caught
" base " from the preceding line.
     15. *gentler*] nobler, better born.
     17. *spoil'd*] ruined.
     17. *friend*] befriend.
     18. *on heaps*] in heaps. Cf. *Troil.*
III. ii. 27,
     " As doth a battle, when they
          charge on heaps ".
Dover Wilson compares *Gesta*, p. 55 :
" tanta crevit congeries occisorum "
etc. Shakespeare may, however,
have had Hall's phrase " on plumpes "
in mind.

SCENE VI.—*Another Part of the Field.*

Alarum.   Enter KING HENRY *and his train with prisoners;*
EXETER *and others.*

K. Hen. Well have we done, thrice-valiant countrymen:
            But all's not done; yet keep the French the field.
Exe. The Duke of York commends him to your majesty.
K. Hen. Lives he, good uncle? thrice within this hour
            I saw him down; thrice up again and fighting;   5
            From helmet to the spur all blood he was.
Exe. In which array, brave soldier, doth he lie,
            Larding the plain; and by his bloody side,
            Yoke-fellow to his honour-owing wounds,
            The noble Earl of Suffolk also lies.   10
            Suffolk first died; and York, all haggled over,
            Comes to him, where in gore he lay insteep'd,
            And takes him by the beard, kisses the gashes
            That bloodily did yawn upon his face;
            And cries aloud, " Tarry, my cousin Suffolk!   15
            My soul shall thine keep company to heaven;

Scene VI

Another . . . Field] Theobald.   Alarum . . . others] Ed.; Alarum. Enter
the King . . . others Dover Wilson; Alarums.   Enter King Henry and
Forces; Exeter and others Capell; Alarum. Enter the King and his trayne,
with Prisoners F.   15. *And*] Q, Pope; *He* F.   *my*] F, Dover Wilson; *dear*
Q, Steevens (1778).

Scene VI

5. *I saw him down*] The French
chronicler Monstrelet records that
York was struck down by Alençon,
and that Henry, trying to raise him,
was struck by Alençon with such
force that part of his crown was
shorn off. Hall and Holinshed both
mention that Alençon " almost felled "
Henry.

8. *Larding*] enriching. Cf. *1H4* II.
ii. 117, where Falstaff " lards the
lean earth ".

9. *honour-owing*] honourable, i.e.
honour-owning. For " owe " meaning " possess ". Cf. *Tp.* III. i. 45.

11. *haggled*] mangled, hacked.

15. *And*] The Q reading is an
obvious improvement on F " He ",
Greg, *Principles*, p. 173. Indeed, it
is difficult to support " He " except,
perhaps, on the supposition that
Exeter pauses at the end of l. 14
overcome by his emotions.

Greg observes that " it is difficult
to suppose that F can be merely
misprinted ". The alternative solu-
tion that Q was drawing on a revised
F text would, however, lead to
complexities better avoided. The
compositor must bear the blame;
perhaps he was faced with so mal-
formed an ampersand that he read
" he ", influenced no doubt by the
verb immediately following.

Tarry, sweet soul, for mine, then fly abreast,
As in this glorious and well-foughten field
We kept together in our chivalry!"
Upon these words I came and cheer'd him up;   20
He smil'd me in the face, raught me his hand,
And, with a feeble gripe, says, " Dear my lord,
Commend my service to my sovereign".
So did he turn, and over Suffolk's neck
He threw his wounded arm, and kiss'd his lips;   25
And so espous'd to death, with blood he seal'd
A testament of noble-ending love.
The pretty and sweet manner of it forc'd
Those waters from me which I would have stopp'd;
But I had not so much of man in me,   30
And all my mother came into mine eyes
And gave me up to tears.

K. Hen.   I blame you not;
For, hearing this, I must perforce compound
With mistful eyes, or they will issue too.   *[Alarum.*
But, hark! what new alarum is this same?   35
The French have reinforc'd their scatter'd men:
Then every soldier kill his prisoners!
Give the word through.   *[Exeunt.*

34. *mistful*] Theobald after Warburton; *mixtfull* F.   38. Exeunt] Rowe
(ed. 3); Exit F.

21. *raught*] reached.
25-7. *and kiss'd . . . love*] For kisses
as seals of love. Cf. *Meas.* IV. i. 5-6.
26-7. *And . . . testament*] Possibly a
reminiscence of "my blood of the
new testament", *Matt.* xxvi. 28.
28. *pretty*] beautiful.
31. *all . . . eyes*] All those womanly
feelings in me inherited from my
mother. Cf. *Tw.N.* II. i. 42-4.
33. *compound*] come to terms. Cf.
IV. iii. 80.

34. *mistful*] The F reading " mixtfull " is difficult to explain. Dover
Wilson suggests that it may be a
" printer's correction, induced by
misunderstanding of ' compound ' ".

35-8. So Hall and Holinshed.

38. The Q preserves a piece of
stage business. Pistol in the Q
version was present throughout this
scene. As he follows the royal train
out, he exclaims, " Couple gorge ".

SCENE VII.—*Another Part of the Field.*

Enter FLUELLEN *and* GOWER.

Flu. Kill the poys and the luggage! 'tis expressly
against the law of arms: 'tis as arrant a piece of
knavery, mark you now, as can be offer't; in
your conscience now, is it not?

Gow. 'Tis certain there's not a boy left alive; and the   5
cowardly rascals that ran from the battle ha' done
this slaughter; besides, they have burned and
carried away all that was in the king's tent;
wherefore the king most worthily hath caused
every soldier to cut his prisoner's throat. O, 'tis   10
a gallant king!

Flu. Ay, he was porn at Monmouth, Captain Gower.
What call you the town's name where Alexander
the Pig was born?

Gow. Alexander the Great.   15

Flu. Why, I pray you, is not pig great? the pig, or
the great, or the mighty, or the huge, or the
magnanimous, are all one reckonings, save the
phrase is a little variations.

Scene VII

Scene VII] Capell Actus Quartus F. Another . . . Field] Theobald.
3. *offer't; in*] Camb.; *offert in* F.   17. *great*] F 2; *grear* F 1.

Scene VII

5–10. *'Tis . . . throat*] This is the
result of the rally led by Bourbon.

13–53. Fluellen constructs a "comparison" following the accepted
rhetorical order. Having compared
the birthplaces of his heroes, he then
compares the localities, and triumphantly concludes with the amusing
"there is salmons in both". Then,
trying to find parallel incidents in
the lives of the two men, he is reduced
to the delicious dissimilarity between
the drunken Alexander killing Cleitus
and the sober Henry turning away
Falstaff. See Baldwin, II. 336–8, for
a full discussion.

But there is more behind it.
Robson, *Alexander the Great*, 1929,
p. 62, suggests that Fluellen's words
may be a "dim parody" of Alexander's belief, according to Arrian
and Strabo, that the Indus and the
Nile were the same river because
there were "crocodiles in both".

Again, while the distinction between
Alexander drunk and Henry sober
is delightfully done, Fluellen is also
obeying Erasmus in that Henry is
shown as superior to the pagan
Alexander. See Introduction, p. xvii.

16–19. *is not . . . variations*] A word
was frequently "varied" by quoting
synonyms as here.

Gow. I think Alexander the Great was born in   20
Macedon: his father was called Philip of Macedon,
as I take it.

Flu. I think it is in Macedon where Alexander is porn.
I tell you, captain, if you look in the maps of the
'orld, I warrant you sall find, in the comparisons   25
between Macedon and Monmouth, that the situa-
tions, look you, is both alike.   There is a river in
Macedon, and there is also moreover a river at
Monmouth: it is called Wye at Monmouth; but
it is out of my prains what is the name of the   30
other river; but 'tis all one, 'tis alike as my fingers
is to my fingers, and there is salmons in both.
If you mark Alexander's life well, Harry of Monmouth's life is come after it indifferent well; for
there is figures in all things.   Alexander, God   35
knows, and you know, in his rages, and his furies,
and his wraths, and his cholers, and his moods,
and his displeasures, and his indignations, and
also being a little intoxicates in his prains, did,
in his ales and his angers, look you, kill his best   40
friend, Cleitus.

Gow. Our king is not like him in that: he never killed
any of his friends.

Flu. It is not well done, mark you now, to take the
tales out of my mouth, ere it is made and finished.   45
I speak but in the figures and comparisons of it:
as Alexander killed his friend Cleitus, being in his
ales and his cups, so also Harry Monmouth, being
in his right wits and his good judgments, turned
away the fat knight with the great-belly doublet: 50

34. *come after*] resembles.
35. *figures*] comparisons, parallels.
35-40. Cf. note to ll. 16-19.
41. *Cleitus*] The close friend and
general of Alexander. During a
banquet at Maracanda in 328 B.C.
Alexander became heated with wine
and boastful of his achievements and
scornful of those of his father, Philip.
Cleitus, also heated with wine,
praised Philip and recklessly taunted

Alexander. In his rage Alexander
killed Cleitus with a spear snatched
from his bodyguard.

50. *great-belly doublet*] The doublet
originally had two thicknesses, hence
its name.   The lower part called
the " belly " could be either " great "
(stuffed) or " thin " (not stuffed). Cf.
Stubbes, *Anatomy of Abuses*, ed. 1879,
p. 55, " Their dublettes are noe lesse
monstrous than the reste ; For now

he was full of jests, and gipes, and knaveries, and
mocks; I have forgot his name.
Gow. Sir John Falstaff.
Flu. That is he. I'll tell you there is good men porn
at Monmouth.   55
Gow. Here comes his majesty.

Alarum. Enter KING HENRY *and* BOURBON *with prisoners;*
WARWICK, GLOUCESTER, EXETER *and others. Flourish.*

K. Hen. I was not angry since I came to France
        Until this instant. Take a trumpet, herald;
        Ride thou unto the horsemen on yon hill:
        If they will fight with us, bid them come down,   60
        Or void the field; they do offend our sight.
        If they'll do neither, we will come to them,
        And make them skirr away, as swift as stones
        Enforced from the old Assyrian slings.
        Besides, we'll cut the throats of those we have,   65
        And not a man of them that we shall take
        Shall taste our mercy.   Go and tell them so.

Enter MONTJOY.

Exe. Here comes the herald of the French, my liege.
Glou. His eyes are humbler than they us'd to be.

56. Alarum ... Flourish] Ed.; Enter King Harry and Burbon with prisoners.
Flourish F; Alarum. Enter King Henry and Forces; Warwick, Gloucester,
Exeter, and others Capell.

the fashion is to have them hang down
to the middest of their theighes ...
being so harde-quilted, and stuffed,
bombasted and sewed, as they can
verie hardly eyther stoupe downe, or
decline them selves to the grounde ".
He later adds that they were " stuffed
with foure, five or six pound of
Bombast at the least ".

58. *trumpet*] trumpeter.

59–67. *Ride ... mercy*] Holinshed
gives this incident, which is not in
Hall (see Appendix, p. 163). The

prisoners referred to in l. 65 were
Bourbon and those who followed him
at the end of IV. v. as Shakespeare's
entry notice, l. 56, makes clear.

63. *skirr*] scurry.

64. *Assyrian slings*] Cf. *Judith* ix. 7,
" The Assyrians ... trust in shield,
speare, and bow, and sling ".

68. According to Holinshed
Montjoy came to Henry in the
morning after the battle and not
on the same day.

K. Hen. How now! what means this, herald? Know'st
    thou not   70
    That I have fin'd these bones of mine for ransom?
    Com'st thou again for ransom?

Mont.   No, great king:
    I come to thee for charitable licence,
    That we may wander o'er this bloody field
    To book our dead, and then to bury them;   75
    To sort our nobles from our common men;
    For many of our princes—woe the while!—
    Lie drown'd and soak'd in mercenary blood;
    So do our vulgar drench their peasant limbs
    In blood of princes; and their wounded steeds   80
    Fret fetlock deep in gore, and with wild rage
    Yerk out their armed heels at their dead masters,
    Killing them twice. O, give us leave, great king,
    To view the field in safety and dispose
    Of their dead bodies!

K. Hen.   I tell thee truly, herald,   85
    I know not if the day be ours or no;
    For yet a many of your horsemen peer
    And gallop o'er the field.

Mont.   The day is yours.

K. Hen. Praised be God, and not our strength, for it!
    What is this castle call'd that stands hard by?   90

Mont. They call it Agincourt.

K. Hen. Then call we this the field of Agincourt,
    Fought on the day of Crispin Crispianus.

Flu. Your grandfather of famous memory, an't please
    your majesty, and your great-uncle Edward the   95

---

80. *their*] Malone; *with* F; *the* Capell.   72, 88, 91. Mont.] Rowe; Her. F.

71. *fin'd these bones*] staked, wagered, etc. Cf. IV. iii. 91 and 123.

72–93. These incidents follow Holinshed fairly closely.

75. *book*] record. Cf. *2H4* IV. iii. 50.

80. *and their*] The F reading " and with " was probably caught from " and with " in the next line (Dover Wilson).

81. *Fret*] chafe.

82. *Yerk*] kick.

83–5. *O . . . bodies*] Cf. *Famous Victories*, Sig. F1ᵛ: "*Herald.* He hath sent me to desire your Maiestie, to give him leave to go into the field to view his poore Country men, that they may all be honourably buried."

87. *peer*] appear.

Plack Prince of Wales, as I have read in the
chronicles, fought a most prave pattle here in
France.

K. Hen. They did, Fluellen.

Flu. Your majesty says very true: if your majesties 100
is remembered of it, the Welshmen did good
service in a garden where leeks did grow, wearing leeks in their Monmouth caps; which, your
majesty know, to this hour is an honourable
badge of the service; and I do believe your 105
majesty takes no scorn to wear the leek upon
Saint Tavy's day.

K. Hen. I wear it for a memorable honour;
For I am Welsh, you know, good countryman.

Flu. All the water in Wye cannot wash your majesty's 110
Welsh plood out of your pody, I can tell you
that: God pless it and preserve it, as long as it
pleases his grace, and his majesty too!

K. Hen. Thanks, good my countryman.

Flu. By Jeshu, I am your majesty's countryman, I 115
care not who know it; I will confess it to all the
'orld: I need not to be ashamed of your majesty,
praised be God, so long as your majesty is an
honest man.

114. *countryman*] F 2; *countrymen* F 1.

97. *a most prave pattle*] If Fluellen
was thinking of Cressy, he should
have said great-grandfather in l. 94
(i.e. Edward III). John of Gaunt,
Henry's grandfather, was six years
old at the time.

101-2. *Welshmen ... grow*] "For
the fact of service done by Welshmen
in a garden of leeks, Fluellen remains
our only authority" (Evans). The
wearing of the leek on St. David's
Day, 1st March, is usually supposed
to commemorate a British victory
over the Saxons on that day in
A.D. 540.

103. *Monmouth caps*] round, brim-
less caps with a high, tapering crown,
originally made in Monmouth (Lin-

thicum, *Costume in Elizabethan Drama*,
p. 226).

105-7. *your majesty ... day*] Dover
Wilson quotes Moore Smith for a
reference to Francis Osborne, *Works*,
8th ed. (1682), p. 610: "Nor did
he [the Earl of Essex] fail to wear a
Leek on St. David's day, but besides
would upon all occasions vindicate
the Welch inhabitants, and own them
for his Countreymen, as Q. Elizabeth
usually was wont, upon the first of
March."

113. *and his majesty too*] "Fluellen
adds these words lest he should
seem disrespectful to God by giving
Him a title lower than that which
he had just given to the King"
(Moore Smith).

Enter WILLIAMS.

K. Hen. God keep me so! Our heralds go with him: 120
  Bring me just notice of the numbers dead
  On both our parts.   Call yonder fellow hither.

  [*Exeunt Heralds with Montjoy.*

Exe. Soldier, you must come to the king.

K. Hen. Soldier, why wearest thou that glove in thy
  cap?   125

Will. An't please your majesty, 'tis the gage of one
  that I should fight withal, if he be alive.

K. Hen. An Englishman?

Will. An't please your majesty, a rascal that swag-
  gered with me last night; who, if alive and ever 130
  dare to challenge this glove, I have sworn to take
  him a box o' th' ear: or if I can see my glove in
  his cap, which he swore as he was a soldier he
  would wear if alive, I will strike it out soundly.

K. Hen. What think you, Captain Fluellen? is it fit 135
  this soldier keep his oath?

Flu. He is a craven and a villain else, an't please
  your majesty, in my conscience.

K. Hen. It may be his enemy is a gentleman of great
  sort, quite from the answer of his degree.   140

Flu. Though he be as good a gentleman as the devil
  is, as Lucifer and Belzebub himself, it is necessary,
  look your grace, that he keep his vow and his
  oath.   If he be perjured, see you now, his reputation is as arrant a villain and a Jack-sauce as 145
  ever his black shoe trod upon God's ground and
  his earth, in my conscience, la!

---

120. *God*] F 3; *Good* F 1.   122. Exeunt . . . Montjoy] added
Malone.   130. *alive*] F; *a' live* Capell.   132. *o' th'*] F 4; *a' th'* F 1.
147. *la*] Capell; *law* F.

131. *take*] strike.   141–2. *as good . . . is*] Cf. *Lr.* III.
140. *sort*] rank, quality.   iv. 138, " The Prince of Darkness is a
140. *quite . . . degree*] of such high gentleman "; i.e. of long and firmly
rank that he cannot in honour accept   established royalty, of the highest
the challenge of anyone of the soldier's rank in hell.
standing.   145. *Jack-sauce*] impudent rascal.

K. Hen. Then keep thy vow, sirrah, when thou meetest
    the fellow.

Will. So I will, my liege, as I live.   150

K. Hen. Who servest thou under?

Will. Under Captain Gower, my liege.

Flu. Gower is a good captain, and is good knowledge,
    and literatured in the wars.

K. Hen. Call him hither to me, soldier.   155

Will. I will, my liege.   [*Exit.*

K. Hen. Here, Fluellen; wear thou this favour for me
    and stick it in thy cap. When Alençon and
    myself were down together I plucked this glove
    from his helm: if any man challenge this, he 160
    is a friend to Alençon and an enemy to our
    person; if thou encounter any such, apprehend
    him, an thou dost me love.

Flu. Your grace doo's me as great honours as can be
    desired in the hearts of his subjects: I would 165
    fain see the man that has but two legs that shall
    find himself aggriefed at this glove, that is all;
    but I would fain see it once, and please God of
    his grace that I might see.

K. Hen. Knowest thou Gower?   170

Flu. He is my dear friend, an please you.

K. Hen. Pray thee, go seek him, and bring him to my
    tent.

Flu. I will fetch him.   [*Exit.*

K. Hen. My Lord of Warwick, and my brother Glou-
    cester,   175
    Follow Fluellen closely at the heels.
    The glove which I have given him for a favour
    May haply purchase him a box o' th' ear;
    It is the soldier's; I by bargain should
    Wear it myself. Follow, good cousin Warwick: 180
    If that the soldier strike him, as I judge

158–9. *When Alençon . . . together*]
See not IV. vi. 5.

168. *and please*] and may it please.
Some prefer to read "an" for F "and"
as in l. 163.

172. *go seek him*] Cf. l. 155. In
this way Henry arranges for Fluellen
and Williams to meet.

178. *o' th'*] F 4; *a' th'* F 1.

By his blunt bearing he will keep his word,
Some sudden mischief may arise of it;
For I do know Fluellen valiant,
And touch'd with choler, hot as gunpowder,   185
And quickly will return an injury:
Follow and see there be no harm between them.
Go you with me, uncle of Exeter.   [*Exeunt.*

SCENE VIII.—*Before King Henry's Pavilion.*

Enter GOWER *and* WILLIAMS.

Will. I warrant it is to knight you, captain.

Enter FLUELLEN.

Flu. God's will and his pleasure, captain, I beseech
you now come apace to the king: there is more
good toward you peradventure than is in your
knowledge to dream of.

Will. Sir, know you this glove?   5
Flu. Know the glove! I know the glove is a glove.
Will. I know this; and thus I challenge it.

[*Strikes him.*

Flu. 'Sblood! an arrant traitor as any's in the universal
world, or in France, or in England.   10
Gow. How now, sir! you villain!
Will. Do you think I'll be forsworn?
Flu. Stand away, Captain Gower: I will give treason
his payment into plows, I warrant you.
Will. I am no traitor.   15
Flu. That's a lie in thy throat. I charge you in his
majesty's name, apprehend him: he's a friend of
the Duke Alençon's.

185. *touch'd*] easily fired. Cf. "touch-wood".

Scene VIII

Before ... Pavilion] added Theobald.   9. *any's*] F 4; *anyes* F 1.

Enter WARWICK *and* GLOUCESTER.

War. How now, how now! what's the matter?
Flu. My Lord of Warwick, here is, praised be God   20
for it! a most contagious treason come to light,
look you, as you shall desire in a summer's day.
Here is his majesty.

Enter KING HENRY *and* EXETER.

K. Hen. How now! what's the matter?
Flu. My liege, here is a villain and a traitor, that,   25
look your grace, has struck the glove which
your majesty is take out of the helmet of
Alençon.
Will. My liege this was my glove; here is the fellow
of it; and he that I gave it to in change pro-   30
mised to wear it in his cap: I promised to strike
him if he did. I met this man with my glove in
his cap, and I have been as good as my word.
Flu. Your majesty hear now, saving your majesty's
manhood, what an arrant, rascally, beggarly,   35
lousy knave it is. I hope your majesty is pear
me testimony and witness, and will avouchment
that this is the glove of Alençon that your
majesty is give me; in your conscience now?
K. Hen. Give me thy glove, soldier: look, here is the   40
fellow of it.
'Twas I, indeed, thou promised'st to strike;
And thou hast given me most bitter terms.
Flu. An please your majesty, let his neck answer for
it, if there is any martial law in the world.   45
K. Hen. How canst thou make me satisfaction?
Will. All offences, my lord, come from the heart:
never came any from mine that might offend
your majesty.

23. King Henry] Rowe; King F.   40. Pope's arrangement; F
divides after *soldier*.   45. *martial*] Pope; *Marshall* F.

22 *as . . . day*] as you could wish for.   37. *avouchment*] i.e. acknowledge.

K. Hen. It was ourself thou didst abuse.   50

Will. Your majesty came not like yourself: you appeared to me but as a common man; witness the night, your garments, your lowliness; and what your highness suffered under that shape, I beseech you, take it for your own fault and not mine: for had you been as I took you for, I made no offence; therefore, I beseech your highness, pardon me.   55

K. Hen. Here, uncle Exeter, fill this glove with crowns, And give it to this fellow.   Keep it, fellow;   60 And wear it for an honour in thy cap Till I do challenge it.   Give him the crowns. And, captain, you must needs be friends with him.

Flu. By this day and this light, the fellow has mettle enough in his belly. Hold, there is twelve pence   65 for you, and I pray you to serve God, and keep you out of prawls, and prabbles, and quarrels, and dissensions, and, I warrant you, it is the better for you.

Will. I will none of your money.   70

Flu. It is with a good will; I can tell you it will serve you to mend your shoes: come, wherefore should you be so pashful? your shoes is not so good: 'tis a good silling, I warrant you, or I will change it.

Enter an English Herald.

K. Hen. Now, herald, are the dead numbered?   75

Her. Here is the number of the slaughter'd French.

[*Presenting a paper.*

K. Hen. What prisoners of good sort are taken, uncle?

Exe. Charles Duke of Orleans, nephew to the king; John Duke of Bourbon, and Lord Bouciqualt: Of other lords and barons, knights and squires,   80 Full fifteen hundred, besides common men.

74. Enter . . . Herald] Malone; Enter Herauld F.   76. Presenting a paper] added Ed.; Kneeling and delivering papers Capell. 79. *Bouciqualt*] Theobald (ed. 2); *Bouchiquald* F.

77. *sort*] rank.   78–108. These lines are a very close paraphrase of Holinshed.

K. Hen. This note doth tell me of ten thousand French
    That in the field lie slain: of princes, in this number,
    And nobles bearing banners, there lie dead
    One hundred twenty-six: added to these,   85
    Of knights, esquires, and gallant gentlemen,
    Eight thousand and four hundred; of the which
    Five hundred were but yesterday dubb'd knights:
    So that, in these ten thousand they have lost,
    There are but sixteen hundred mercenaries;   90
    The rest are princes, barons, lords, knights, squires,
    And gentlemen of blood and quality.
    The names of those their nobles that lie dead:
    Charles Delabreth, high constable of France;
    Jacques of Chatillon, admiral of France;   95
    The master of the cross-bows, Lord Rambures;
    Great Master of France, the brave Sir Guichard
        Dauphin;
    John Duke of Alençon; Anthony Duke of Brabant,
    The brother to the Duke of Burgundy;
    And Edward Duke of Bar: of lusty earls,   100
    Grandpré and Roussi, Faulconbridge and Foix,
    Beaumont and Marle, Vaudemont and Lestrale.
    Here was a royal fellowship of death!
    Where is the number of our English dead?

                        [Herald shows him another paper.

    Edward the Duke of York, the Earl of Suffolk,   105
    Sir Richard Ketly, Davy Gam, esquire;
    None else of name; and of all other men
    But five and twenty. O God, thy arm was here;

101. *Faulconbridge*] Dover Wilson; *Fauconbridge* F.   *Foix*] Capell;
Foyes F.   104. Herald . . . paper] added Capell.   108. F divides
after *twenty* beginning a fresh line with *O God*; F 2, 3, 4 prefix this with
"King".

82. *ten thousand French*] So Hall and
Holinshed. The latest estimate is
7,000 (Jacob).

84. *banners*] i.e. bearing coats-of-
arms.

102. *Lestrale*] Holinshed gives the
name as "Lestrake".

105. *Earl of Suffolk*] Michael de la
Pole, b. 1394, succeeded to the earl-

dom on his father's death at the siege
of Harfleur.

106. *Ketly*] "Kikely" Holinshed.

106. *Davy Gam*] David ap Llewellyn
of Brecon, called Gam (i.e. squinting).

108. *five and twenty*] So Hall and
Holinshed, the latter, however, gives
other estimates. The latest estimate
is between 400 and 500 (Jacob).

And not to us, but to thy arm alone,
Ascribe we all!   When, without stratagem,   110
But in plain shock and even play of battle,
Was ever known so great and little loss
On one part and on th' other?   Take it, God,
For it is none but thine!

Exe.   'Tis wonderful!

K. Hen. Come, go we in procession to the village: 115
And be it death proclaimed through our host
To boast of this or take that praise from God
Which is his only.

Flu. Is it not lawful, an please your majesty, to tell
how many is killed?   120

K. Hen. Yes, captain; but with this acknowledgment,
That God fought for us.

Flu. Yes, my conscience, he did us great good.

K. Hen. Do we all holy rites:

Let there be sung " Non nobis " and " Te Deum"; 125
The dead with charity enclos'd in clay.
And then to Calais; and to England then;
Where ne'er from France arriv'd more happy men.

[*Exeunt.*

112–13. *loss . . . other? Take*] Pope; *losse? . . . other, take* F.
115. *we*] F 2; *me* F 1.   124. *rites*] Pope; *Rights* F.   127. *Calais*] Rowe;
Callice F.

---

115. *village*] Maisoncelles.

125. " *Non nobis* " and " *Te Deum* "] Holinshed, closely following Hall, states that Henry caused " his prelats and chapleins to sing this psalme: *In exitu Israel de Aegypto*, and commanded euerie man to kneele downe on the ground at this verse: *Non nobis, Domine, non nobis, sed nomini tuo da gloriam*. Which doone, he caused *Te Deum*, with certeine anthems to be soong." Noble points

out that in the Vulgate " In exitu Israel " includes " Non nobis, Domine ".   Shakespeare, however, knowing that they were separate psalms in the Anglican Psalter, presents them in that form here.

126. *The dead . . . clay*] Dover Wilson refers to Stow's *Annals*, p. 351*a* for the source of this.

126. *charity*] i.e. Christian burial. Cf. IV. i. 144–5.

Lines as real soldiers
— taking newspaper off
each other

ACT V

Enter CHORUS.

Vouchsafe to those that have not read the story,
That I may prompt them: and of such as have,
I humbly pray them to admit th' excuse
Of time, of numbers, and due course of things,
Which cannot in their huge and proper life   5
Be here presented. Now we bear the king
Toward Calais: grant him there; there seen,
Heave him away upon your winged thoughts
Athwart the sea. Behold, the English beach
Pales in the flood with men, with wives, and boys,   10
Whose shouts and claps out-voice the deep-mouth'd sea,
Which, like a mighty whiffler, 'fore the king
Seems to prepare his way: so let him land,

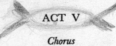

Chorus

7. *Calais*] Rowe; *Callice* F.   10. *with wives*] F 2; *Wiues* F 1.

ACT V

Chorus

Five years pass between Agincourt and the negotiations resulting in the Treaty of Troyes described in this act. While the Chorus depicts Henry's return to Calais, his landing at Dover, his entry into London, and mentions the visit of the Emperor Sigismund, it says nothing of Henry's second campaign which began on 1 August 1417.

3–4. *admit* . . . *Of*] " excuse us in our treatment of " (Dover Wilson).

9–13. *Behold* . . . *way*] Probably based on Pseudo-Elmham, *Vita*, p. 71, " Rege vero apud villam de Dowere in natalis soli patriam applicante, reverencia debita & occursu solenni populus innumerus religiosorum virorum, ecclesiasticorum & secularium, tanti principis congratulantes victoriae, festivis gaudiis, processione devota, graciarum accione multiplici, ipsius felicem adventum celebrant & honorant . . . ipsique de portibus burgenses ad regem in terram suis brachiis deportandum, profundi pelagi latices prae gaudio non horrentes, usque ad regis cimbam per medium fluctuum devenerunt."

10. *Pales in*] hems in.

10. *wives*] women.

12. *whiffler*] " one of a body of attendants armed with javelin, battle-axe, sword, or staff, and wearing a chain, employed to keep the way clear for a procession " (*O.E.D.*).

And solemnly see him set on to London.
So swift a pace hath thought that even now   15
You may imagine him upon Blackheath;
Where that his lords desire him to have borne
His bruised helmet and his bended sword
Before him through the city: he forbids it,
Being free from vainness and self-glorious pride;   20
Giving full trophy, signal and ostent,
Quite from himself, to God. But now behold,
In the quick forge and working-house of thought,
How London doth pour out her citizens.
The mayor and all his brethren in best sort,   25
Like to the senators of th' antique Rome,
With the plebeians swarming at their heels,
Go forth and fetch their conqu'ring Cæsar in:
As, by a lower but by loving likelihood,
Were now the general of our gracious empress,   30
As in good time he may, from Ireland coming,
Bringing rebellion broached on his sword,
How many would the peaceful city quit
To welcome him! much more, and much more
     cause,
Did they this Harry.   Now in London place him;   35
As yet the lamentation of the French
Invites the King of England's stay at home;

29. *lower but by loving*] F; *lower but loving* Camb. after Seymour.

17–22. *Where . . . God*] So Holinshed, see Appendix, p. 163.
18. See IV. vi. 5 note.
21. *signal*] token.
21. *ostent*] display.
23. *quick forge*] Thought was associated with the elements air and fire. Dover Wilson compares *2H4* IV. iii. 107–8, " quick, forgetive, full of nimble fiery and delectable shapes ".
25. *sort*] array.
29. *As . . . likelihood*] as by a humbler but lovingly anticipated possibility.
30. *the . . . empress*] An allusion to the expedition commanded by Robert Devereux, Earl of Essex, which left England on 27 March 1599, to suppress Tyrone's rebellion in Ireland. He returned in September unsuccessful and in disgrace. Dover Wilson notes the " skill and caution " of this compliment: " after the reference to Caesar to call Elizabeth ' empress ' puts Essex neatly in his place ".
32. *broached*] spitted.
34–41. These lines are awkward and clumsy and corruption has been suspected.
36–7. *As yet . . . home*] as the French are still occupied in mourning their defeat, Henry has no reason to leave England.

The emperor's coming in behalf of France,
To order peace between them; and omit
All the occurrences, whatever chanc'd,   40
Till Harry's back-return again to France:
There must we bring him; and myself have play'd
The interim, by rememb'ring you 'tis past.
Then brook abridgement, and your eyes advance,
After your thoughts, straight back again to France. 45
                                                        [*Exit.*

SCENE I.—*France.   The English Camp.*

Enter FLUELLEN *and* GOWER.

Gow. Nay, that's right; but why wear you your leek
    to-day?   Saint Davy's day is past.
Flu. There is occasions and causes why and wherefore
    in all things: I will tell you, asse my friend,
    Captain Gower. The rascally, scauld, beggarly,   5
    lousy, pragging knave, Pistol, which you and your-
    self and all the world know to be no petter than
    a fellow, look you now, of no merits, he is come
    to me and prings me pread and salt yesterday,
    look you, and bid me eat my leek. It was in a   10
    place where I could not breed no contention with
    him; but I will be so bold as to wear it in my
    cap till I see him once again, and then I will tell
    him a little piece of my desires.

Enter PISTOL.

Gow. Why, here he comes, swelling like a turkey-   15
    cock.

Scene 1

France . . . Camp] added Camb.

38. *The emperor's coming*] The Holy
Roman Emperor Sigismund came to
England on 1 May 1416.

Scene 1

5. *scauld*] scurvy, scabby.
9. *yesterday*] Presumably St. David's
day.

Flu. 'Tis no matter for his swellings nor his turkey-cocks. God pless you, Aunchient Pistol! you scurvy, lousy knave, God pless you!

Pist. Ha! art thou bedlam? dost thou thirst, base Trojan   20
To have me fold up Parca's fatal web?
Hence! I am qualmish at the smell of leek.

Flu. I peseech you heartily, scurvy, lousy knave, at my desires and my requests and my petitions to eat, look you, this leek; because, look you, you   25 do not love it, nor your affections and your appetites and your disgestions doo's not agree with it, I would desire you to eat it.

Pist. Not for Cadwallader and all his goats.

Flu. There is one goat for you. [*Strikes him*] Will   30 you be so good, scauld knave, as eat it?

Pist. Base Trojan, thou shalt die.

Flu. You say very true, scauld knave, when God's will is. I will desire you to live in the mean time and eat your victuals: come, there is sauce for it.   35 [*Strikes him.*] You called me yesterday mountain-squire, but I will make you to-day a squire of low degree. I pray you, fall to: if you can mock a leek you can eat a leek.

Gow. Enough, captain: you have astonished him.   40

Flu. I say, I will make him eat some part of my leek, or I will peat his pate four days. Bite, I pray

---

20–2. Pope's arrangement. Prose F.   27. *disgestions*] F; *digestions*
Rowe.   36. Strikes him] added Pope.

19. *bedlam*] mad. A corruption of Bethlehem, the name of a hospital for lunatics in London.

20. *Trojan*] a slang term for a person of low character.

21. *fold . . . web*] kill you.

21. *Parca*] i.e. Parcae, the three Fates who, in classical legend, wove the web of a man's destiny cutting off the thread when the pattern was completed and so ending his life.

29. *Cadwallader*] The last of the

British kings, also the ancestor of Queen Elizabeth.

29 *goats*] a term of contempt associated with Wales.

36–7. *mountain - squire*] squire of worthless land. A term of contempt.

37–8. *squire of low degree*] (*a*) a quibble on low in contrast with "mountain" l. 36, (*b*) a reference to the title of a medieval metrical romance.

40. *astonished*] dumbfounded, stunned.

you; it is good for your green wound and your
ploody coxcomb.

Pist. Must I bite?   45

Flu. Yes, certainly, and out of doubt and out of question too and ambiguities.

Pist. By this leek, I will most horribly revenge. I
eat and eat, I swear—

Flu. Eat, I pray you. Will you have some more   50
sauce to your leek? there is not enough leek to
swear by.

Pist. Quiet thy cudgel; thou dost see I eat.

Flu. Much good do you, scauld knave, heartily. Nay,
pray you, throw none away; the skin is good   55
for your broken coxcomb. When you take
occasions to see leeks hereafter, I pray you,
mock at 'em; that is all.

Pist. Good.

Flu. Ay, leeks is good. Hold you, there is a groat   60
to heal your pate.

Pist. Me a groat!

Flu. Yes, verily and in truth, you shall take it; or I
have another leek in my pocket, which you shall
eat.   65

Pist. I take thy groat in earnest of revenge.

Flu. If I owe you any thing I will pay you in cudgels:
you shall be a woodmonger, and buy nothing
of me but cudgels. God bye you, and keep
you, and heal your pate.   [*Exit.*   70

Pist. All hell shall stir for this.

Gow. Go, go; you are a counterfeit cowardly knave.
Will you mock at an ancient tradition, begun
upon an honourable respect, and worn as a

48–9. *revenge . . . swear*—] Camb.; *reuenge I eate and eate I sweare.*   F, Dover
Wilson.   69. *bye*] Moore Smith; *bu'y* F.   73. *begun*] Capell; *began* F.

43. *green*] raw.

48–9. *By . . . swear*] Simpson,
Shakespearean Punctuation, p. 12, defends the F punctuation on the
grounds that the cudgel supplies a very

satisfactory dramatic punctuation.
Dover Wilson follows F.

54. *do you*] may it do you.

62. *Me a groat!*] Pistol is offended
at the offer of fourpence.

74. *respect*] reason, consideration.

memorable trophy of predeceased valour, and 75
dare not avouch in your deeds any of your
words? I have seen you gleeking and galling at
this gentleman twice or thrice. You thought,
because he could not speak English in the native
garb, he could not therefore handle an English 80
cudgel: you find it otherwise; and henceforth
let a Welsh correction teach you a good English
condition. Fare ye well.   [*Exit.*

Pist. Doth Fortune play the huswife with me now?
News have I that my Doll is dead i' th' spital 85
Of malady of France;
And there my rendezvous is quite cut off.
Old I do wax, and from my weary limbs
Honour is cudgell'd. Well, bawd I'll turn,
And something lean to cut-purse of quick hand. 90
To England will I steal, and there I'll steal:
And patches will I get unto these cudgell'd scars,
And swear I got them in the Gallia wars.   [*Exit.*

84–91. Pope's arrangement. Prose F.   85. *Doll*] F; *Nell* Capell
after Johnson.   86. *malady*] Pope; *a malady* F. *France;*] *France; mine
hostess too* Farmer's suggestion.   89. *cudgelled*] Camb.; *cudgeld* F.   93.
swear] F 3; *swore* F 1.

---

75. *predeceased valour*] Cf. iv. vii.
102.

77. *gleeking*] mocking.

77. *galling*] jeering.

84. *huswife*] hussy.

85. *Doll*] See Introduction, p.
xxxviii.

85. *spital*] hospital.

86. *malady of France*] venereal disease.

87. *rendezvous*] Cf. *1H4* iv. i. 57,
" A rendezvous, a home to fly unto ".

90. *And ... to*] with a leaning
towards the profession of.

92–3. *And ... wars*] One of the
" slanders of the age ". Cf. iii. vi.
68–83.

SCENE II.—*Troyes in Champagne. An Apartment in the* FRENCH *King's Palace*

Enter, at one door, KING HENRY, EXETER, BEDFORD, GLOUCESTER, WARWICK, WESTMORELAND, *and other Lords; at another, the* FRENCH KING, QUEEN ISABEL, *the* PRINCESS KATHARINE, ALICE, *and other Ladies, the* DUKE OF BURGUNDY, *and his Train.*

K. Hen. Peace to this meeting, wherefore we are met!
Unto our brother France, and to our sister,
Health and fair time of day; joy and good wishes
To our most fair and princely cousin Katharine;
And, as a branch and member of this royalty,   5
By whom this great assembly is contriv'd,
We do salute you, Duke of Burgundy;
And, princes French, and peers, health to you all!

Fr. King. Right joyous are we to behold your face,
Most worthy brother England; fairly met: 10
So are you, princes English, every one.

Q. Isa. So happy be the issue, brother England,
Of this good day and of this gracious meeting,
As we are now glad to behold your eyes;
Your eyes, which hitherto have borne in them,   15
Against the French, that met them in their bent,
The fatal balls of murdering basilisks;
The venom of such looks, we fairly hope,

Scene II

Troyes . . . Palace] Malone; Enter . . . Train Camb.; Enter at one doore, King Henry, Exeter, Bedford, Warwicke, and other Lords. At another, Queene Isabel, the King, the Duke of Bourgongne, and other French F.
7. *Burgundy*] Rowe; *Burgogne* F.   12. *England*] F 2; *Ireland* F 1.

Scene II

The events of this scene took place in May, 1420.

1. *Peace . . . met*] "Peace, for which we are here met, be to this meeting" (Johnson).

12. *England*] F "Ireland" suggests that the manuscript spelling was "Ingland".

16. *bent*] (*a*) glance, (*b*) line of fire.

17. *balls*] (*a*) cannon balls, (*b*) eye-balls.

17. *basilisks*] (*a*) large cannon, (*b*) mythical reptiles that slew by a glance of their eyes. They were supposedly hatched by a serpent from the eggs of a cockerel.

Have lost their quality, and that this day
Shall change all griefs and quarrels into love.   20
K. Hen. To cry amen to that, thus we appear.
Q. Isa. You English princes all, I do salute you.
Bur. My duty to you both, on equal love,
    Great Kings of France and England! That I have
        labour'd
    With all my wits, my pains, and strong endeavours,   25
    To bring your most imperial majesties
    Unto this bar and royal interview,
    Your mightiness on both parts best can witness.
    Since then my office hath so far prevail'd
    That face to face, and royal eye to eye,   30
    You have congreeted, let it not disgrace me
    If I demand before this royal view,
    What rub or what impediment there is,
    Why that the naked, poor, and mangled Peace,
    Dear nurse of arts, plenties, and joyful births,   35
    Should not in this best garden of the world,
    Our fertile France, put up her lovely visage?
    Alas! she hath from France too long been chas'd
    And all her husbandry doth lie on heaps,
    Corrupting in it own fertility.   40
    Her vine, the merry cheerer of the heart,
    Unpruned dies; her hedges even-pleach'd,

19. *have*] plural by attraction to "looks".

19. *quality*] power.

23. *on*] based on, arising from.

24–8. After the murder of John the Fearless, Duke of Burgundy, by the Dauphin, Philip his son came to terms with Henry and an alliance was made between them in December 1419. Henry made it clear what his ultimate aims were, and to these Philip agreed.

27. *bar*] place for judgement.

31. *congreeted*] exchanged greetings. Cf. I. ii. 182, "congreeing".

33. *rub*] obstacle. See note to II. ii. 188.

33–62. Noble draws attention to a general resemblance between these lines and *Isa.* xxxii. 10–20.

39. *on heaps*] See IV. v. 18.

40. *it*] its. The usual genitive form of "it" was "his", but Shakespeare occasionally uses the form "it". Cf. *Tp.* II. i. 163, "of it own kind".

41. *Her vine . . . heart*] Cf. *Ps.* civ. 15, "wine that maketh glad the heart of man", and *Judges* ix, "And the vine said unto them, Should I leave my wine, which cheereth God and man?"

42. *even-pleach'd*] evenly layered. Trimmed with branches partly cut through and intertwined to form a compact hedge. The word "plash" with this meaning is still found in Lincolnshire dialect. Cf. *Ado,* I. ii. 11, "thick-pleached".

Like prisoners wildly overgrown with hair,
Put forth disorder'd twigs; her fallow leas
The darnel, hemlock and rank fumitory   45
Doth root upon, while that the coulter rusts
That should deracinate such savagery;
The even mead, that erst brought sweetly forth
The freckled cowslip, burnet, and green clover,
Wanting the scythe, all uncorrected, rank,   50
Conceives by idleness, and nothing teems
But hateful docks, rough thistles, kecksies, burrs,
Losing both beauty and utility.
And as our vineyards, fallows, meads, and hedges,
Defective in their natures, grow to wildness,   55
Even so our houses and ourselves and children
Have lost, or do not learn for want of time,
The sciences that should become our country,
But grow like savages, as soldiers will
That nothing do but meditate on blood,   60
To swearing and stern looks, diffus'd attire,

---

45. *fumitory*] F 4; *Femetary* F 1.   50. *all*] Rowe (ed. 3); *withall* F.
54-5. *as ... wildness,*] Capell; *all ... wildness.* F.   61. *diffus'd*] F 3;
defus'd F 1.

---

44. *fallow leas*] arable land lying
unsown.

45. *darnel*] ryegrass.

45. *darnel ... fumitory*] Shakes-
pear's accurate observation is supported by modern text-books on
British Flora, where both darnel and
fumitory are described as " weeds of
cultivation ", i.e. they grow most
prolifically on cultivated land. Cf.
Lr. IV. iv. 3–6,

   " Crown'd with rank fumiter and
        furrow weeds,
   With burdocks, hemlock, nettles,
        cuckoo-flowers,
   Darnel, and all the idle weeds
        that grow
   In our sustaining corn."

46. *coulter*] the knife that precedes
the ploughshare.

51. *Conceives by idleness*] Cf. the
proverb " Idleness is the mother of
vice ".

51. *nothing teems*] produces nothing.

52. *kecksies*] kexes. The dry hollow
stems of various plants such as
hemlock or alexanders. Here possibly
the plants themselves.

54-5. *as ... wildness*] Capell's emendation is clearly right since these lines
summarize ll. 40–53 to form a comparison with ll. 56–62.

55. *Defective ... wildness*] At the
Fall all the natural world degener-
ated with man and became corrupt
(see Perkins, *Works*, 1613, III. 575).
" Elizabethan thought conceived of
cultivation, culture, civilization as
attempts to restore ' nature ' to its
pristine excellence" (Dover Wilson).

56. *houses*] households.

60. *meditate on blood*] Cf. IV. i.
145-6, " when blood is their argument ".

61. *diffus'd*] disordered.

And every thing that seems unnatural.
Which to reduce into our former favour
You are assembled; and my speech entreats
That I may know the let, why gentle Peace			65
Should not expel these inconveniences,
And bless us with her former qualities.

K. Hen. If, Duke of Burgundy, you would the peace,
Whose want gives growth to th' imperfections
Which you have cited, you must buy that peace			70
With full accord to all our just demands;
Whose tenours and particular effects
You have, enschedul'd briefly, in your hands.

Bur. The king hath heard them; to the which as yet
There is no answer made.

K. Hen.				Well then the peace,			75
Which you before so urg'd, lies in his answer.

Fr. King. I have but with a cursitory eye
O'erglanc'd the articles: pleaseth your grace
To appoint some of your council presently
To sit with us once more, with better heed			80
To re-survey them, we will suddenly
Pass our accept and peremptory answer.

K. Hen. Brother, we shall. Go, uncle Exeter,
And brother Clarence, and you, brother Gloucester,
Warwick and Huntingdon, go with the king;			85
And take with you free power to ratify,

68. *Burgundy*] Rowe; *Burgonie* F.
75–6. F divides after *made, urg'd.*
F; *cursorary* Q 3, Pope.

72. *tenours*] Theobald; *Tenures* F.
77. *cursitory*] Dover Wilson; *curselarie*

63. *reduce*] lead back, return.
63. *favour*] appearance.
65. *let*] hindrance.
68. *would*] desire.

72. *tenours*] general trends. The F spelling " Tenures " is a normal variant.

77. *cursitory*] Dover Wilson notes that " cursorary " the Q 3 reading is " not found elsewhere in English, whereas ' cursitory ' or ' cursetory ' (of which F is an obvious misp.) is a

recognized seventeenth century word = cursory ".

82. *Pass ... answer*] formally pronounce our agreed and final reply.
82. *Pass*] give, usually associated with undertaking, promise, assurance or similar word. Cf. *Tit.* I. i. 468–9.
82. *accept*] accepted (see *O.E.D.*).
82. *peremptory*] decisive, final. The pairing of this word with " accept " is interesting, since L " emere " from which peremptory is derived is normally defined by " accipere ".

Augment, or alter, as your wisdoms best
Shall see advantageable for our dignity,
Any thing in or out of our demands,
And we'll consign thereto.   Will you, fair sister,   90
Go with the princes, or stay here with us?

Q. Isa. Our gracious brother, I will go with them.
Haply a woman's voice may do some good
When articles too nicely urg'd be stood on.

K. Hen. Yet leave our cousin Katharine here with us: 95
She is our capital demand, compris'd
Within the fore-rank of our articles.

Q. Isa. She hath good leave.

　　　　　　　[Exeunt all but King Henry, Katharine, and Alice.

K. Hen.　　　　　　　Fair Katharine, and most fair,
Will you vouchsafe to teach a soldier terms
Such as will enter at a lady's ear   100
And plead his love-suit to her gentle heart?

Kath. Your majesty shall mock at me; I cannot speak
your England.

K. Hen. O fair Katharine! if you will love me soundly
with your French heart, I will be glad to hear   105
you confess it brokenly with your English tongue.
Do you like me, Kate?

Kath. Pardonnez-moi, I cannot tell wat is " like me."

K. Hen. An angel is like you, Kate, and you are like
an angel.   110

Kath. Que dit-il? que je suis semblable à les anges?

Alice. Oui, vraiment, sauf votre grace, ainsi dit-il.

K. Hen. I said so, dear Katharine, and I must not blush
to affirm it.

---

93. *Haply*] F 4; *Happily* F 1.   98. Exeunt . . . Alice] Delius; Exeunt
omnes.   Manet King and Katherine F.

93. *Haply*] The F " Happily " is a
normal variant spelling. Cf. IV. vii.
178. F " haply ".

94. *When . . . on*] when minutely
argued trivialities are insisted upon.

98–298. For the wooing scene in
the *Famous Victories* see Appendix,
p. 165. These scenes may have
arisen from a very early tradition.
Jacob, p. 158, refers to a contempor-

ary popular song in which Katharine,
after " bemoaning her fate and repel-
ling her English husband ", cries

　Retourne-toi, embrasse-moi
　Mon cher Anglais!
　Puisque Dieu! nous a assemblés,
　Faut nous aimer.

108. *wat*] There seems no reason
for adopting Rowe's emendation
" vat ".

Kath. O bon Dieu! les langues des hommes sont 115
pleines de tromperies.

K. Hen. What says she, fair one? that the tongues of
men are full of deceits?

Alice. Oui; dat de tongues of de mans is be full of
deceits: dat is de princess. 120

K. Hen. The princess is the better Englishwoman.
I' faith, Kate, my wooing is fit for thy understanding; I am glad thou canst speak no better
English; for if thou couldst, thou wouldst find
me such a plain king that thou wouldst think I 125
had sold my farm to buy my crown. I know
no ways to mince it in love, but directly to
say, " I love you ": then if you urge me farther
than to say, " Do you in faith? " I wear out
my suit. Give me your answer; i' faith, do: 130
and so clap hands and a bargain. How say
you, lady?

Kath. Sauf votre honneur, me understand well.

K. Hen. Marry, if you would put me to verses, or to
dance for your sake, Kate, why you undid me: 135
for the one, I have neither words nor measure,
and for the other, I have no strength in measure,
yet a reasonable measure in strength. If I could
win a lady at leap-frog, or by vaulting into my
saddle with my armour on my back, under the 140
correction of bragging be it spoken, I should
quickly leap into a wife. Or if I might buffet
for my love, or bound my horse for her favours,
I could lay on like a butcher and sit like a jack-
an-apes, never off. But, before God, Kate, I 145

---

116. *pleines*] Pope; *plein* F.

139. *vaulting*] F 3; *vawting* F 1.

120. *dat ... princess*] that is what
the princess says.

121. *The princess ... Englishwoman*]
i.e. because she sees through flattery.

131. *clap hands*] join hands to seal
an agreement.

137. *I ... measure*] I am not
good at treading a measure, i.e.
dancing.

139–40. *by vaulting ... back*] Cf.
1H4 iv. i. 104–10.

142. *leap into*] achieve, win. Equi-
vocal.

144–5. *sit ... off*] sit like a monkey
on horseback, so tightly as not to be
thrown off.

144–5. *jack-an-apes*] monkey (see
O.E.D.).

cannot look greenly nor gasp out my eloquence, nor
I have no cunning in protestation; only downright
oaths, which I never use till urged, nor never break
for urging.   If thou canst love a fellow of this
temper, Kate, whose face is not worth sun-burning,   150
that never looks in his glass for love of any thing
he sees there, let thine eye be thy cook.   I speak
to thee plain soldier: if thou canst love me for
this, take me; if not, to say to thee that I shall
die, is true; but for thy love, by the Lord, no;   155
yet I love thee too.   And while thou livest, dear
Kate, take a fellow of plain and uncoined con-
stancy, for he perforce must do thee right, because
he hath not the gift to woo in other places; for these
fellows of infinite tongue, that can rhyme them-   160
selves into ladies' favours, they do always reason
themselves out again.   What! a speaker is but a
prater; a rhyme is but a ballad.   A good leg will
fall, a straight back will stoop, a black beard will
turn white, a curled pate will grow bald, a fair   165
face will wither, a full eye will wax hollow; but
a good heart, Kate, is the sun and the moon; or
rather the sun, and not the moon; for it shines
bright and never changes, but keeps his course
truly.   If thou would have such a one, take me;   170
and take me, take a soldier; take a soldier, take
a king.   And what sayest thou then to my love?
speak, my fair, and fairly, I pray thee.

---

146. *look greenly*] look sheepishly.

150. *not ... sun-burning*] " so ugly
that the sun cannot make it more so "
(Dover Wilson). Cf. *Troil.* I. iii.
281–2, " The Grecian dames are sunburnt, and not worth the splinter of
a lance ".   A sunburnt face was considered unbecoming.

152. *thine eye ... cook*] let your eye
present me more attractively than I
am.

157. *uncoined*] not   minted   and

therefore not in circulation (among
the ladies).

163. *but a ballad*] Ballads were
extremely popular among the Eliza-
bethans, but were despised by the
judicious.   Thus in *I Return from
Parnassus*, Luxurio plans to forsake the
poverty of Parnassus for the plenty
of ballad-making: " To London Ile
goe, for there is a great nosde ballet-
maker deceaste, & I am promised to
be the rimer of the citie " (ll. 412–13).

Kath. Is it possible dat I sould love de enemy of
    France?   175

K. Hen. No; it is not possible you should love the
    enemy of France, Kate; but, in loving me, you
    should love the friend of France, for I love
    France so well that I will not part with a village
    of it; I will have it all mine: and Kate, when 180
    France is mine and I am yours, then yours is
    France and you are mine.

Kath. I cannot tell wat is dat.

K. Hen. No, Kate? I will tell thee in French, which
    I am sure will hang upon my tongue like a new- 185
    married wife about her husband's neck, hardly
    to be shook off. Je quand sur le possession de
    France, et quand vous avez le possession de moi
    —let me see, what then? Saint Denis be my
    speed!—donc votre est France, et vous êtes 190
    mienne. It is as easy for me, Kate, to conquer
    the kingdom as to speak so much more French:
    I shall never move thee in French, unless it be
    to laugh at me.

Kath. Sauf votre honneur, le Français que vous 195
    parlez il est meilleur que l'Anglais lequel je
    parle.

K. Hen. No, faith, is't not, Kate; but thy speaking
    of my tongue, and I thine, most truly-falsely,
    must needs be granted to be much at one. But, 200
    Kate, dost thou understand thus much English?
    Canst thou love me?

Kath. I cannot tell.

K. Hen. Can any of your neighbours tell, Kate? I'll
    ask them. Come, I know thou lovest me: and 205
    at night, when you come into your closet, you'll
    question this gentlewoman about me; and I know,

196. *il est*] Pope; *il & F. meilleur*] Hanmer; *melieus* F.

174–5. *Is it ... France?*] Cf.
Famous Victories, Sig. G2ʳ,
    " How should I loue thee, which
        is my fathers enemye? "

199. *truly-falsely*] " in good faith
but in bad " French and English
(Deighton).

200. *at one*] alike, in sympathy.

Kate, you will to her dispraise those parts in me
that you love with your heart: but, good Kate,
mock me mercifully; the rather, gentle princess, 210
because I love thee cruelly. If ever thou beest
mine, Kate, as I have a saving faith within me
tells me thou shalt, I get thee with scambling, and
thou must therefore needs prove a good soldier-
breeder. Shall not thou and I, between Saint 215
Denis and Saint George, compound a boy, half
French, half English, that shall go to Constantinople and take the Turk by the beard?
shall we not? what sayest thou, my fair flower
de-luce?   220

Kath. I do not know dat.

K. Hen. No; 'tis hereafter to know, but now to
promise: do but now promise, Kate, you will
endeavour for your French part of such a boy, and
for my English moiety take the word of a king 225
and a bachelor. How answer you, la plus belle
Katharine du monde, mon très cher et divin
déesse?

Kath. Your majesté 'ave fause French enough to de-
ceive de most sage damoiselle dat is en France. 230

K. Hen. Now, fie upon my false French. By mine
honour, in true English, I love thee, Kate: by
which honour I dare not swear thou lovest me;
yet my blood begins to flatter me that thou dost,
notwithstanding the poor and untempering effect 235

---

212. *saving faith*] Cf. 1 *Pet.* i. 9,
"the end of faith, the salvation of
your souls", and *Luke* vii. 50, "Thy
faith hath saved thee".

213. *scambling*] See I. i. 4.

216–18. *compound a boy ... beard*]
Ironically Henry VI.

217–18. *Constantinople*] Actually not
captured by the Turks until 1453,
thirty-one years after Henry's death.
The Turks were active in their
attacks on Christendom during the
sixteenth century, and the expressed

wish of all Christian kings was
to recapture Constantinople. Cf.
Daniel, *Civil Wars*, II. 126–7, where
Daniel laments that if only Henry
V's claim had been lawful, Essex
would now have led England's armies
against "the Easterne Powres".

227–8. *mon ... déesse*] Presumably
some of Henry's "fause French"
(Dr. Packer).

235. *untempering*] "without power
to soften a lady's heart" (Moore
Smith). Cf. II. ii. 118.

of my visage.　Now beshrew my father's ambition!
he was thinking of civil wars when he got me:
therefore was I created with a stubborn outside,
with an aspect of iron, that when I come to woo
ladies I fright them.　But, in faith, Kate, the　240
elder I wax the better I shall appear: my comfort
is, that old age, that ill layer-up of beauty, can
do no more spoil upon my face: thou hast me, if
thou hast me, at the worst; and thou shalt wear
me, if thou wear me, better and better.　And　245
therefore tell me, most fair Katharine, will you
have me?　Put off your maiden blushes; avouch
the thoughts of your heart with the looks of an
empress; take me by the hand, and say, "Harry
of England, I am thine": which word thou shalt　250
no sooner bless mine ear withal, but I will tell
thee aloud, "England is thine, Ireland is thine,
France is thine, and Henry Plantagenet is thine";
who, though I speak it before his face, if he be
not fellow with the best king, thou shalt find the　255
best king of good fellows.　Come, your answer
in broken music; for thy voice is music, and
thy English broken; therefore, queen of all,
Katharine, break thy mind to me in broken
English: wilt thou have me?　260

Kath. Dat is as it shall please de roi mon père.

K. Hen. Nay, it will please him well, Kate; it shall
please him, Kate.

Kath. Den it sall also content me.

K. Hen. Upon that I kiss your hand, and I call you　265
my queen.

---

242. *ill layer-up*] ill-preserver,
wrinkler.　Cf. *2H4*, v. i. 93–4, "you
shall see him laugh till his face be
like a wet cloak ill laid up".

244. *wear*] possess and enjoy as
one's own.　Cf. *Ado*, v. i. 82.

256. *king of good fellows*] Part of the
proverb "The king of good fellows
is appointed for the queen of beggars"
(*Ox. Dict. Prov.*, p. 337.)　The French,
of course, were begging for peace.

257. *broken music*] music arranged
in parts to be played by different
instruments.

259. *break*] open.　Cf. *1H4* I. iii.
82, "But we shall meet, and break
our minds at large".

265.　The episode of the kiss is
probably based on Pseudo-Elmham,
Vita, p. 222.

At their first meeting Henry
kissed Katharine, whereupon "virgo,

Kath. Laissez, mon seigneur, laissez, laissez! Ma foi,
    je ne veux point que vous abaissiez votre grandeur,
    en baisant la main d'une de votre seigneurie
    indigne serviteur: excusez-moi, je vous supplie, 270
    mon très puissant seigneur.

K. Hen. Then I will kiss your lips, Kate.

Kath. Les dames et demoiselles, pour être baisées
    devant leur noces, il n'est pas la coutume de
    France.   275

K. Hen. Madam my interpreter, what says she?

Alice. Dat it is not be de fashion pour les ladies of
    France—I cannot tell wat is baiser en Anglish.

K. Hen. To kiss.

Alice. Your majesty entendre bettre que moi.   280

K. Hen. It is not a fashion for the maids in France to
    kiss before they are married, would she say?

Alice. Oui, vraiment.

K. Hen. O Kate! nice customs curtsy to great kings.
    Dear Kate, you and I cannot be confined within 285
    the weak list of a country's fashion: we are the
    makers of manners, Kate; and the liberty that
    follows our places stops the mouth of all find-
    faults, as I will do yours, for upholding the nice
    fashion of your country in denying me a kiss: 290
    therefore, patiently and yielding. [*Kissing her.*]
    You have witchcraft in your lips, Kate: there is
    more eloquence in a sugar touch of them than in
    the tongues of the French council; and they

268. *abaissiez*] Camb.; *abbaise* F.   268. *grandeur*] F 2; *grandeus* F 1.
269–70. *la main . . . serviteur*] Camb.; *le main d'une nostre Seigneur indignie
seruiteur* F.   273. *baisées*] Theobald; *baisee* F.   274. *noces*] Dyce;
nopces F.   *coutume*] Rowe; *costume* F.   278. *baiser*] Hanmer; *buisse* F.
Anglish] F.   284. *cursty*] Arden; *cursie* F.   291. Kissing her]
added Rowe.

pax a justicia sumens oscula, vir-
ginales vultus exuere nesciens, mox
castissimam faciem roseo coepit
rubore perfundi, ac omni gestu vir-
gineo suae virginitatis insignia de-
monstrare ".
    274. *noces*] the F " nopces " is an
older form of the word.

278. *Anglish*] Surely preserves
Alice's pronunciation.

284. *nice*] fastidious.

286. *list*] barriers.

287–8. *that follows our places*] that
royalty is permitted.

should sooner persuade Harry of England than a 295
general petition of monarchs. Here comes your
father.

Re-enter the FRENCH KING, QUEEN, *and French Lords*;
BURGUNDY, EXETER, WESTMORELAND *and English Lords.*

Bur. God save your majesty! My royal cousin, teach
you our princess English?

K. Hen. I would have her learn, my fair cousin, 300
how perfectly I love her; and that is good
English.

Bur. Is she not apt?

K. Hen. Our tongue is rough, coz, and my condition
is not smooth; so that, having neither the voice 305
nor the heart of flattery about me, I cannot so
conjure up the spirit of love in her, that he will
appear in his true likeness.

Bur. Pardon the frankness of my mirth if I answer
you for that. If you would conjure in her, you 310
must make a circle; if conjure up love in her in
his true likeness, he must appear naked and blind.
Can you blame her then, being a maid yet rosed
over with the virgin crimson of modesty, if she
deny the appearance of a naked blind boy in 315
her naked seeing self? It were, my lord, a hard
condition for a maid to consign to.

K. Hen. Yet they do wink and yield, as love is blind
and enforces.

Bur. They are then excused, my lord, when they see 320
not what they do.

---

297. Re-enter . . . Lords] Ed.; Enter the French Power, and the English
Lords F.

294–6. *they . . . monarchs*] Cf.
Famous Victories, Sig. F3ᵛ,
"For none in the world could
sooner haue made me debate
it,"
and Sig. F4ʳ,
"none in the world could sooner

haue perswaded me to It then
thou."

304. *condition*] disposition, tem-
perament.

310–12. *If . . . blind*] Cf. *Rom.* II. i.
24–6.

318. *blind*] lustful (Dover Wilson).

K. Hen. Then, good my lord, teach your cousin to
consent winking.

Bur. I will wink on her to consent, my lord, if you
will teach her to know my meaning: for maids, 325
well summered, and warm kept, are like flies at
Bartholomew-tide, blind, though they have their
eyes; and then they will endure handling, which
before would not abide looking on.

K. Hen. This moral ties me over to time and a hot 330
summer; and so I shall catch the fly, your cousin,
in the latter end, and she must be blind too.

Bur. As love is, my lord, before it loves.

K. Hen. It is so: and you may, some of you, thank
love for my blindness, who cannot see many a 335
fair French city for one fair French maid that
stands in my way.

Fr. King. Yes, my lord, you see them perspectively,
the cities turned into a maid; for they are all
girdled with maiden walls that war hath never 340
entered.

K. Hen. Shall Kate be my wife?

Fr. King. So please you.

K. Hen. I am content; so the maiden cities you talk
of may wait on her: so the maid that stood in 345
the way for my wish shall show me the way to
my will.

Fr. King. We have consented to all terms of reason.

K. Hen. Is't so, my lords of England?

West. The king hath granted every article: 350
   His daughter first, and then in sequel all,
   According to their firm proposed natures.

---

332. *too*] F 2; *to* F 1.   340. *never*] added Rowe.   351. *then*]
added F 2.

326. *well summered ... kept*] well
nurtured and delicately reared.

326. *summered*] i.e. pastured, grazed
in pastures rich with summer growth.

326–8. *like flies ... eyes*] Like flies
sluggish in the colder weather of
late August.

327. *Bartholomew-tide*] St. Bartholomew's day, 24th August.

330. *This ... over*] This kind of
argument restricts me.

338. *perspectively*] through a glass
so cut to produce a picture from a
confused pattern, or like a picture so
devised to give different views from
different angles.

344–5. *so ... her*] as long as she
brings these cities as a dowry.

Exe. Only he hath not yet subscribed this:
    Where your Majesty demands, that the King of
    France, having any occasion to write for matter 355
    of grant, shall name your highness in this form,
    and with this addition in French, Notre très cher
    filz Henry, Roy d'Angleterre, Héritier de France;
    and thus in Latin, Præclarissimus filius noster
    Henricus, Rex Angliæ, et Hæres Franciæ. 360
Fr. King. Nor this I have not, brother, so denied,
    But your request shall make me let it pass.
K. Hen. I pray you then, in love and dear alliance,
    Let that one article rank with the rest;
    And thereupon give me your daughter. 365
Fr. King. Take her, fair son; and from her blood raise
       up
    Issue to me; that the contending kingdoms
    Of France and England, whose very shores look pale
    With envy of each other's happiness,
    May cease their hatred, and this dear conjunction 370
    Plant neighbourhood and Christian-like accord
    In their sweet bosoms, that never war advance
    His bleeding sword 'twixt England and fair France.
All. Amen.
K. Hen. Now welcome, Kate: and bear me witness all, 375
    That here I kiss her as my sovereign queen.

                                [*Flourish.*

Q. Isa. God, the best maker of all marriages,
    Combine your hearts in one, your realms in one!
    As man and wife, being two, are one in love,
    So be there 'twixt your kingdoms such a spousal 380
    That never may ill office, or fell jealousy,

374. All] Rowe; Lords F.

354–60. This follows Holinshed closely. See Appendix, p. 163.

355–6. *for . . . grant*] in any matter connected with grants of land or titles.

359. *Præclarissimus*] Hall has " praecharissimus ", a form of the correct " praecarissimus ", but in the edition of 1550 it is misprinted as " praeclarissimus ". Holinshed repeats the error from Hall (1550) and Shakespeare follows Holinshed.

368. *pale*] i.e. because of the white cliffs.

370. *dear conjunction*] solemn union. Cf. II. ii. 181, " dear offences ".

371. *neighbourhood*] neighbourliness. Cf. I. ii. 154.

381. *office*] dealing, acts.

Which troubles oft the bed of blessed marriage,
Thrust in between the paction of these kingdoms,
To make divorce of their incorporate league;
That English may as French, French Englishmen, 385
Receive each other!   God speak this Amen!
All. Amen.
K. Hen. Prepare we for our marriage: on which day,
  My Lord of Burgundy, we'll take your oath,
  And all the peers', for surety of our leagues.   390
Then shall I swear to Kate, and you to me;
And may our oaths well kept and prosp'rous be!
                             [Sennet.   Exeunt.

Enter CHORUS.

Thus far, with rough and all-unable pen,
  Our bending author hath pursu'd the story;
In little room confining mighty men,
  Mangling by starts the full course of their glory.
Small time, but in that small most greatly lived   5
  This star of England: Fortune made his sword,
By which the world's best garden he achieved,
  And of it left his son imperial lord.
Henry the Sixth, in infant bands crown'd King
  Of France and England, did this king succeed;   10
Whose state so many had the managing,

---

383. *paction*] Theobald; *Pation* F 1; *Passion* F 3.   390. *peers'*]
Capell; *Peeres* F.

---

383. *paction*] compact.

389–90. *we'll ... leagues*] So Hall
and Holinshed. In *Famous Victories*,
Sig. G2ʳ, the Dauphin and Burgundy
take the oath on the stage. In the
play mentioned by Nashe both the
French king and the Dauphin swear
fealty (see Introduction, p. xxxiii),
though Nashe may not be reporting
accurately.

392. Sennet] a set of trumpet

notes sounded at the entrance or
exit of a procession.

Chorus

Note that this epilogue is a regular
Shakespearian sonnet.

2. *bending*] i.e. " stooping to your
clemency", *Ham.* III. ii. 160 (Steevens).

4. *by starts*] by arbitrary selection
or omission.

7. *world's best garden*] Cf. v. II. 36.

That they lost France and made his England bleed:
Which oft our stage hath shown; and, for their sake,
In your fair minds let this acceptance take.

[*Exit.*

14. Exit] added Capell.

13. *oft ... shown*] If, as seems
likely, *I Henry VI* is the play referred
to by Henslowe, *Diary*, ed. Greg, I.

13–15, and Nashe, *Pierce Pennilesse*
(*Works*, ed. McKerrow, I. 212), it was
an extremely popular play.

14. *this*] this play.

APPENDIX I

Only a selection of extracts can be given here; for a comprehensive collection the reader is referred to W. G. Boswell-Stone, *Shakespeare's Holinshed*, 1896. Comments are added to show the relationship of each passage with Hall's *Union of the Two Noble Families*, 1548. The passages enclosed in square brackets do not occur in those words in Hall.

I. i. 1–19 [Holinshed, III. 545].

[In the second yeare of his reigne], king Henrie called his high court of parlement, the last daie of Aprill in the towne of Leicester, in which parlement manie profitable lawes were concluded, and manie petitions mooued, were for that time deferred. Amongst which, one was, that a bill exhibited in the parlement holden at Westminster in the eleuenth yeare of king Henrie the fourth (which by reason the king was then troubled with ciuill [discord] came to none effect), might now [with good deliberation] be pondered, and brought to some good conclusion. The effect of which supplication was, that the temporall lands deuoutlie giuen, and disordinatlie spent by religious, and other spirituall persons, [should be seized into the kings hands, sith the same] might suffice to mainteine, to the honor of the king, and defense of the realme, fifteene earls, fifteene hundred knights, six thousand and two hundred esquiers, and a hundred almessehouses, for reliefe onelie of the poore, impotent, and needie persons, and the king to haue cleerelie to his coffers twentie thousand pounds, with manie other prouisions and values of religious houses, which I passe ouer.

This bill was much noted, and more feared among the religious sort, whom [suerlie] it touched [verie neere, and therefore] to find remedie [against it, they determined to assaie all waies to put by and ouerthrow this bill: wherein they thought best to trie if they might mooue the kings mood with some sharpe inuention, that he should not regard the] importunate petitions of the commons.

With the exception of "should . . . same" all the bracketed portions are summaries of Hall, the rest is taken word for word from him.

I. ii. 33–95 [Holinshed, III. 545–6].

Both Hall and Holinshed relate that the Archbishop's speech was delivered in Parliament.

"[Herein did he much inueie against the surmised and false fained law Salike, which the Frenchmen alledge euer against the kings of England in barre of their iust title to the crowne of France.] The verie words [of that supposed law] are these, *In terram Salicam mulieres ne succedant*, [that] is to saie, into the Salike land let not women succeed. Which the [French] glossers [expound] to be the realme of France, [and that] this law [was made by] king Pharamond; [whereas yet their owne authors affirme, that the land Salike is] in Germanie, betweene the riuers of Elbe and Sala; [and that when] Charles the great [had ouercome] the Saxons, [he placed] there certeine Frenchmen, which hauing [in disdeine the dishonest maners] of the Germane women, made a law, that the females should not succeed to any inheritance with that land, which [at this daie] is [called Meisen], [so that, if this be true, this] law [was not] made for the realme of France, [nor] the Frenchmen possessed the land Salike, till foure hundred and one and twentie yeares [after the death of] Pharamond, the [supposed maker] of this Salike law, for this Pharamond deceassed in the yeare 426, and Charles the great [subdued] the Saxons, [and placed the Frenchmen in those parts beyond the riuer of Sala], in the yeare 805.

Moreouer, it appeareth by their owne writers, that king Pepine, which deposed Childerike, claimed the crowne of France, as heire generall, for that he was descended of Blithild, daughter to king Clothair the first: Hugh Capet also, who vsurped the crowne vpon Charles duke of Loraine, the sole heire male of the line and stocke of Charles the great, to make his title seeme true, and appeare good, [though in deed it was starke naught,] conueied himselfe as heire to the ladie Lingard, daughter to king Charlemaine, sonne to Lewes the emperour, that was son to Charles the great. King Lewes also the tenth otherwise called saint Lewes, being verie heire to the said vsurper Hugh Capet, could neuer be satisfied in his conscience how he might iustlie keepe and possesse the crowne of France, till he was persuaded and fullie instructed, that queene Isabell his grandmother was lineallie descended of the ladie Ermengard daughter and heire to the aboue named Charles duke of Loraine, by the which marriage, the bloud and line of Charles the great was again vnited and restored to the crowne & scepter of France, so that more cleere than the sunne it openlie appeareth, that the title of king Pepin,

the claime of Hugh Capet, the possession of Lewes, yea and the
French kings to this daie, are deriued and conueied from the
heire female, though they would [vnder the colour of such a
fained law], barre [the kings and princes of this realme of England of their right and lawfull inheritance.]

[The archbishop further alledged out of] the booke of Numbers
this saieng: When a man dieth without a sonne, let the inheritance
descend to his daughter.

In the first paragraph Holinshed has summarized Hall and
slightly altered his order. His phrasing too, is different, but the
unbracketed portions give some idea of the matter common to
both. In the second and third paragraph he follows Hall very
closely.

II. ii. 167–81 [Holinshed, III. 548].

[Having thus] conspired the death and destruction of me,
which am the head of the realme and gouernor of the people,
[it maie be (no)doubt] [but] that you likewise haue [sworne] the
confusion of all that are here with me, and also the [desolation]
of your [owne] countrie. [To what horror (O Lord) for any
true English art to consider, that such an execrable iniquitie
should euer so bewrap you, as for] pleas[ing of] a forren enemie
to imbrue your hands in] your bloud [and to ruine your owne
natiue soile.] [Reuenge herein touching my person, though I
seeke not; yet for the safegard of you my deere freends, & for
due preseruation of all sorts, I am by office to cause example to
be shewed. Get ye hence therefore, ye poore miserable wretches,
to the receiuing of your iust reward, wherein Gods maiestie
giue you grace of his mercie and repentance of your heinous]
offenses.

Holinshed begins by paraphrasing Hall freely, and then in the
last two sentences he adds matter of his own.

II. iv. 132–3 [Holinshed, III. 548].

[[Henry] wrote to him that yer ought long he would tosse
him some London balles that perchance should shake the walles
of the best court in France]

No parallel in Hall.

III. iii. 45–7 [Holinshed, III. 550]

To whome the Dolphin answered, that the kings power was not
yet assembled, in such number as was conuenient to raise so
great a siege

Verbatim from Hall.

III. vi. 41 [Holinshed, III. 552]

A souldier [took] a pix out of a church, for which he was apprehended, & the king not once remooued till the box was restored, and the offendor strangled.

Hall gives more details. He notes that the soldier "vnreuerently dyd eate the holy hostess within the same conteigned".

III. vi. 146–68 [Holinshed, III. 552]

King Henrie [aduisedlie] answered: Mine intent is to doo as it pleaseth God, I will not seeke your maister at this time; but if he or his seeke me, I will [meet] with them [God willing]. If anie of your nation attempt once to stop me in my iournie now towards Calis, at their ieopardie be it; and yet [wish I not anie] of you so vnaduised, as to be the occasion thet I [die] your tawnie ground with [your red bloud]

Slightly summarized from Hall whose last sentence reads, ". . . I in my defence shall colloure and make redde youre tawny grounde . . .".

IV. iii. 16–67 [Holinshed, III. 553]

[It is said, that as he heard one of the host vtter his wish to another thus: I would to God there were with vs now so manie good soldiers as are at this houre within England! the king answered: I would not wish a man more here than I haue, we are indeed in comparison to the enimies but a few, but if God of his clemencie doo fauour vs, and our iust cause, (as I trust he will) we shall speed well inough. But let no man ascribe victorie to our owne strength and might, but onelie to Gods assistance to whome I haue no doubt we shall worthilie haue cause to giue thanks therefore. And if so be that for our offenses sakes we shall be deliuered into the hands of our enimies, the lesse number we be, the lesse damage shall the realme of England susteine: but if we should fight in trust of multitude of men, and so get the victorie (our minds being prone to pride,) we should thervpon peraduenture ascribe the victorie not so much to the gift of God, as to our own puissance, and thereby prouoke his high indignation and displeasure against vs: and if the enimie get the vpper hand, then should our realme and countrie suffer more damage and stand in further danger. But be you of good comfort, and shew your selues valiant. God and our iust quarrell shall defend vs, and deliuer these our proud aduersaries with all the multitude of them which you see (or at the least the most of them) into our hands.]

The corresponding speech in Hall is rather different in tone, but Shakespeare takes ideas from both. Hall does not record the wish for more men.

IV. vii. 59–67 [Holinshed, III. 555]

[Some write, that the king perceiuing his enimies in one part to assemble togither, as though they meant to giue a new battell for preseruation of the prisoners, sent to them an herald, commanding them either to depart out of his sight, or else to come forward at once, and give battell: promising herewith, that if they did offer to fight agine, not onelie those prisoners which his people alreadie had taken; but also so manie of them as in this new conflict, which they thus attempted should fall into his hands, should die the death with redemption.]

Not in Hall.

v. Chorus 17–22 [Holinshed, III. 556]

[The king, like a graue and sober personage, and as one re-membring from whom all victories are sent, seemed little to regard such vaiue (sic) pompe and shewes as were in triumphant sort deuised for his welcomming home from so prosperous a iournie: in so much that he would not suffer his helmet to be caried with him, whereby might haue appeared to the people the blowes and dints that were to be seene in the same.]

Not in Hall.

v. ii. 354–60 [Holinshed, III. 574]

Also that one said father, during his life, shall name, call and write vs in French in this manner: *Nostre treschier filz Henry roy d'Engleterre heretere de France*. And in Latine in this maner: [*Præclarissimus*] *filius noster Henricus rex Angliae & hæres Franciae*.

Almost verbatim from Hall. See v. ii. 359 note.

APPENDIX II

THE GIFT OF THE TENNIS BALLS

There is no historical evidence that the Dauphin sent a gift of tennis-balls to Henry coupled with insulting remarks about his youthful frivolity. The legend, however, is found in the *Brut*, ed. de Brie, p. 374, and in Lydgate's *Poem on Henry V's Expedition* (Nicolas, *Chronicle of London from 1089 to 1438*, 1827, p. 216) and in Elmham's *Liber Metricus*, all of which are contemporary documents. The truth of the matter is probably contained in the version given by Strecche ("Chronicle of John Strecche for the Reign of Henry V, 1414–1422", ed. F. Taylor in *Bulletin of the John Rylands Library*, XIV, 1932, p. 16).

Verumtamen isti Gallici, superbia excecati, nociva non previdentes, *nunciis regis Anglorum* verba fellis eructantes, eisdem indiscrete *predixerunt quod* Henrico regi Anglorum, quia iuvenis erat, *mitterent* parvas pilas ad ludendum et pulvinaria mollia ad cubandum quousque in virile creverit in futuro.

Certain French nobles *foretold the English ambassadors that . . . they would send* Henry, king of the English, because he was a youth, little balls to play with and soft cushions to lie on. . . .

In other words, it was the kind of jesting threat that might easily arise on such occasions, particularly on this occasion if the French in annoyance were "belching words of bile".

Emmerig, *Englische Studien*, 1908, XXXIX pp. 362–401 noted a parallel with the story in Pseudo-Callisthenes that Darius, king of Persia, had sent to Alexander the Great "a strap for his castigation and a ball for his amusement". The story was apparently repeated in the Alexander romances.

It may well be that the incident recounted by Strecche was seized upon as an example of French impudence in full awareness of the Alexander story and used as propaganda (see Jacob, pp. 71–3).

APPENDIX III

Sig. F3^{v}.

The French king and his lords withdraw to consider the terms of the treaty.

Hen. 5. With a good will my good brother of France.
　　Secretary deliuer him a coppie.
　　My lords of England go before
　　And I will follow you. 　　　　　　　　　　*Exeunt Lords.*
　　　　　　　　　　Speakes to himselfe
Hen. 5 Ah Harry, thrice vnhappie Harry.
　　Hast thou now conquered the French King,
　　And begins a fresh supply with his daughter,
　　But with what face canst thou seeke to gaine her loue,
　　Which hath fought to win her fathers Crowne?
　　Her fathers Crowne said I, no it is mine owne:
　　I but I loue her, and must craue her,
　　Nay I loue her and will haue her.
　　　　　　　　　Enters LADY KATHEREN *and her ladies.*
　　But here she comes:
　　How now faire Ladie, Katheren of France,
　　What newes?
Katheren. And it please your Maiestie,
　　My father sent me to know if you will debate any of these
　　Vnreasonable demands which you require:
Hen. 5. Now trust me Kate,
　　I commend thy fathers wit greatly in this,
　　For none in the world could sooner haue made me debate it
　　If it were possible:
　　But tell me sweete Kate, canst thou tell me how to loue?
Kate. I cannot hate my good Lord,
　　Therefore far vnfit were it for me to loue.
Hen. 5. Tush Kate, but tell me in plaine termes,
　　Canst thou loue the King of England?
　　I cannot do as these Countries do,
　　That spend halfe their time in woing:

Tush wench, I am none such,
But wilt thou go ouer to England?

Kate. I would to God, that I had your Maiestie,
As fast in loue, as you haue my father in warres,
I would not vouchsafe so much as one looke,   Sig. F4ʳ.
Untill you had related all these vnreasonable demands.

Hen. 5. Tush Kate, I know thou wouldst not vse me so
Hardly: But tell me, canst thou loue the king of England?

Kate. How should I loue him, that hath dealt so hardly
With my father.

Hen. 5. But ile deale as easily with thee,
As thy heart can imagine, or tongue can require,
How saist thou, what will it be?

Kate. If I were of my owne direction,
I could giue you answere;
But seeing I stand at my fathers direction,
I must first know his will.

Hen. 5. But shal I have thy good wil in the mean season?

Kate. Whereas I can put your grace in no assurance,
I would be loth to put in any dispaire.

Hen. 5. Now before God, it is a sweete wench.

                    She goes aside, and speaks as followeth.

Kat. I may thinke my selfe the happiest in the world,
That is beloued of the mightie King of England.

Hen. 5. Well Kate, are you at hoast with me?
Sette Kate, tel thy father from me,
That none in the world could sooner haue perswaded me to
It then thou, and so tel thy father from me.

Kat. God keepe your Maiestie in good health.

                              Exit KAT.

Hen. 5. Farwel sweet Kate, in faith, it is a sweet wench,
But if I knew I could not haue her fathers good wil,
I would so rowse the Towers ouer his eares,
That I would make him be glad to bring her me,
Upon his hands and knees.

                              Exit KING.

And later. Sig. G2ʳ:

Fr. King. Wherein is it that we may satisfy your Maiestie?

Hen. 5. A trifle my good brother of France.
I meane to make your daughter Queene of England,
If she be willing, and you therewith content:
How saist thou Kate, canst thou loue the King of England?

Kate. How should I loue thee, which is my fathers enemy?

Hen. 5. Tut stand not vpon these points,
    Tis you must make vs friends:
    I know Kate, thou art not a litle proud, that I loue thee:
    What wench, the King of England?

French King. Daughter let nothing stand betwixt the

Sig. G2ᵛ

    King of England and thee, agree to it.

Kate. I had best whilst he is willing,
    Least when I would, he will not:
    I rest at your Maiesties command.

Hen. 5. Welcome sweet Kate, but my brother of France,
    What say you to it?

French King. With all my heart I like it,
    But when shall be your wedding day?

Hen. 5. The first Sunday of the next moneth,
    God willing.

            Sound Trumpets.

                     Exeunt omnes.

APPENDIX IV

In *Studies in Bibliography*, VIII (1956), pp. 67–93, A. S. Cairncross presents a detailed case for the use of Q3 and Q2 as copy for F. A few bibliographical links between Q and F had been noted previously by Price, Pollard, Greg and Duthie, especially between Q3 and F, but no significance had been attached to them. Cairncross claims that extensive use was made of Q3, corrected by reference to an authoritative manuscript, and supplemented by Q2 or by manuscript transcripts where the corrections would have been too numerous to accommodate on a Q3 page, or where Qq had omitted lengthy passages or whole scenes. The correcting, he thinks, was carried out in the printing-house from a manuscript provided by Heminge and Condell. The corrector as well as correcting the Q text used scissors and paste methods, so that the copy for F comprised corrected passages of Q3 and Q2, pasted cuttings from Q2, and manuscript slips and sheets. Some ingenious reconstructions of the suggested process are given in a series of plates. The purpose of this was to provide the printers with printed copy which, it is stated, they preferred to manuscript copy, and perhaps to hasten the return of the manuscript to the playhouse.

Cairncross's article is too detailed to be examined here in full; it should be read by all students concerned with the provenance of the text. What follows is an indication of the parts of the play that he considers derive from Q2, from manuscript, and from Q3, and a selection from his evidence together with an appraisal of its value.

The following passages are claimed to show traces of F dependence on Q2: II. iii. 44–II. iv. 75; possibly III. vii. 126–IV. i. 65 (4 Chorus and IV. i. 1–34 are omitted by Q); IV. i. 64–110; IV. i. 299–IV. iii. 29 (IV. ii. omitted by Q); IV. iii. 73–116; possibly IV. vii. 27–67; IV. vii. 171–IV. viii. 37; IV. viii. 110–V. i. 16 (5 Chorus omitted by Q). Altogether they represent some nine pages of the quarto. With some of these one may venture to disagree. There would appear to be no necessity to use Q2 to supplement II. iii. 44–65; the additions and corrections to II. iv. 1–75 indicated on p. 87 may be thought too complicated to commend themselves to a printer; and similar weight of corrections makes the use of manuscript more likely at III. vii. 126–57 than passages from Q2.

Certain scenes and passages in F have no counterpart in the quartos and would therefore have to be provided in manuscript: the Prologue, Epilogue, all four Choruses; I. i.; I. ii. 115–35; III. i.; III. ii. 69–143; III. iii. 11–41, 51–8; III. v. 26–60; III. vii. 27–41, 69–81, 131–57; IV. i. 1–34, 236–94; IV. ii.

A few other passages would have required so much correction that a manuscript transcript might have been used: III. ii. 1–69; III. iv; v. ii. The rest of F is assumed by Cairncross to be based on Q3 with perhaps some small manuscript additions.

Evidence of F dependence on Q2 consists of spellings, speech-headings, punctuation, and readings common to Q2 and F as distinct from Q3, and more rarely Q1, and usually drawn from passages of approximately the same number of lines as occurs on a quarto page. Some six passages provide most of the instances.

(a) In II. iv. 21–65 the following are cited: forth, F Q2, foorth Q1, 3; France: F, *France*: Q1, 2, *France* Q3; busied F Q1, 2, troubled Q3; King'd F, Kingd Q2, kingd Q1, 3; phantastically F Q2, fantastically Q1, 3; Embassador F Q1, 2, Ambassador Q3.

F, however, always uses the form "forth", and comparison with Q3 "foorth" is valueless; "busied" is clearly the correct reading as against Q3's alteration; "Embassador", again, is the normal F spelling in the text (except I. ii. 3), and it occurs where there is no corresponding Q text in I. i. 91 and 3 Chor. 28.

(b) IV. i. 65–81; fewer F, lewer Q1, 2, lower Q3; aunchient F, auncient Q2, ancient Q1, 3; bable F Q1, 2, babble Q3; *Gow.* F Q2, *Gour.* Q1, *Gower.* Q3.

F "fewer" can hardly be a "conjectural emendation" by F corrector of Q2 "lewer" since the corrector was assumed to be using an authoritative manuscript. The compositor might have emended it if the corrector had failed to observe the misprint. In view of the well-known idiom "to speak few" (*N.E.D.*, "few" 1g.), F reading has some support in spite of "loud" and "lower" later in the scene.

F spelling "aunchient" has nothing to do with Q2. It is used in Fluellen's speeches alone and in his speeches always (the variant "annchiant" occurs once). Altogether there are eight instances, and for five of these the corresponding quarto forms are "ancient", "auncient", and "antient". In the speeches of other characters F uses "ancient", although at II. i. 3, 27 Q2 has "auncient". Such F consistency runs counter to Cairncross's theory.

(*c*) IV. iii. 4–16; *Exe.* F Q1, 2, *Ex.* Q3; all are F Q1, 2, are all
Q3; Lord F Q1, 2, Lords Q3; *the King* F Q2, *King* Q1, 3.

The speech-heading *Exe.* is the form normally used by F;
there are only three exceptions, *Exeter.* and *Exet.* (twice). F "all
are" is the correct reading, Q3 "are all" is an unnecessary alteration. F "Lord" is demanded by the context; Q3 "Lords" is
erroneous. F S.D. *the King* is the normal form apart from ceremonial entries where F uses *King Henry*. *King* is used once only, at
IV. viii. 23, where the quartos have *the King*.

(*d*) IV. iii. 90–113. The colons common to F and Q2 after
"back", "famed", "fly" are put forward as evidence. This is most
unreliable. The use of colons here is normal F practice; any other
stop would be unusual. (See below.)

(*e*) IV. viii. 1–31: *Gower* F Q1, 2, *Captaine Gower* Q3; toward
F Q1, 2, towards Q3; now, what's F, now, what is Q1, 2, now?
What's Q3; in person Q3, F Q1, 2 omit; in his F Q1, 2, in's Q3.

Of these "towards", "in person", "in's" are arbitrary variants
of Q3, and are neither improvements nor corrections. S.D. *Gower*
is used by F throughout, the form *Captain Gower* does not occur.
F "now, what's" (the article has misreadings here) is normal F
usage. In F " How now" does not have a question mark when, as
here, it is immediately followed by a question (cf. III. ii. 89; III.
vi. 1–2; IV. vii. 70).

(*f*) IV. vii. 110–v. i. 14; other, F, other. Q1, 2, other? Q3;
God F Q1, 2, O God Q3; proclaymed F, proclaimed Q1, 2,
proclaim'd Q3; sault F Q1, 2, salt Q3.

Q3 "other?" is correct; but F does not appear to be following
Q2, where there is no question mark. The question-mark in F is
misplaced at the end of the previous line. The readings "God"
and "proclaymed" are necessitated by the metre. The spelling
"sault" is claimed to be unique in F, but so is "scauld" in the
same passage (v. i. 5, 31). Like "aunchient" this may well be a
attempt to represent Fluellen's pronunciation.

Perhaps the strongest evidence for the use of Q2 copy is at II. iii.
50, "the word is 'Pitch and pay' ". Both F and Q2 read "world",
while Q1, 3 read "word", which would appear to be the correct
reading. In spite of this the assertion that F depended in places
on Q2 copy must be considered very doubtful.

The evidence offered in support of F dependence on Q3 is
more extensive. A list of the "main verbal links" in which F
has failed to correct errors in Q3 is given on p. 69. Of thirteen
such links, some need be no more than coincidence, for example,
II. ii. 177 ye Q1, 2, you, F Q3; IV. v. 19 inough Q1, 2, enow F

Q3; iv. vii. 160 of from his Q1, 2, from's Q3, from his F; v. i. 15 Here a Q1, 2, Heere he F Q3.

75 brother Q1, 2, brother of F Q3; iv. vii. 93 Cryspin, Cryspin Q1, 2, Crispin Crispianus F Q3 have stronger claims to acceptance. Even so a case can be made that F "brother of" is a legitimate phrase used in *Famous Victories*, Sig. f 3ᵃ, and in *King John*, II. i. 547; III. i. 161; and that "Crispin Crispianus" is metrically more satisfactory than "Cryspin, Cryspin", and is anticipated in part by F Crispin Crispian iv. iii. 57, which has no equivalent in the quartos. Yet whether these last F readings are erroneous or not, their correspondence with Q3 is striking.

The list of correspondences between Q and F stage directions carries weight, but it is pertinent to point out that some F stage directions differ from Q where there would be no reason for any change, and agreement would be expected; that the appearance of "manet" (v. ii. 98) in all quartos and F, where Cairncross suggests that no quarto copy was used, is odd; and that F "Enter two Bishops", I. ii. 6, may have nothing to do with the quartos, but is a repetition of F entry notice at I. i, "Enter the two Bishops of Canterbury and Ely", a passage omitted by the quartos.

Two pieces of evidence cited by Cairncross on p. 71 strongly support his theory of F's use of Q3; in fact, no alternative explanation seems possible. At IV. viii. 108 F ends the line after "twenty", and makes a fresh line with "O God, thy arm was here", indenting it to the point at which speech-headings are begun. This indentation, as Cairncross points out, is apparently a "survival of the deletion in the text of Q2 or Q3 of the erroneous speech-prefix *King*".

In II. i. 40 F "*Nym.* Pish", Q3 "*Nym.* Push" are both printed within the last line of the preceding speech.

Further evidence adduced from speech-headings is less satisfactory.

II. i. 101 *Pi.* F Q3. The normal F form is *Pist.*, but here the shortened form is clearly due to the need to justify a crowded line. IV. vii. 85–139. Stating that this is the only F passage which departs from the normal speech-heading *King.*—incorrectly for at I. ii. 259 F has *Kin.*, Qq *King.*—Cairncross collates eight speech-headings showing identity of variants *Kin.* or *King.* between F and Q3. This is misleading. There are, in fact, eleven speech-headings, *King.* or *Kin.*, in this passage, and two of the three additional speech-headings show F and Q3 in disagreement: l. 99 *Kin.* F, *King* Q3; l. 128 *Kin.* F, Qq omit.

The appearance of the speech-heading *Welch.* for Fluellen eight times consecutively in III. ii. 72–143, where there is no corresponding text in the quartos, may indicate a change from Q3 copy to manuscript copy (p. 72). It has, however, been suggested in the Introduction (p. xxxvii) that this scene was added to the original play, and there seems to be no reason to withdraw that suggestion; in which case the speech-headings may be sufficiently explained without the need to postulate a change from quarto to manuscript copy.

The use of the speech-heading *Woman*, II. iii. 34, in place of the normal *Hostess* is claimed to indicate dependence on manuscript material because of a gap in Q3 (p. 72). There is no gap of any consequence in Q3 at this point; the quarto version of the Hostess's speech is reasonably full. Yet there is a good deal of evidence from spellings (see Introduction, p. xxxvii) thát this whole scene is close to Shakespeare's autograph.

It is difficult to imagine, for example, a printing-house corrector or compositor A introducing such spellings as F "Deules" (l. 32) for Q3 "diuels". By way of analogy, what explanation can be given of the speech-headings at I. ii. 259, *Kin.* F, *King.* Qq, and II. ii. 29 *Kni.* F, *Gray.* Qq, other than that F compositor was influenced by copy not derived from the quartos, in places where the theory would have him follow Q3?

The evidence of mislineation common to F and Q is more significant (pp. 72–3). Three passages are quoted: II. iv. 127–32; IV. i. 305–8; IV. viii. 40–3; and a further passage, IV. iii 120–1 is referred to on p. 76.

Inferences (p. 74) drawn from the increasing tendency to favour "d" rather than "t" as the unvoiced weak past participle endings in the period 1590–1623 have slight value. As Cairncross writes, such spellings were arbitrary, and therefore a large proportion of agreements between Q and F must be expected.

The peculiar spellings common to both texts are more convincing: Owse (I. ii. 164) and "crasing" (IV. iii. 105) in particular.

The two compositors A and B who set up F text have spellings which they prefer (p. 75), but their variations from such habitual spellings cannot always be ascribed to the influence of Q copy. In IV. i. 115 F "beleeue", set up by A who prefers "belieue", is omitted by Q. Similarly, A is not consistent in his use of "here" or "heere", and again the inconsistency is independent of Q. Incidentally "theeues", I. ii. 177, referred to on p. 75, is not in a passage set up by A, and cannot therefore be regarded as a variant from his usual form "thieues".

The coincidence of colons between F and Q noted on pp. 72, 77, 86, 90 is unreliable evidence. The colons appear to be in unusual positions, but elsewhere F places a colon before a relative (I. ii. 39–40, 51–2; 194–5, etc.), and a colon before "for" is normal F practice (I. ii. 17–18, 23–4, 97–8, 145–6, 155–6, etc.).

The sections of the article dealing with the suggested process by which copy was prepared for F (pp. 77–92) also contain illustrations of how some F errors may have arisen. F errors arising out of deletions in the copy and of transposition could, of course, have originated equally well from a heavily corrected manuscript. In the corrected facsimiles which follow, some extremely ingenious explanations of the possible origin of doubtful or peculiar F readings are put forward. The suggestion that F "will avouchment" (IV. viii. 37) may have sprung from Q2 speech-heading *Soul.* corrected to *Will.* is an attractively neat proposal. So, too, the suggestion that F "cudgeld", v. i. 92, was erroneously caught from the marginal additions and corrections made on the quarto page, and that its omission restores the correct metre (p. 83) is very ingenious. It is possible, however, that "will I" in the same line was "caught" by the compositor from "will I" in the previous line, and should be omitted. This also restores the metre, and makes rather better sense, for the retention of "cudgeld" makes quite clear to the audience that Pistol has no honourable scars, but only those inflicted by Fluellen.

While Cairncross's main contention that F made some use of Q3 copy is acceptable, it is clear that much of the evidence can bear alternative interpretation and needs careful sifting. There are, too, some difficulties that have been indicated above: the apparent use of manuscript copy where there was no significant gap in Q; the possible use of Q copy where the theory postulates the use of manuscript copy; and the occasional odd speech-heading or stage direction that remains unexplained.

The theory does not throw any light on the odd position of F *Actus Quartus*, nor on the interchanging in F of IV. iv and v. It is strange, too, that, if the printers had a manuscript copy of the play in their possession, they did not print directly from it. They may, indeed, have preferred printed copy, but the labour of correcting a quarto would have been considerable, and the resulting copy with its corrections, additions, pasted slips, and sheets would have been tedious and very difficult to follow. That Q3 affected F is established beyond doubt, but it is not shown that the means by which Q3 affected F was the use by F of a corrected Q3 as copy.

NOTE ON "'AND A' BABBLED OF GREEN FIELDS'"
(II. iii. 17)

There has recently been an outburst of conjecture. In general Theobald's emendation has been attacked on the ground that it throws doubt on the reliability of the Folio text, and that it is mere eighteenth-century sentimentality. Attempts have been made, therefore, to interpret the F reading "Table" as it stands. Hotson has pressed the interpretation, "and a spitten image off Grenville", with reference to Sir Richard Grenville's death of Flores, with much learning and ingenuity. (*Times Literary Supplement*, 1956, p. 212.) Mrs Hulme offers two interpretations after substituting "on" for "and". The first proposes that "pen", "table", "green fields" bear sexual imagery in keeping with the Hostess's bawdiness in II. i. The second interpretation attaches a heraldic significance to "table" "green field" (*Notes and Queries*, CCI. (1956), 283–7; *Essays in Criticism*, VI. (1956), 117–19. See also *E in C.*, VI. 486–91; VII. 222–6.)

FINIS